GODIVA ROCKS
BY PETE CHAMBERS

Dedicated to all those musicians in Coventry & Warwickshire
who rocked or who are about to rock.

FOREWARD BY HORACE PANTER

Put the words Coventry and Music together and most people will come up with 2-Tone - The Specials and The Selecter. Others might then go on to say King, or even The Primitives. Some might go back further and say The Sorrows?, or even, God forbid, Frank Ifield. These were the ones that made it. There were loads of bands that didn't. Some of them, admittedly didn't particularly want to. They were happy playing out one or two nights a week and occasionally aspiring to the dizzy heights of a gig in Leicester or even Birmingham..

Ever since I have lived in Coventry there has been a local scene. It's had its ups and its downs, but its always been there. For me, nothing is more fulfilling than playing music. Whether it's at The Hope & Anchor in Whitefriars Street or The Whiskey A Go-Go on Sunset Boulevard. These days its more likely to be the former than the latter, but to be honest, the former is preferable. As Rufus Thomas famously said, "It ain't what you got, It's what you DO with what you got!" OK So you can play, What choo gon do about it! The local scene has always been about people learning. Breaking out of the bedroom with a desire to play; the often frustrating search for the right like-minded fellow travellers and experiencing that magical feeling that happens when a bunch of musicians play together, cease to be individuals and become a BAND. It has been my great privilege to have been present at some of these occasions.

The local scene doesn't just rely on the bands. Non-muso figures loom large in the City's musical mythology. The General Wolfe (Ken Brown), Greg Crabbe's club at The Colin Campbell, the Rockhouse/Backbeat rehearsal complex, all these people/places have helped to shape the local music scene and make it happen. Coventry has its fair share of unsung heroes, people who left town to join bands based elsewhere, but there must be a lot of people who you pass in the precinct who one time or another had dreams of being a Keith Richard or a Johnny Rotten and very nearly realised them on stage upstairs at The Golden Cross or The Bear. You may also pass the next generation of Coventry heroes. Wish them well.

HORACE PANTER, FORMER BREAKER, SPECIALS, AND GENERAL PUBLIC, JANUARY 2004

INTRODUCTION BY PETE CHAMBERS

Hello and welcome to my most involved project so far, Godiva Rocks. With this book I hope to give the reader a broad view of popular music in Coventry and Warwickshire. As my expertise as it were lies in rock and pop, I have based this book around those genres, but still giving a sideways glance at some other musical forms in the local area.

Having been a Coventry music Journalist for some 8 years in the 80's, with The Coventry Weekly News and later having my own Coventry Gazebo in Brum Beat. I have collected records, tapes, posters, badges, handbill, fanzines from many Coventry bands and artists all this helping with my task at hand. This project has been on the back burner nearly 20 years, for I had intended to run a series in Brum Beat entitled the 'Coventry Charters', looking at each local act that charted. Many local musicians kindly helped, but sadly due to lack of publishing space it never happened, all my research wasn't wasted, as I passed on a lot of it to Pete Frame for his wonderful book *The Rock Gazetteer*. Now of course I have updated it and used it in this volume. In my time I have also been a band manager, photographer and studio bound artist (though never in a big way). As you will discover I have a manically eclectic taste in music, and I have actually heard most of the artists I talk about in this book (obviously some have proved impossible). Thanks to all the artists who lent and gave me recordings of their stuff and their wonderful contributions.

Is it all here? Well for the most part I hope! It's certainly the most involved book about all Coventry music, (yeah I know there has been a few just on Two Tone alone, but never the entire scene). Obviously I have included some artists that the reader may not have included if they had written this book themselves, or put certain artists in the B or C list when you feel they should be in the A list. Well if you disagree, get in touch.

(I have also left out a few Hospital related incidents that would be in poor taste to include). So even though I have spent hours, days, and months researching this volume there is bound to be stuff I have missed, and facts I have left out. For those of you who are wildly shouting, "He's missed out so and so" or you think your mate's grunge metal band or your brother's brass band should be included. I would ask you to get in touch and let me know the missing artists or facts. So any updated version we can have a more complete record of the areas sounds. Likewise if you are in a band and feel you should have got more coverage, let me know why. I can't promise anything, but you never know. If you just have a story to tell (be you 11 or 80 years old), or you would like to sell my book in your shop/pub. PLEASE contact me I would LOVE to hear from you. If you have photos to send and a written contribution send it via e-mail *(please note that by sending me a contribution you are allowing it for use in any future book by Pete Chambers without requiring any financial (or any other) compensation to your self).*

E-mail me at **godivarocks@yahoo.co.uk**

Or ring me on **07963 953586** (this phone is normally off so leave your number or text me **I will** get back).

Website **http://rocksgodiva.tripod.com/**

USING THIS BOOK

OK I'm not insulting your intelligence, this is just a guide to how things work. Right who's included? Well it's impossible to include everyone who ever had a musical connection with Coventry & Warwickshire, my rationale for inclusion is an obvious one. Charted artists, artists with record deals, well-known artists, influential artists and any artist with a shelf life of more that two months.

Right the body of each main entry is a biographical entry on each artist, sometimes I have included details of previous bands and future bands. This is to make things fit a little better and prevents tons of entries. Some entries are generic and include one artist and all their body of work in various groups. You will see I do go on about chart entries a lot, this is not because I am obsessed with the charts (far from it) but it does tend to put an artist into perspective and provide a kind of measuring stick if you like.

DO YOU WANT TO MAKE THE "COVENTRY SOUND"?...
Then come and 'SELECT' from our 'SPECIALS
ARIA GUITARS
New stocks just arrived, superb instruments from **£124**
INTERMUSIC AMPS
These must be the best value on the market, a 120-watt combo with built-in reverb sustain and phaser. Flight-case construction, **£285**
DRUM KITS
5-Drum Outfits, complete with all stands and pedals, from **£228**
These are just three examples of the vast range of sound equipment we keep in stock. All leading makes of amplifiers, electric and acoustic guitars, basses, drums and disco gear available.
Pay by Access, Barclaycard, etc. or low-deposit finance arranged.
Tel. Coventry 457175 or call in and see us at
the sound centres
98-100, Clay Lane, Coventry

If you see a (12) after a song title it means of course it got to that number in the charts. Band names and main artists tend to be in **bold type,** while song titles are usually in *Italics.* That's the general rule but not always. A band that has no real local connection will not be bold or Italics type. Obviously where there is a link you will see this (SEE SPECIALS). Again I have tried to keep them to a minimum, mostly though they are unavoidable.

THE COVENTRY SOUND-A MYTH OR REALITY

Godiva Rocks, well if you look at the Broadgate clock she sure does (though not as much as she did). In this book she always will rock. It's easy to knock this great City of ours, but as you will see we have a lot to be proud of. Not just the city, for this book is about Warwickshire music as well, Rugby, Nuneaton, Leamington and Kenilworth have all been just as important. The whole area has something to be proud of, so lets stop knocking our successes and applaud our local musical heroes. Being smack in the middle of England it was reasonable to assume that any resultant music in such an area would be a either a non descript blandness that was not akin to either the north, or the south. That neither related to the sounds from east or west. Just a grey uninspired singular anomaly. Or on the other hand, it could be argued that topographic factors could have melded together in such a way as to create a big bang that would be the *Coventry Sound*. As it happens we got both. From the late 50s and the early 60s, Coventry had little or no identity of it's own. The legendary Larry Page was to search in vain for a *Coventry Sound*. Because the required permutations were not as yet in place, but they were taking shape. I am certainly not trying to rubbish the Coventry artists of that time. However a *Coventry sound* was never likely to come from Frank Ifield and his strong pull to the antipodeans and the R&B sound of The Sorrows who were pretty much on their own chart-wise. Both were top acts, with the preverbal bucket loads of talent, but it was to take something else to create a local identity!

What we need is a great big melting pot, that's what Coventry and area were about to get. With the influx of Asians and West Indians, it would be only a matter of time until an authentic *Coventry Sound* was a reality. The permutations were coming into place and although many still doubt its existence the *Coventry Sound* would come on line in a Ska-tastic way in 1979 for The Specials and the rest of the 2 Tone collective. Believe me I was there, I was writing about the music, I could see a whole shed load of local talent suddenly using ska rhythms in their music. Without question we had The *Cov Sound*, and everyone else wanted a piece of it. So once again lets stop pretending that it never happened and be proud that for a couple of years at least we were cool and we were hip!

Nowadays the *Cov sound* has swung towards our Asian roots, with Covasians Taz and Panjabi MC showing us the way with probably the greatest dance music ever.....Bhangra. Less distinct I know but still unquestionably a *Coventry Sound all the same.* The question is where will it go next? Celtic influences? Polish rap with a Polka beat who really knows, whatever the direction it heads it will be our music from our Great City and towns, and it will take a decade or two before we realized it ever existed.

Pete Chambers, Summer 2004.

The best thing to happen to Coventry since Lady Godiva

We take a fascinating look at the Rock City of the Year. Home of the Specials and Selecter, Coventry's changing fast. We check out the studios, gigs and garages. Is there another New Wave breaking or is the tide simply turning? Read the news behind the notes this week and every week in:

MUSICIANS ONLY

...plug in and read. Every Wednesday. 20p

GODIVA ROCKS THE 'A' LIST

ADORABLE

Here's a Cov band that almost had it all in their hands. Piotr Fijalkowski (vocals, guitar), Robert Dillam (guitar), Kevin Gritton (drums) and Wil snidely (bass). Formed in 1990 out of the remnants of small-time Cov bands **Bubblegum Flesh** and **The Candy Thieves**. With more than a tip of the hat to Echo and The Bunnymen (and Ian McCulloch in particular). Outspoken sure, talented definitely, things looked amazing for them when they signed to the Oasis label Creation (signing in a Coventry Pub). Their first single *Sunshine Smile* won rave reviews and the number one spot on the Indie chart. Followed by the album *Against Perfection* charting at number 70 in 1993. Sadly for the lads their continued arrogance and record company squabbling effectively killed off their initial momentum and their subsequent album *Fake* failed to shine and eventually the band were dropped from a Creation that had become owned by Sony music. Leaving Piotr Fijalkowski to go off and form **Casino** then **Polak** who for this venture he bizarrely dropped the Polish spelling of his name to the English Peter. Pete's favourite football teams by the way are Coventry City & Poland unsurprisingly.

ALTERNATIVE SOUNDS

In 1979 things changed for the better for Coventry music lovers with the advent of our first (and best) fanzine **Alternative Sounds**. Punk based fanzines like the original *Sniffin Glue* had heralded the new trend. Instead of just watching local bands, you at last had something tangible, you could read about your faves, find out where and when they were playing again. In short the music scene had organised itself.

I will always be indebted to the **Alternative Sounds** creator/Editor **Martin Bowes**. Without him I doubt whether I would have ever bothered putting pen to paper to write that first letter to the fanzine or do my first review on Bad Manners. (Yeah I admit it, I was watching Bad Manners at the Dog and Trumpet while one of the best bands in the world namely The Clash played at Tiffanys). At just 20p you got 20 pages full of great stuff. OK here's what you got in issue 6. A gig review of the Wild Boys at the Swanswell and interviews with The Swell Maps, Gods Toys and Dave Vanian of the Damned. Loads of gigs (in those days I had to pick where to go on what night, you always had a choice). Singles reviews: Nag,Nag,Nag from Cabaret Voltaire, great stuff they say and a great Cov area bands list. Still a great read 25 years on, I'm glad I kept a few issues. There were 18 issues of the fanzine running from 1979 to 1981 plus a copy of the fanzine was also given away with *The Sent From Coventry* compilation album.

More 'zines followed like **Adventures in Reality**, a worthy second to **Alternative Sounds**. Others included **The Cordial Knot, Private Enterprise, Damn Latin, Rough Justice, Suck Language, Torn** and **Coventry 222**. When **Alternative Sounds** finally came to an end, Martin gave up writing about music and started to create it with his own band **Attrition** (SEE ATTRITION).

ANY GIVEN DAY

A glorious blend of hard-hitting power chords and spot on vocal deliveries make this Rugby five piece the current darlings of the area. They have updated the spirit of the 70's punk band The Rezillos and made it their very own, they call in 'punk 'n' roll'. Already a German tour has been undertaken and the USA is on the horizon. Their superb album *Perverts and Pornstars* (mine's never out the player) is picking up some great reviews, and it's about time Rugby had some new chart stars (no offence there Sonic & Jason). This band really does rock, but you probably wouldn't want to take Libby (and her bottle of Jack Daniel's) home to meet your parents!

ROB ARMSTRONG

Nowadays Rob is best known as being a master luthier (that's a string instrument maker to you and me). Back in 1968 however Rob was a member of the hardworking folk/jugband **The Idiot Grunt Band,** a folk ensemble (SEE FOLK) that toured Germany and included Rod Felton and John McIntosh in its ranks. A year later they became the **New Modern Idiot Grunt Band.** By 1972 Rob had joined a new unit called **Music Box.** They released an album entitled *Songs of Sunshine* on Westwood Records (now very collectable). The band included all round muso' Colin Armstrong who nowadays runs *Armstrongs Books & Collectables* in *Albany Road*. A later venture including a spell with **Quite Riot** along side Former **Bonzo Dog Do Dah Band** guitarist **Bubs White** (Bubs, has also sessioned for The Scaffold, Jim Capaldi, Viv Stanshall and Red Express, he lives near Rob in the Stoke area of Coventry). In September 2000 Rob released his most accomplished album *A* His backing band for this project reads like folk who's who, with Dave Pegg, Martin Allcock, Gordon Giltrap, Martin Jenkins, Vikki Clayton and Bubs White. Currently Rob writes and records a song a week in collaboration with **Bubs White** who also produces the projects. Rob also uses many of his songs to showcase his superb guitars.

He began making fine stringed instruments in 1971, Although he never advertises. His reputation as a master of his craft has seen him sell acoustic guitars to the likes of George Harrison, Alvin Lee, Joe Brown, Gordon Giltrap, Mark 'Bedders' Bedford (of Madness), Martin Barre (of Jethro Tull who also happened to have studied architecture at Lanchester Polytechnic in the 60's) and Dave Swarbrick (SEE DAVE SWARBRICK). He reckons he's made 714 instruments to date. Taking about 2-3 weeks to make each instrument from wood that's at least 25 years old. He uses no power tools, preferring to make each one totally by hand. Its no wonder then that when reviewed in Guitar magazines his pieces usually achieve top marks; praise indeed!

ATTRITION

Formed in the early eighties by **Alternative Sounds** editor Martin Bowers (SEE ALTERNATIVE SOUNDS). **Attrition** were and still are hard to pigeon-hole. 'Industrial', 'Goth' or whatever you want to call their brand of electronic based music is of no interest to the band or indeed their legion of hard core fans. Their dark rhythms have never given purchase to the inconsequential and glib side of music, it could be argued they are an acquired taste, but once acquired it's never to be relinquished.

The band comprising of Martin Bowers (vocals, keyboards) as the central member with various personnel coming and going. Some of the more permanent members have been Ashley Niblock (keyboards) and Julia Waller (vocals). With some 18 albums and 14 singles to their name their body of work has been constant, with the 1985 album, *Smiling at the Hypogonder Club* being a classic among classics. With The *Attrition Of Reason* and *The Realms Of Hungry Ghosts* also well worth a listen. Martin currently teaches music technology in Coventry. Check out the website at **www.attrition.co.uk**

GODIVA ROCKS SOUND BYTE FROM-Martin Bowers (Attrittion & Alternative Sounds) "Time flies. (like an insect...up and down the wall..)" as Howard Devoto once said. ..his band Magazine were one of the legion of punk and post punk bands that inspired a younger me to get up and do something. to say something. I published 18 issues of my fanzine "Alternative SOUNDS" between 1979 - 1981. Coventry had a vibrant music scene. the Specials were the public face but we had so many good bands. i helped put together an album of them in 1980. "Sent from Coventry". Memories. I remember meeting an excited Terry Hall in Woolworths... he'd just picked up a copy of the "Top of the pops" covers album which included a Specials song... in 1980 the BBC came to town and filmed me and others for an edition of the youth TV programme "Something else"... They say that music journalists are frustrated musicians and i my case it was true. I needed more and i started my own band. Attrition. As a non-musician punk inspired me and the electronic/industrial scene afterwards focused me... i still don't play anything traditional but touring the world and 50,000 albums later i am now teaching a new generation of non-musicians how to create electronic noises of their own

BAIT

Coventry based rock band formed from former Coventry University students. Theirs is a blend of guitar based harmonic rock that is hard to pigeonhole, although something akin to the Doobie Brothers meets The Eagles is probably something near. They have released four albums, *Not In My Back Yard*, *Live 15-09-01*, *Shut Up and Take A Seat* and their best and most focused album so far *South of the Delta*. Current line-up is Chris Johnson, Andy Pitcher, Nick Nugent and John Chivers. Andy and John are also members of the part-time folk-rock outfit **Godivaride** who released the wondrous album *The Magnificent Mr Moonflange* in 2001.

BANCO DE GAIA

Banco De Gaia (literally meaning Bank of the World) or Toby Marks to you and me, based in Leamington, he along with The likes of the Chemical Brothers and The Orb has made himself one of the leading forces on the ambient trance dance scene. His diverse musical background (having played Bhangra, Heavy Rock, classical and Jazz) has given him and his music a sense of unpredictability and constant development. His creations move with atmospheric backdrops, subliminal decoration, always evocative, always inventive.

The master of 'Chill out' began his creative path with his own Planet Dog label. Using the sounds he had heard on his travel he perceived the groundbreaking album *Maya* charting at 34 in 1994. By 95 he had moved on musically and the masterful *Last Train to Lhasa* attained a credible 31 in the national album charts. The mid nineties brought *Live at Glastonbury*, *Big Men Cry* and *Igizeh* (partly recorded inside the pyramid at Giza). Followed by batch of compilations and remixes. He still continues to grow musically (currently working with vocalist to Jennifer Folker on the single *Zeus No Like Techno*). Although his output of late is less than prolific His diversity with his chosen genre can never be too overstated.

THE BEATLES

Of course not from Coventry, but they do have a few connections with the area. The moptops played Coventry on three occasions. First as nobodies they played on 17th November 1962 at the Matrix Ballroom on Fletchamstead Highway (a young Pete Waterman was in the audience that night) (SEE PETE WATERMAN). They were supported by Coventry outfit Lynne Curtis and the Mustangs. (Lynne released a solo single in 65 on Decca entitled *House For Sale*). They played Nuneaton's *Co-op Hall* the following week (SEE NUNEATON). They returned to Cov as a support band to Helen Shapiro on 24th February 1963.to play at the Coventry Theatre. Strangely some 10 months later they played again (this time as stars) at the Coventry Theatre on 17th November 1963. Exactly a year to the day of the Matrix concert! It would seem by all accounts that the Matrix gig was badly attended. With the audience blissfully unaware of what those four lads would soon become. It's even mentioned in the Beatles *Let it Be* feature film. Between the songs *Dig it*

GODIVAROCKS@YAHOO.CO.UK

and *Two of Us,* Paul talks to a pretty uninterested John about George's worries of playing live again. Paul says to John, "When we came back from Hamburg and did Leicester De Montford Hall or wherever it was, Coventry. You know we played the ballroom and we had the worst first night thing, we were all nervous, it was terrible". Two weeks before they had indeed been playing the Star Club in Hamburg, Coventry was about the third time they had ventured so far South.

John came to Coventry again on 15th June 1968 with Yoko Ono (mid way through recording *The White Album*, between the tracks *Blackbird* & *Revolution 9* to be exact). They attended 'The National Sculpture Exhibition' in the grounds of Coventry Cathedral (SEE COVENTRY CATHEDRAL). This was to be the couples first time out in public together and first joint 'artistic' venture, entitled '*Acorns For Peace,* or *Living Art-Two Acorns*, (the event was immortalised in the Beatles song *Ballad of John and Yoko*, Lennon sings, "Fifty acorns tied in a sack"). They had previously sent a selection of world leaders two acorns to be planted for peace. As Coventry Cathedral was (and still is) a dominion of reconciliation and world peace, it was an obvious place for the couple to 'perform' their peace-art. They turned up in John's Rolls Royce (complete with TV, video recorder and Telephone) with a trailer attached, an odd sight indeed. On the trailer was a round white circular metal seat to sit on and contemplate the growing of the acorns. They planted two acorns (that were in white plastic cups) in the centre of it, with one facing East, one West. Symbolising the meeting of John & Yoko, and the meeting of their two different cultures.

JOHN & YOKO AT COVENTRY
Photo courtesy of the Coventry Weekly News.

The day was filled with problems, when the couple's sculpture was removed from in front of the Chapel of Unity to the Cathedral gardens. Fabio Barraclough who was the assistant of art at Rugby School and the chief organiser of the event, claimed that it was Cannon Stephen Verney who had the sculpture moved because he objected to exhibiting their work on consecrated ground because of their extra-marital relationship. He later refuted this. On top of that, John and Yoko were not allowed to be mentioned in the main catalogue, so they produced their own, even this was not allowed to be distributed. (So I'm really happy to actually own a copy of the said catalogue). John and especially Yoko were livid, and in the privacy of the Deanery she forced The Cannon to ring leading artists to prove that their work was indeed 'art'!

THE SAGA OF THE ACORNS

ORIGINALLY PLANTED HERE BY JOHN & YOKO

REPLANTED (AND STOLEN) FROM HERE

Within two days the acorns and the plaque (bearing the legend, John by Yoko-Yoko by John) on the sculpture were stolen (if E-bay had been around then, one wonders how many hundreds of supposedly genuine 'peace' acorns would have been up for sale?). *The Telegraph* even got an anonymous call from someone claiming to be the acorn thieves. The myths of that Saturday in June continue, some say the couple were so upset they sent some more acorns and they were put under 24 hour security (or armed guard as one US site claims). Some say they never sent replacements. Staff at The Cathedral maintain the trees grew for some 25 years then died. Certainly there seems to be no sign of this in their original position.

GODIVAROCK@YAHOO.CO.UK

There is a school of thought that suggests that if replacements had been planted we probably wouldn't have been privy to it anyway, a valid point. Though there doesn't seem to be any evidence of oak trees in the Cathedral area. Following the event a very angry Lennon wrote a letter to the Cannon calling him to be a hypocrite claiming, "Jesus would have loved the piece as it is", the letter was sold many years later for £9,400 to *The Hardrock Cafe* group. The sculpture its self was later removed by Lennon's chauffeur Les and taken back down to London on the trailer, apparently John and Yoko are seen sitting on it briefly in the film *Imagine*. In 1984 when *Strawberry Fields* was being built in Central park New York (a place I was lucky enough to visit, how I wish I had taken some acorns). Yoko mentioned that sixteen years earlier she and John had planted acorns in the precincts of Coventry Cathedral. That acorn was now symbolically a tree. So no matter what, the Cathedral at Coventry is an important part of the John and Yoko legend. In 1985 the film *John and Yoko-A Love Story*, starring **Mark McGann** and *Kim Myori*, features a good re-enactment of the Coventry visit, its a good video to. Speaking of re-enactments the story of the Acorns, or rather The Bench was part of the *City Stories* dramas performed by **Theatre Absolute**. They took place in Priory Gardens in June 2004. Written by Chris O'Connell the story of the Lennon's visit is given a comedic slant, a replica of the white metal bench was also made for this production. So did You steal the acorns, do you know who did, I would love to know, contact me with totally anonymity.

THE 2004 BENCH

Paul too had the occasion to mention not just Coventry, but the Cathedral. Paul's second solo album 'Ram' was released in 1971, he also recorded a full orchestral version of it called *Thrillington* under the name of Percy 'Thrills' Thrillington. His fictitious biography begins Percy "Thrills" Thrillington was born in Coventry Cathedral in 1939. Obviously the city made a lasting impression on the guys. I also remember reading in the *Cov Telegraph* a long time back that John had brought a house for a guy called Jonathan Hague in Leaminton in the 60's that he used to go to art school with. In 1984 Yoko had given £1000 to Coventry's rape Crisis Centre. Just for completeness, Coventry born DJ **Brian Matthew** had the fab four on his BBC radio shows many times in the 60's, and even appeared on their *Live at the BBC* album (SEE BRIAN MATHEW). In 2000 Ringo's son Zak Starkey, played at the *Coliseum* (SEE VENUES) with former Smiths guitarist Johnny Marr. Finally Cov Guitar maker Rob Armstrong (SEE ROB ARMSTRONG) made 2 custom guitars for George Harrison. Oh and on the Beatles bootleg *Alf Together Now* (Alf Bicknell was the Fab 4's handy man) there is a track entitled *Are You In Coventry*, it's only 4 seconds long so I guess its someone just asking are you in Coventry, why I don't know.

CHUCK BERRY

Chuck Berry was born in Holbrooks, Coventry in 1926, **NO**, of course he wasn't I'm just fooling, he was actually born in San Jose California 1926. He does however have a strong connection to our City. On February 3rd 1972 during his UK tour Berry took part in The Lanchester Arts Festival. OK lets clear up a couple of fallacies here and now. The concert was indeed part of The Lanch Music Festival (SEE VENUES), but the main acts (Pink Floyd and Berry) used The higher capacity Locarno for the shows, not The student Uni' hall (as often mooted). The concert was also not attended by 35,000 people as Berry states in his autobiography. That would be a bit of a fire risk, not least for the people walking on the ceiling with chewing gum attached to their feet..

GODIVAROCKS@YAHOO.CO.UK

His backing band for the tour were Onnie McIntyre (Guitar), Robbie McIntosh (drums, not to be confused with the Pretenders/McCartney Guitarist of the same name), Nick Potter (bass) and Dave Kaffinetti (piano) Both McIntosh and McIntyre would soon form The Average White Band, (McIntosh would die 20 months later). The first half of the show was taken up by Berry classics ike Sweet little Sixteen and Maybellene. The second half would see Berry perform his 'Musex' starting with a 'rude' version of *Reelin'* & *Rockin'* and onto an epic version of a new song *My Ding A-Ling*. Audience participation always a mainstay for Berry is used to maximum effect on this rather tawdry fourth grade innuendo ridden composition (based on a previous Berry song entitled *My Tambourine)*. Splitting the Coventry audience into gender groups, with the girls singing, "My" followed by the boys singing "Ding A-Ling" and then the girls, "I want you to play with", the boys again singing "My Ding A-Ling". It caused a stir with the likes of Mary Whitehouse, and other 'moral' judges of our society at the time. Especially as it hit the Number one spot in the UK and US. Bizarrely Berry's first Number one's in either country. Musos' still shake their heads in disbelief to think that this remains Berry's only chart topper. So despite a stream of classic rock and roll songs this 'novelty' song is the one the public always remember. My Ding A-Ling staying in the American charts for one year. The follow up *Reelin'* & *Rockin'* also recorded at Cov made no 18 in the UK and 27 in the US charts.

My Ding A-Ling originally 11.28 long on *The London Sessions* album was heavily edited down to 4.13 for the single (although I suspect that the album track may also have been edited, judging by the speed the audience seemed to learn their 'bits'). *The London Sessions* album featured studio recordings on side one and a live 23 minute Coventry set on side two, made up of the three tracks *Reelin' n Rockin'*, *My Ding A-Ling* and *Johnny B Goode*. More live tracks were intended for the album, but technical problems with the Pye mobile studio meant that only these three tracks saw the light of day. Berry himself insists he had no idea the concert was being recorded, hard to imagine he had missed the Pye mobile truck and audience mikes that must have been set up for such a recording, (but as mentioned above he also claimed the audience numbered 35,000). Word has it the Lanch demanded a share of the subsequent profits, (Berry received over £250,000 from the first Ding A-Ling royalty cheque alone), but they never got as anything. Berry was so ecstatic with the audience's reaction the show over-ran, this is also documented on the record at the end of *Johnny B Goode*, when the compere begs the audience to vacate the venue, they ignore him and continue chanting, "We Want Chuck". Much to the annoyance of the 2,000 rain soaked Pink Floyd fans waiting outside in The Precinct for the next concert. Chuck Berry at the time referred to the gig "as a defining moment in his career" he later however dismissed it, (a typical Berry trait) claiming he didn't remember Coventry especially. Another thing worth mentioning concerns the fact that *My Ding A-Ling* has more Coventry people actually singing on it than any other record. (I am aware there has been a couple of Sky Blue songs where the crowd can be heard, but those have been merely 'bolted on' to the final cut). In the audience that night were top journalists Tony Stewart from the NME and the 'god' of rock scribes Charles Sharr Murray. So was a certain Mel Preece who works for Coventry firm Astleys, I mention this only because Astleys deem it important enough to include it on their website for some strange reason. One other strange occurrence is I used Central Library whilst researching this item, it suddenly occurred to me that I was in the actually building where the song was recorded, weird!

A GODIVA ROCKS TRIVIA BOX
In the last quarter of 1972 Coventry was to rule the proverbial roost in the homegrown hits department. **Lieutenant Pigeon's** *Mouldy Old Dough* made the number one spot in the UK on the 14th October, staying there for 4 weeks in total. It was replaced by Gilbert O'Sullivan's Clair for 2 weeks. Then on November 25th **Chuck Berry's** *My Ding A-Ling* went to Number one and took up tenancy for 4 weeks. Meaning in that 10 week run, 8 weeks were taken up by songs recorded in Coventry. *Mouldy Old Dough* in a Kingsway front room and *My Ding A-Ling* at the Locarno! If that's not enough trivia for you then you may like too know that for two weeks while *Mouldy Old Dough* topped the charts in the UK. *My Ding A-Ling* was topping the charts in America. So both number ones either side of the pond were recorded in good old Coventry, makes you kinda' proud don't it!

GODIVAROCKS@YAHOO.CO.UK

BHANGRA

I remember listening to Bhangra music way back in the eighties, many of my friends (Asian and non-Asian) found it odd that a white guy could get off on this stuff. I look at it like this. I love all kinds of music, and the swirling sounds and driving beats, were to me just as 'moving' as the rock music I was always listening to. It didn't matter if it was performed by **The Sahotas, Queen, Genesis** or **XLNC**, it was still great music to enjoy, and to me that's all that matters. I freely admit I have always been a bit of a cultural tourist. It really is great stuff, next time you hear Bhangra listen to it's sound, not just the vocal line, but all of it, hear the sounds, feel the beat. Take it in, you will find that it can be just as stimulating as listening to dance music, because that's what is! Don't be prejudice just feel the Bhangra beat! Because this is the latest 'Coventry Sound'. Indeed the last two Coventry acts (as I write this) to chart have both been Covasians (**Taz and Panjabi MC**) (SEE STEREO NATION, SEE PANJABI MC). They are fiercely loyal to their City, shouldn't Coventrians also be loyal to it's musicians?

PARTNERS IN RHYME

Indian music is very complicated, not just to play but there are so many schools and off-shoots that just calling it *Indian music* is a bit like calling The *Taj Mahall* a mausoleum. Bhangra originated in the 15th Century from folk dances of the Punjab, based around the sounds of the two-headed dhol drum that gives Bhangra it's distinctive sound. Of course as Indian migrants came to the UK, they brought with them their culture, including Raga and Bhangra. It's understandably that it would eventually take on 'Western' elements that would combine to create the fusion Bhangra we know today. The name is said to derive from the Panjabi word 'bhang' meaning hemp! Despite it's Panjabi roots Bhangra has been adopted by many other Indian ethnic groups including Gujaratis. Some of the early traditional Bhangra performers were **Deedar Singh Pardesi, Mohinder Kaur Bhamra** and the band **Bhujangy** It was't until the late 70's however when 'pop-Bhangra' emerged mainly as cover bands playing the latest Bollywood songs for weddings. Eventually they would emerge as original acts writing their own material, giving the British-Asian youth a genre that was all their very own. With the likes of **Kuldip Manak, Bhujangy, Hans Raj hans, Joi, Alaap, XLNC, B21, Sangeeta** and **DCS**. Bhangra then went Desi, basically a fusion of Bhangra and Hip-hop beats. Pioneered by the great **Bally Sagoo** and **Apache Indian** and popularised by Coventry artists like **Taz & Stereo Nation** and **Panjabi MC**. Even **Specials** man Neville Staples has sang on Bhangra records and **Fun Boy 3** did an Urdu version of *Our Lips Are Sealed*.

Other names on the local scene include the mighty **Silinder Pardesi** a master in Bhangra. Originally from Birmingham but based in Coventry for many years. Won The Asian Song Contest in 1986 and he and **The Pardesi Music Machine** have released a steady flow of high grade Bhangra albums. His music is stimulating and tremendously dynamic. Despite the winning of awards for his singles *Shake Yer Pants* and *Balbeero Bhabi.*, Silinder can still mix it with the likes of Pavarotti at the 1997 Moscow celebrations, such is the diversity of his art and love of classical Indian music. His body of work includes *Pump Up The Bhangra, Shabad Gurbani and Geet Guran De and Nashay Diay Band Botlay*. **Partners In Rhyme** seem to be a permanent fixture in the official Bhangra charts. Not surprising really they produce some of the finest bhangra you are ever likely to hear, hard thumping drums mixed with delicate harmonies. This Coventry duo Hardip and Prem have been setting alight the indi-pop scene for many years. Singing in both Hindi and Urdu even venturing into Islamic based Qawwali music (with the legend that was **Nusrat Fateh Ali Khan** as their mentor). **PIR** like many bhangra/desi acts are never afraid to diversify, and use what sounds best, despite it's country or culture of origin. Their original dance fusion music is testament to this. Their albums have included *House Of All Nations, Distant Voices, Timeless* and the quite wonderful *Replay*.

SILINDER PARDESI

Then we have **Shinda Sureela** a Coventry based singer who favors a more traditional approach to Bhangra his output includes, *Duniya da Experience, Dhoilia and Khabraan*. Someone to look out for in the future is **Hanson Khan** a young singer and dancer, and a future force in desi music or even *Bollywood*. With smoldering good looks and ability to rap unaccompanied he has hopefully a bright future on the Bhangra scene. Also look out for two Coventry Car workers Ownkar Tamber (from Wolverhampton) & Wayne Arundel (from Wyken) have recorded a single entitled *Lifetime and A Day* under the name **Dual Flava.**

One guy who is already a force on the local Asian scene is **Baldev Mastana** one of the world's finest Bhangra producers. Not just a producer but an engineer, lyricist and all round teacher of Bhangra. He's also a real gentleman whose music seems to be a spiritual part of him. No wonder that he has been the kingpin of the Midlands scene for over 20 years. Working from his fabulous *World Music Recording Studios* in Foleshill Coventry,(SEE STUDIOS) it is through his skills that the likes of **Shinda Sureela, Awaaz Group, Mangal Singh, J Deep** and **Balwinder Safri & The Safri Boyz** have attained their highs in the world of quality Bhangra. Baldev's message to the world is "Music never ends". .**Mitch Hyare** is probably the greatest dhol (drum) player in the world today. He too was born in Coventry. Born **Mahaveer Hyare** now lives in California and fronts two bands Lethal Dholis and Daku Knox, has also played with **Panjabi MC** and **Stereo Nation** (SEE PANJABI MC) (SEE STEREO NATION). Apart from that he also produces hip-hop for the likes of **e40**. It's good to know that Coventry is one of the few major Bhangra centers in the country and indeed the World!

BALDEV MASTANA

PAULINE BLACK

Born Pauline Vickers in Romford, Essex on October 24th 1953. Studied biochemistry at the Lanchester Poly. She dropped out (or was asked to leave, depending on which version you want to believe) and went on to work as a radiographer at Walsgrave hospital. Her early musical career was spent singing in local folk clubs. She joined **Hard Top 22** in 1978, who quickly became **The Selecter** (SEE THE SELECTER). Pauline fronted the Two-Tone band (SEE TWO TONE) in her familiar black suit, trilby hat giving it loads of bottle, such was her gutsy stage presence and powerful vocals.. Clocking up 3 hits (*On my Radio, Three Minute Hero and Missing Words*).

When the Selecter split Pauline released an unsuccessful solo single, a cover of Jimmy Cliff's *I Can see Clearly Now*, on Chrysalis records. By 1984 she had teamed up with Neville Staples and Lynval Golding (SEE THE SPECIALS, SEE THE FUN BOY THREE). They went by the name of **Pauline Black and Sunday Best**, releasing the one single *Pirates of the Airways*, a tip of the hat to high rise pirate radio stations. Also on the record was the rhythm section of the band Lynval was managing at the time **After Tonight.**

Pauline went on to concentrate on the 'other' strings to her bow, namely acting and TV presenting. She presented her own Channel 4 show *Black on Black*, and kids show *Hold Tight*. Acting-wise she appeared in *the Bill, the Vice* won the Time Out Award for Best Actress in 1990 for her portray of Billie Holiday. Presented a one-woman show. On top of that she presented Radio 5 show Black to the Future and wrote a novel entitled *Goldfinches*. She formed the band **Supernaturals**, including in it's ranks Drummer Rob Hill formerly of the **Squad, The Mix** and the **Pink Umbrellas** (SEE THE SQUAD, SEE PINK UMBRELLAS) and John Shipley on Guitar (ex-**Swinging Cats**, SEE SWINGING CATS). After stints of supporting the Joboxers and the Communards, in band fighting commenced that would split the group. She joined a hurriedly reformed **Selecter** (SEE THE SELECTER) put together to supported Bad Manners on tour. Eventually releasing 4 albums under the Selecter banner. In 2000 she formed the **Ska Divas** with Special AKA vocalist **Rhoda Daka** (SEE THE SPECIALS) and Jennie Bellestar of the Bellstars. She continues to be part of The 'acoustic' **Selecter** and a very familiar face of our City.

PAGE 12   GODIVAROCKS@YAHOO.CO.UK   PAGE 12

POLLY BOLTON

Born in Leamington Spa April 27th 1950 **Polly Bolton** has one of the purist female voices in the business today, forever in demand a session singer as well as fronting her own band. Curious then that Polly's initial ambition was to be a zoologist working with gorillas, rather than musicians (although some would say it's a fine line) It was while she was at college she met up with successful Coventry Folk Band **Dando Shaft** (SEE DANDO SHAFT). They had already released their first album *An Evening With*, by the time Polly joined. Switching to RCA for a further two albums *Dando Shaft* & *Lantaloon*, they went on to achieve some measure of success. When they split in 1973 Polly went off to America to sing with Blue Aquarius a soul come jazz band, eventually ending up in a no hope covers band. She returned to the UK making the superb single *The Year of the Child* on Horizon Records with the Coventry Cathedral Choir (commemorating the International Year of the Child 1979). This was to be her last musical endeavour for some seven years, swapping singing for market gardening, even writing three books on the subject!

She made a return to the business in 86 to work with former **Dando Shaft** vocalist (and former partner) Kevin Dempsey on *The Cry of Love*, and collaborations with folk legend and Albion Band supremo Ashley Hutchings (particularly memorable was the epic *By Gloucester Docks I Sat Down and Wept* album). She released *No Going Back* her first solo album in 1989, produced by Ashley Hutchings. Teaming up in 1991 with the Breton musical genius Alan Stivell on his *the Mists of Avalon* album. The Polly Bolton band was formed soon after with John Shepherd (Keyboards) and Steve Dunachie (Fiddle) producing albums *Songs From a Cold Open Field* in 1991 and The Loveliest of Trees in 1996. Her musical collaborations continue as does her Singing workshops at Oak Barn in Shropshire. Such is the unique talent of this superb vocalist.

CAPEL BOND

Born in Gloucester in 1730 he moved to Coventry at 19, and was hugely influential in Coventry music in the 18th Century. Became organist at Holy Trinity and organized concerts and created a music Society. His only surviving music is *Six Concertos in Seven parts* and *Six Anthems in Score*.

THE BROKEN DOLLS

Leamington/Coventry sextet who through Radio One's Unsigned Band Contest running on *The Jo Whiley Show* have picked up "the next local band to sign" baton. Indeed they made it into second place (with The Love Gods winning it). Saying that most of the feedback on the Radio One site was about this band. By the time this book comes out I hope that a major has picked them up. Well too late, before the book was finished they had signed to DJ Fat Boy Slim's label *Southern Fried Records* for a 5-album deal and played Glastonbury! Listen out for *Rock 'n' Roll* It's an infectious slice of nouveau rock that pumps along relentlessly. It's absolutely blooming marvellous, all you have heard about them is true, yes, they really are that good. Expect an album early 2005.

THE EDGAR BROUGHTON BAND

Originally from Warwick, formed out of the local band Tony and The Talons. Based in London from 1968. The band comprised of brothers Edgar (guitar, vocals) and Steve (drums) Broughton and bassist Arthur Grant. Signing to Blackhill Enterprises (who also handled the Floyd) and EMI's 'progressive' label Harvest. The trio's brand of real raucous rebellious rock hit the spot to the disenchanted types of the late sixties. They delighted in rubbing the establishment up the wrong way. Often playing free, but always playing with total commitment whatever the cause. They were once banned from playing an open-air concert In Warwick, so as a protest they played from the back of a moving lorry down Warwick's (SEE WARWICK) main High street!

After a slow start with their first and one of their best albums *Wasa Wasa* They went on to clock up their first hit single in April of 1970 with the confrontational *Out Demons Out* (borrowed from the radical American band The Fugs) reaching 39 in the charts. Likewise their classic album *Sing Brother Sing* made it to number 18. Their biggest (and last hit) single *Apache Dropout (on Harvest Records)* adapted the guitar hook from the Shadows classic Apache and the rest from another radical US band Captain Beefheart. It rose to number 49, went out the charts for a month and re-entered at 35. It went out of the chart once again and re-entered at 35, finally leaving the charts one more time to re-enter at 33! The band still plays together and it now includes Edgar's son Luke on synthesiser. The good news is that age has not mellowed them at all.

CLASSICAL

By far Coventry's finest composer in the classical school is **Dr. Arthur Wills OBE**. He was born in Coventry in 1926. He became director of Music at Ely Cathedral in 1958 till 1990. Not just a composer, he is an accomplished organist to boot. His music has taken him all over the world, to Australia, Europe, Hong Kong and America. One of his finest works is an opera based on **George Orwell's** *1984*. Such is his greatness there is The *Arthur Wills Ely Music Shop* (obviously in Ely) that is the only shop in history devoted to a living composer. Opera singer **Omar Ebrahim** began singing as a choirboy at Coventry Cathedral (SEE COVENTRY CATHEDRAL). The baritone has sung with *The Ensemble Modern* performing Frank Zappa songs and countless other modern operas. He also teachers music vocal studies at Trinity College. Conductor **Simon Over** was born in Kersley and was Director of Music at *St. Margaret's* at *Westmister Abbey*. He now leads the Southbank Sinfonia. as well as the Parliament Choir (consisting of MP's and Peers). Concert pianist **Denis Matthews** was born in Coventry in 1919, as part of The Liverpool Philharmonic Orchestra he has performed works by Beethoven, Mozart and John Field. He was the subject of a celebrated painting by Juliet Pannett in the 1950's, in now hangs in *The National Portrait Gallery*.

Dr. A WILLS

Three modern local composers are **Brian Ferneyhough** from Coventry (born1943*)* **Robin Holloway** from Leamington (born1943*)* and **Andrew March** from Nuneaton (born 1973) Brian studies at the Birmingham School of Music and later in Amsterdam. He has won prizes for his compositions *Sonatas for String Quartet*, *Encircle* and *Missa Brevis*. He has been Professor of Music at the University of California, San Diego since 1987. He has won many awards in his career, his compositions, very much in the 'modern' style of the genre include *Time and Motion Study No. 1*, *Time and Motion Study No. 2 and Unity Capsule*. **Robin Holloway** was at St. Paul's Cathedral it was here that he began composing. He later went onto King's college Cambridge. He became full lecturer of the Cambridge Music Faulty in 1980. His compositions include *Concerto No. 2 for Orchestra* and *Sea-Surface Full of Clouds (cantata), Op. 28*. **Andrew March** wrote his first piece in 1991, he accepted a place in *The Royal College of Music* in 1992. He received a total of five prizes for compositions including the John Longmire Prize. His full-scale compositions have included *Easdale* and *Nymphéas*.

ROBIN HOLLOWAY

The University of Warwick Symphony Orchestra is very much a come along and play affair. No person is disadvantaged or turned away because of their choice of degree discipline or ability. They recently performed at a 50 million pound wedding in India of the sons of India's richest man Subrata Roy. The 100-piece orchestra all flew out to perform to over 30,000 guests including The Indian Prime minister and Boris Becker. **The City of Coventry Youth Orchestra** with 75 members is a full symphony orchestra. Made up of people in full time education.

GODIVAROCKS@YAHOO.CO.UK

Major choirs in the area are **The City of Coventry Male Voice Choir**, and **The Royal Leamington Spar Bach Choir**. **The City of Coventry Male Voice Choir** began 50 years ago as an amalgamation of singers from Coombe Social Club and miners from Binley Colliery. They have raised a lot of cash over the years for charities like Myton Hospice and one close to my heart Parkinsons Disease (something my step-son Kev battles with). Good for them. **The Royal Leamington Spar Bach Choir** is a mixed choir, a lively group of singers whose key word is 'entertainment'! Toronto Composer **Phiip McConnell** was from Coventry. He is the artistic *Director of The Toronto Sinfornietta* and Musical Director of *The Toronto District Youth Orchestra*.

Gloucestershire's **Herbert Norman Howells** wrote Sequence *for St Michael; Coventry Antiphon; Stabat Mater & The Coventry Mass (SEE COVENTRY CATHEDRAL)*. **John Steane**, who writes for *Gramophone, Musical Times* and *Opera News*. Lives in Coventry. **Music on the Web (UK)** is a major classical website based in Coventry, it has been reviewing some 200 albums and concerts per month for the last five years. They are now part of *Classic Link*. Find them at www.musicweb.uk.net. Then we have **M.B Sunderland** in Earlsdon who specialise in sheet music. The Town of Leamington hosts a classical music festival at the Pump Rooms (SEE LEAMINGTON). **Steven Mead** one of the worlds finest euphonium players lives in the village of Fenny Drayton near Nuneaton. Finally **Dktr** is a Coventry based experimental musician in the Electro-classical mode.

CLUB BANDS

While this book majors of course on the more mainstream popular acts, it would be remiss of me to ignore some of the hardest workers in the business. Namely club acts; tirelessly entertaining the CIU bingo hordes, in their chapels of ale and the sacred cheese and onion batches. Not all club acts are of the Vic Reeves club singer variety, although they still very much exist, (I still can't listen to Vanity Fairs "Hitching A Ride" without thinking of the Stoke-ex WorkingMan's Club.) The following acts however have more polish than a preverbal Cherry Blossom factory.

While many of these acts are transient in nature, a few names have remained pretty constant. Undisputed all round nice guy and king of the "Country and Irish" sound in the area is **Bob Brolly** MBE. From Ireland to Coventry, from **Calvery** to solo projects, from Mercia Sound to local BBC his charm and genuine Irish warmth has endeared itself to legions of the Sanatogen brigade. His MBE is testament to his convivial radio manner and tireless fundraising (over half a million pounds at the last count). The previously mentioned **Calvary**, (later **Bob Brolly's Calvery**) were for the most part an M&B promotion covers-band. Included in it's ranks trumpet maestro John Gissane, son of the now sadly departed Pat Gissane of another quality club act in the best Irish showband style **The Pat Gissane Showband** (who always wore purple suits for some reason).

BOB BROLLY MBE

No list of Coventry club outfits however would be complete without **Smakee**. Barry Walker and his band have entertained for what seems like an eternity, from the early days as **Eyes of Blue**, they have branched out to eclipse the cabaret circuit, finally settling (for now anyway) to be part of the tribute-band movement, choosing ABBA as their role models. Previous members have included Paul Hooper (SEE INDIAN SUMMER, SEE ROGER LOMAS, SEE THE FORTUNES) and Rick Medlock (SEE I).

Here is a perfect demonstration of the "transient in nature" comment above the following is the band list of one Mick Sturdy a club musician from 1959 to 2001, it reads like a *CIU* who's who. **The Barry James Band, The Sapphires, The Lloyd Group, The Vincent Brothers, The Doug Martin 4, Volume Three, The Dave Robinson 5, Sounds Complete** and **Capitol**.

SMAKEE

GODIVAROCKS@YAHOO.CO.UK

THE COLOURFIELD

After the demise of the successful, Fun Boy Three (SEE FUN BOY THREE). Former **Specials** front man (SEE THE SPECIALS) Terry Hall set about forming yet another trio in the shape of the Colourfield. With Terry on vocals and guitar, Karl Shale (from the bands **Solid Action** and **Aching Tongue**) on Bass and Toby Lyons on Guitar/organ formerly of **The Swinging Cats** (SEE THE SWINGING CATS). The boys were set to go with their first release *The Colourfield* in the early part of 84, reaching a 43. Terry's voice was still unmistakable, but there was a whole new maturity to the **Colourfields** sound. The summer saw their second single released entitled *Take* with Echo and the Bunnymens Pete De Freitas on drums. A wonderful slice of sarcastic bitterness, something Terry Hall has always been good at. Sadly it floundered at 70 in the charts.

1985 was a better year with the release of *Thinking of You* this was to be their most successful single clocking in at number 12. A great song with a class video to boot, featuring Katrina Phillips on vocals, it worked at all levels. As did the their first album 'Virgins and Philistines' (12). Some may say it was scrappy and lacked direction, but didn't the **Colourfield** always delight into turning that into an asset? They headlined *Covaid* (SEE FESTIVALS) in October and UK and US tours followed, by 1968 they were to add drummer Gary Dwyer and Lose Karl Shale (Karl was to join **Vagabond Joy**). Their second album *Deception* (95) was to be virtually 'Terry Hall and his backing band Colourfield'. The single *Castles in the Air* (51) their last 'hit' had been lifted from it, February 86 saw them play at Warwick Arts Centre. After their last singles *Running Away* and *She* (a cover of a Monkees song) failed to chart, the end was on the cards, and Halls itchy feet was to take him to pastures new (SEE TERRY HALL).

COVENTRY BY NAME

This section looks at songs with a Coventry connection, be it obvious or tenuous. Well as far as obvious goes, *The Coventry Carol* has to be the team leader. Written in the 15th century, it comes from the play *The Pageant of The Shearmen and Tailors* as part of the 'Coventry Cycle' Mystery Plays (and does the lesser know carol *As I Rode This Endless Night-The Coventry Shepherds Carol*). Traditionally performed on the Cathedral steps by (Coventry's first) locals musicians known as 'waits' (usually a quartet led by a trumpeter). Covering the Nativity story and the Annunciation to the Massacre of the Innocents. Just in case you can't place this traditional Christmas Carol here's the first line: *Lullay, Thou little tiny Child, By, by, lully, lullay.Lullay,* There is no known record of the songs' composer but the lyrics are credited to Robert Croo. Although there is evidence that these are a second set of lyrics. Sadly most of the transcripts of the *Coventry Cycle Pageant were* destroyed and Thomas Sharp in his Dissertation on the Pageants at Coventry produced the only surviving record in 1825. It is believed that the plays were performed to Richard III in 1484 and Henry VII in 1584.

The song has been performed by many great and diverse artists over the years including: Joan Baez, Charlie Byrd, Charlotte Church, John Denver, Morgan Fisher (ex Mott The Hoople), Kenny Loggins, Phil Mazanera (ex Roxy Music),Liberace, Loreena McKennitt, Bett Midler, Alison Moyet, Elaine Paige,Sir Harry Secombe, John Taylor (Duran Duran), Kate Winslet a Spanish version entitled *Coventry Espangnol* by Stover & Wells and our own The St Michael's Singers (SEE COVENTRY CATHEDRAL).

The *Coventry Carol* is of course a song about well; killing babies basically, and I'm afraid Coventry profile don't get any better. Take the song *Coventry* from the 'Oi' band **The Business**. Based on events that occurred when the band was stopped by the police on Walsgrave Road on their way to a gig at The Lanch (SEE VENUES). It begins, "*A switch blade flashes on a Coventry night, a kids lying there, he didn't want to* fight He said I didn't do it and threw up his hand, everyone knows where the blame it should land. Always on the outside of whatever side there was, The lights go down in Coventry, the lights go down in Coventry". A good song no doubt (with loads of lyrics borrowed from Bob Dylan's Desire album), shame it portrays the city in such a negative light (**Headcase** and **The Hybrid Kids** also covered it). Our shoddy reputation continues thanks to Munich art band **Chicks on Speed.** They too have a song called *Coventry*, and it goes, *"Russell Lives in Cov that's a really brutal place, It's in the middle of England, right into your face"!* Well thanks for that, I'm sure that the Coventry tourist Office will be in touch.

Never mind Ah, it gets better **The Men They Couldn't Hang** were *Going Back to Coventry* and even Queen's *Don't Stop Me Now* mentioned Lady Godiva (more about her later). So it can't be all-bad. Then we are reminded of The Specials darker moments in the likes of *Concrete Jungle* and *Ghost Town*, bleak to say the least. Well at least Former Van der Graaf Generator front man Peter Hammill's *Planet Coventry* was a metaphorical place inhabited by those who have suffered the fate of being 'sent to Coventry'. **Greg Davis** was 'sent to Coventry' as a child hence his avant garde electro offering also called *Coventry*. Then there's the Dixieland tune *Coventry Rag*. Midlands trad' folkies **The Boatmen** recorded the track *Coventry Lass*. Charlie Harper of the UK Subs mentions Cov in his solo single *Barmy London Army*. A blatant **2 Tone** bandwagon jumper (SEE 2 TONE) has to be *Send Me to Coventry*, by **The Mob** there were 9 of them, including **Rob Jackson** (SEE ROB JACKSON). It's a song that really has no right to be so catchy. With lyrics such as, *"I can see no naked lady, riding on her horse now"*, and, *"C-O-V-E-N try our new horizon"*, a blatant plug for **Horizon studios** (SEE STUDIOS) probably not it was recorded at **Woodbine Studios**! The Mob was the brainchild of **Arun Bhandari**. Who not long before the Two Tone explosion was fronting a rock band called **Stiletto** doing a blooming good Phil Lynott impersonation at the **Dog and Trumpet** (SEE VENUES). This is certainly my favourite Coventry song of the time, a kitsch classic. Another catchy little cash-in (although I doubt that literally) was *Sent to Coventry* by the **Clean Looking Boys**, I have the single, but can't remember anything else about the band. Drums and Bass dance act Tango have also recorded a track entitled *Sent To Coventry*. In 1980 Cherry Red released the Compilation LP *Sent From Coventry*, showcasing local talent from the city, including **The End, The Mix, Machine, Protégé** and **The Clique**. **Archie Leyton** Is probably responsible for writing the more songs about Cov than anyone else. They include *I Was Born In Coventry, In The Heart of Dear Old England* and a Gang Show favourite *Come to Coventry*. He has also written *The Brandon Bees Song* and a Sky Blue Song. Colin Armstrong who was a member of folk band **Music Box** (SEE ROB ARMSTRONG), recorded a CD about the rebirth of Coventry in *New City Songs*.

King (SEE KING) always proud to be from Coventry, sang in *Fish*, *"I've been looking for the heart of town but the ring roads lead me round and round"*, sound familiar? Then go on to put it all in perspective and sing, *"Celtic brothers in the stream, hooked and sent to Coventry"*. (Lyrics courtesy of P.King and King Songs/EMI Songs). **Squad** (SEE SQUAD) were hanging around Radford in the 1979 single *Millionaire*, and **Lieutenant Pigeon** (SEE LIEUTENANT PIGEON) put the Scott Joplin-like *Gosford Street Rag* on the 'B'-side of their Rockabilly Hotpot 45. **Reg Dixon** (SEE REG DIXON)) wrote and sang a song entitled *Send Me To Coventry (My HomeTown)*. Dave Peppers local band **Blitz Kreig Zone** was an obvious hint to Coventry. There's a local band called **Jordan Well**. Even actor **Dirk Bogarde** got in on the act, releasing a spoken word single entitled *Dirk Bogarde Reads Coventry Verse*. This 1980 offering included the spoken works, *St Michael's Cathedral* and *A Coventrian in the Eighties*, rousing stuff! South African jazz ensemble **Cape-Jazz** often played a track called *Coventry Road*. Then we have all the Football songs, but that's another story (SEE COVENTRY CITY FC).

Cov lad Declan Bennett (SEE DECLAN BENNETT) has a band called **Sumladfromcov.** There's no mistaking where local hiphop band **C.O.V.** (or **The City of Villainz**) come from. Then there's a couple of bands called **Coventry** too, one of them comes from Seattle and plays punk folk, the other a now long defunct rock band that included Quiet Riot drummer Frankie Banali in it's ranks. They came from Ft Lauderdale in Florida, and were originally called **Coventry Carol**. Some more US bands with Coventry in their name are **Coventry Road** a jazz, rock, blues and reggae band from New York. Louisiana had a folk group called **The Coventry Singers**. There's also a guy who calls himself **Coventry Jones**. He's based in

Milwaukee, but originally came from England. My favourite however has to be the Milwaukee Death Metal band called **The Coventry Sacrifice**. Their name is based on the unconfirmed report that Winston Churchill knew about the pending blitz on Coventry during WWII, but chose to sacrifice the City rather than reveal that the German codes had been cracked. They seem to be pretty tied-up in the 'legend' as their first EP was entitled *Moonlight Sonata,* the German codename for the raid. (Vincent Leeds is another US act who tell a similar tale in their Track *Coventry Cross).* Last in the Cov' section but by no means the least are **The Coventry Automatics**, an early epithet for the **Specials** (SEE THE SPECIALS).

What about Coventry's most famous daughter Godiva! Well I can't talk about Godiva without mentioning our own Coventry Ambassador the lovely Pru Poretta, a lady that has done more to promote Coventry than many who think they have! Right enough said, onto Godiva. The song that springs to everyone's minds (yeah I can hear you singing it now) is *Lady Godiva* by **Peter And Gordon.** This was to be the duos last UK hit, peaking (no pun intended it's the wrong spelling anyway) at number 16 in September 1966. The song updated the story, turning the 'Lady' Godiva into a cheap stripper. Rumour has it that the Lord Mayor of Coventry at the time was so incensed by it that he had the song banned in the area! The duo also released an album entitled *Lady Godiva* . **Herb Albert** did an instrumental version, so he got away with it. Another less than favourable song about Cov's first lady is the **Velvet Underground's** dark and harrowing *Lady Godiva's Operation,* Yuk, the **Fatima Mansions** did a cover of this too. Continuing with the negatives, we also have the *Engineers drinking song,* being very rude about our Godiva; think Rugby song and you're about there. Then you have *Lady Godiva and Me* by the slightly odd 3 piece from Los Angeles **Grant Lee Buffalo** and *Henry and Godiva at the bar* by **Deadstar.** Would be Spinal Tap rockers **Lizzy Borden** also did a song called *Godiva.*

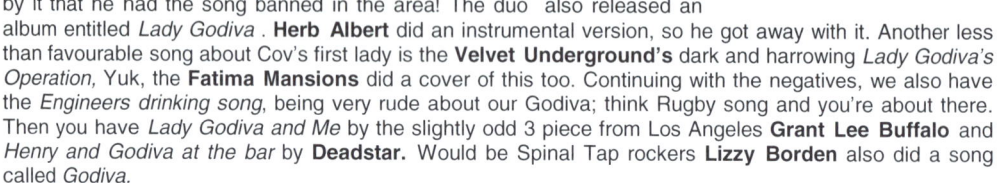

Much nicer songs about the naked one are *Lady Godiva* by **Boney M** (another biographical song from the makers of, Ma Baker & Rasputin). The elegant *Lady Godiva's room by* **Simply Red***, Dr Hook's Hey Lady Godiva.* **Mother love bone** had an instrumental entitled *Lady Godiva's Blues.* Cov's **Ludicrous Lollipops** did a song called *Godiva* on the B-side of their *A Part* single. Then there was the Jazzy *Lady Godiva* performed by **Young Holt Unlimited. Every Brilliant Eye** had the song *Herr Godiva* on their *Died Pretty* Album. *Godiva* was also a song from punk bassman Pete Conway better known as **Flour.** Then we have local part-time folk rock outfit **Godivaride** (who are half of the Cov based **Bait**) (SEE BAIT). In 1907 Vitezslav Novak wrote a classical piece entitled *The Lady Godiva Overture.* She also gets a mention in *My Girl* by **Aerosmith,** and in the theme tune from the US TV show *Maude. Waiting for Godiva* was the name of an album by **Sauce.** Then there is a Swiss heavy metal band called **Godiva** and a Celtic/folk punk group from Germany called **Lady Godiva.** Phew! What a popular gal! Finally Peeping Tom, well **Toots & The Maytals, Mike Patton,Tommy Smith, Artie White, Ronnie Singh** and **Placebo** all had songs entitled *Peeping Tom.* Coventry beat-masters **The Peeps** (SEE THE PEEPS) obviously took their name from the world's most famous voyeur. Sorry If I've missed any.

COVENTRY CATHEDRAL

Apart from being a world site for peace and reconciliation, Coventry Cathedral is a centrepiece of our City, for Christians and non-Christians alike, it is the heart of Coventry. After September 11th, it was the first place, I and many other people felt compelled to go. Many Coventrians have not set foot in the place for years, but it's still theirs and ours. The new Cathedral was consecrated in 1962. The great **Benjamin Britten** had written his famous *War Requiem* for the pageant. (It was performed there again in November 2000, to mark the 60th anniversary of the bombing of the city). Perhaps overshadowed a little by Britten, was **Sir Arthur Bliss** who had also written for the consecration with his 50 minute long *The Beatitudes.* **Brian Easdale** also wrote for the occasion, producing *Missa Coventrensis* for choir and congregation and the mighty Cathedral organ. Not forgetting **Michael Tippett's** *King Priam,* effectively a mini opera of Homer's Iliad. (SEE CLASSICAL). More up to date was **Derek Nisbit** a regular writer for the Belgrade Theatre (SEE VENUES) with the likes of *Mysteries 2003* performed in the Old Cathedral's ruins. He was also commissioned to write for the Cathedral for the Coventry Millennium. Celebrations as a prelude to the celebrated tightrope walk by

Ramon Kelvink. **Dame Kiri Te Kanawa**, has performed at the Cathedral, releasing a live album and video of the event, entitled *Carols from Coventry Cathedral*. German Electro duo **Tangerine Dream** also played at the Cathedral in 1975. Essentially an experimental band but chose to overdub large parts of their Coventry concert for the 'Live' album *Ricochet*. An odd thing for a so-called spontaneous art band to do. **King** (SEE KING) with Cheggers, made a Saturday Superstore appearance in the ruins. **Duke Ellington** has also played at The Cathedral as part of his *Sacred Concert tour* in 1966 (SEE JAZZ).

In 1995 Virgin boss *Richard Branson* presented the Cathedral with the sculpture entitled *Reconciliation*, depicting a young man and woman kneeling in embrace, (it can be found in The Ruins of the Old Cathedral). Coventry Cathedral in turn presented a similar statue to Berlin. While Hiroshima and Belfast also have replicas of this very pertinent work. It's worth mentioning here that despite the fact St Michael's was destroyed by the Luftwaffe in 1940, killing 568 people, after the war Coventry accepted Germany's offer of help to rebuild the Cathedral, rather than retribution. I had an American friend over a few years back, and he was absolutely knocked-out by this act of Humanity, one more reason why Coventry people are special.

KING AT THE CATHEDRAL RUINS

Leamington's **Polly Bolton** (SEE POLLY BOLTON), released a single (*The Year Of the Child*) with the Cathedral choir. The B-side featured **The Coventry Cathedral Choristers** singing Do *You Hear What I Hear*. Then we have **The St. Michael's Singers**. A mixed choir of 90 voices, they were formed in 1963.They have appeared with the **Halle Orchestra**, and took part in commemorations of the fiftieth anniversary of the bombing of Dresden, performing Mozart's Requiem conducted by the late **Yehudi Menuhin** in Coventry Cathedral. They have even sung with American Catholic singer **John Michael Talbot** on his Signatures Album. The man at the helm is conductor **Paul Leddington Wright**. Their recordings include, *Royal Coventry, Coventry Christmas* (no prizes for guessing at least one song on there) and *Coventry Praise*. David Foster Lepine, David Poulter, Christopher Bowers-Broadbent, Graham Barber, David M Patrick and Wayne Marshall have all released albums of music played on the mighty Cathedral organ. The organ was built by the world famous Durham organ makers *Harrison and Harrison* in 1962, many believer it to be the greatest organ made in the 20th century. It has four manuals and 73 stops. Then we have **the Beatles** connection (SEE THE BEATLES), with a visit of John and Yoko planting acorns in the Cathedral grounds, also Paul's fictional character *Percy Thrillington* supposedly born in the Cathedral. The Cathedral also releases Christian music under it's own Record Label *Coventry Music*.

COVENTRY CITY FC

In 1987 after some 104 years The Sky Blues did the unthinkable, and won the most coveted prize in English domestic football, the FA Cup of course. Beating Spurs 3-2 in one of the best finals ever, complete with Houchen's flying header. What a time that was, houses painted sky blue, not a Man U or Liverpool top in sight. For those few months Cov City were the glamour side we always wished they were. Of course every team in the final had to have a single to commemorate the occasion. With luck would have it Coventry City's 1987 FA Cup Final Song was not of the laughable cringe-worthy abominations we normally hear. Ok so it wasn't The Beatles, but *Go For It* did the job. It was written by Steve and Heather Taylor from Holbrooks and recorded in their living room. It outsold copies of the Madonna *Who's That girl* by ten to one in Coventry record shops. The song was sung on Wogan and Blue Peter and got to 61 in the charts. Before *Go For It*, the most famous Sky blue song was, *Let's All Sing Together (the Sky Blue Song)*. Jimmy Hill and City Director at the time John Camkin wrote the unforgettable words to the Sky Blue song in the autumn of 1962,using the *Eton Boating song* as its tune. In December of that year, Hill staged a press conference at the Coventry Theatre to launch the song and was assisted by comic legends Sid James and Frankie Howerd and was sung at the home game against Colchester the following Saturday. Hill, then persuaded Ted Heath and his Orchestra to record a version of the song. This became an anthem for City supporters and was played to announce the arrival of the City team on the pitch both before and at half time up until 2002. It is still played on occasions before matches played at Highfield Road.

Then we have the 15 Sky Blue Classics CD. OK, lets be honest no matter how much of a City fan you are, this CD is not good, I haven't met a city fan yet who likes it. Crass embarrassing, waste of time, yeah that about sums it up. Having said that it is Cov and it is music (sort of), so it has to be looked at (I will keep it short). It opens with *Go For It*, then takes a nose dive big time. There's **Alan Randall** Nuneatons finest George Formby impersonator,(SEE NUNEATON) singing *The Coventry City Song*, It doesn't really work, neither does **Dave Willetts** (SEE DAVE WILLETTS) singing *Go For It* and *Let's All Sing Together (the Sky Blue Song)*. Dave has a powerful refined classical voice. It's a disgrace that one of the City's great singers should have been reduced to singing this nonsense. *Sky Blue Army* and *Stand Up For The Sky Blues* are on there too plus the usual suspects, I think that covers it, let's move on.

In August 2001, B.A. Roberston who had football related chart hits with *Knocked It Off* and *We Have A Dream* With the Scottish World Cup Squad, wrote a song for his son and for Coventry City supporters called "It's For Life". Unfortunately for the Scot, Coventry Supporters took an instant dislike to it and the playing of the song was quickly axed. Probably the most awful of all the City songs is a thing called *Coventry Boy* by Motorpsycho from their 1998 double album entitled *Trust Us*. How they managed to get a deal heaven knows. Stranger than that, the band is from Norway! One very obscure footie' related band was **The Nardiellos,** named in honour of City's Welsh player of the 70's Don Nardiello, apparently this Cov/ Leamington covers band lasted one gig. Former City player Dion Dublin is the subject of three non-football facts, they are 1. Yes he is an accomplished Sax player, 2. No he is NOT the son of the Showaddywaddy drummer Romeo Challenger (Romeo does however have a sporting son Ben who is an Olympic athlete) and 3. I couldn't possibly say in a family book like this. Ex-City & current Swedish/Celtic goalkeeper Magnus Hedman is married to Swedish pop star Magdelena Graaf. Former City favourite Mickey Quinn who is now an 'expert' for *TalkSport Radio* appeared on their 4-4-2 England Euro 2004 single *Come on England* (to the tune of Come On Eileen), what next Ernie Hunt singing *When I'm Cleaning Windows?*

Many of the songs and chants sung by Coventry City supporters are adaptations of chart hits of the day with the best being a rendition of the Beatles Classic *Hey Jude (Sky Blues)*. One song I always will remember being sung at Highfield Road, was Steams (later Covered by Bananarama), *Na Na Hey Hey Kiss Him Goodbye*. The City fans used to sing "Na na na na, na na na na hey hey Roy Barry", I will always remember thinking to my shame, why are they singing Rolf Harris! Doh! As for musical city fans, well the **King** (SEE KING) boys were all fans even doing a pre-match concert at Harry Roberts Testimonial. As for **The Specials** (SEE THE SPECIALS) apart from Lynval Golding who's a big city fan, never really had much to do with football (Terry Hall is a Man U fan) although they used to get the crowd to chant C.C.F.C. during *The Liquidator*. Steve Johnson of Lieutenant Pigeon (SEE LIEUTENANT PIGEON) appeared on a promo photo in the green and black striped away top, so I guess he's a fan. Vince Hill is a fan. Pete Waterman supports Cov' and Walsall. Former Westlifer Brian McFadden is a Cov City fan. Kev Monks chairman of The successful *Coventry City Ladies Football* team, had approached Brian's wife Kerry (and former Atomic Kitten) to join them as a player. That now looks unlikely since she became Queen of the Jungle in the TV show *I'm a Celebrity Get Me out of Here!*

DAVID CONWAY

Coventry born harmonica player(March 16th 1957). In 1961 he became a part of the famous harmonica comedy troop **The Monarchs** (then **The 3 Monarchs**) who had a 7-week run at The Coventry Theatre supporting The Springfield's. On leaving in 1968 he teamed up with his wife Pauline and they began touring together as **Dave & Pauline "Music worth Watching"** something they have continued for over 29 years. David has recently written a book about The Coventry Theatre.

PAGE 20   GODIVAROCKS@YAHOO.CO.UK   PAGE 20

DANDO SHAFT

A unique progressive folk band, that refused to use 'electric' instruments. The five piece from Coventry consisted of Kevin Dempsey (acoustic guitar/vocals). Martin Jenkins (vocals, mandolin/fiddle/ guitar), Ted Kay (tabla/ percussion), Roger Bullen (bass), and Dave Cooper (guitar/vocals). Dempsey had previously been with blues band **The Bo'Weevils** (SEE TIM JAMES) They released their first album *An Evening With Dando Shaft* on Youngblood records in 1970 (on Decca in the U.S.), plus their first single *Cold Wind*. The album was well received, Overseen by producer Miki Dallon (who also produced **The Sorrows** and **Don Fardon** (SEE THE SORROWS, SEE DON FARDON). so much so that they then signed for RCA's Neon label (alongside Cov outfit **Indian Summer** (SEE INDIAN SUMMER).

Their second effort *Dando Shaft* in 1971 was to showcase even more of the bands incredible musicianship, and the inclusion of Polly Bolton on vocals (SEE POLLY BOLTON) gave their music an extra dimension. If ever an unplugged folk band could be 'heavy', then **Dando Shaft** were it. They used Bulgarian influences (a long time before Kate Bush) and Adopted 'jazz-like' time signatures. Their songs appeared simple yet at the same time complex. They released their third album *Lantaloon* on RCA in 1972 (and their second single *Sun Clog Dance*). Although it could not match the second classic album, it still cut the mustard, but due to the lack of commercial success RCA dropped the band from its label. Bolton and Dempsey (who were an item at the time) went of to America. While Jenkins joined **Hedgehog Pie** and Kay went to folk rock outfit **Wave**. That's not where the story ends though, in 1977 the band reformed for one more album *Kingdom* on Rubber Records. From that Jenkins and Dempsey joined Dave Swarbrick (SEE DAVE SWARBRICK) in **Whippersnapper** Never giving up on a good thing they reformed again for a week in 1989! Currently Dempsey has toured with Mary Black and is working on his own album *Freehand* in collaboration with Joe Broughton.

CAROL DECKER

Often assumed to be of Nuneaton or Shrewsbury birth, Carol was actually born in Liverpool Sept. 10, 1957. She moved to Nuneaton at an early age. Spending a lot of time in Coventry. Her Mother and brother still live in Nuneaton. She made her name as the fiery lead singer of the soft rock act T'Pau (named after a female Vulcan in the original Star Trek series). The bands first hit *Heart and Soul* got to number 4 in 1987. They dominated the charts in autumn 1987, with *China in Your Hands* staying at number One for five weeks and their Album *Bridge of Spies* also attaining the number one position. The band were catapulted to the position of rock stadium giants almost over night. Decker's powerful voice and good looks wooed audiences whenever they played.

More hits followed, including *Valentine* (9) and *I Will Be With You* (14) and *Whenever You Need Me* (16). Their second album *Rage* also netted a number 4 slot in 1988. By the early nineties however the cracks began to show and T'Pau's reign came to an end (although the name would be briefly resurrected again by Carol in 1997). Carol continues to perform and write as a solo artist, also appearing in the play *Mum's The Word* and the film *Nine Gay Guys*. She came back to her roots in March 2001 when she played Jumpin Jaks at Coventry's SkyDome.

DELIA DERBYSHIRE

Delia Derbyshire was one if not the most important pioneers in electronic music. The name may not be familiar but her music definitely is! Delia was born in Coventry, in 1937. She attended Coventry Grammar and went on to achieve a degree at Cambridge in Mathematics and music. A perfect combination for her chosen career. Originally rejected at Decca records in 1959 because they didn't employ women in their studios. She went on to join the BBC's Radiophonic Workshop. Her most famous creation was the *Theme from Doctor Who*. She didn't actually write the piece that was Ron Grainer's job. Such was her ability though, Grainer was astounded to hear what she had done with his composition, asking her, "Did I really write this?" It of course became one of the most well know themes songs in British history.

Through her career she was to mix with the creative minds of the 60's (Brian Jones, Paul McCartney, George Martin and the great Karlheinz Stockhausen). The 70's (Pink Floyd, John and Yoko). Right up to the new breed of electro artists with her influences on such forward thinking artists as Sonic Boom (SEE SPACEMAN 3) and The Chemical Brothers. Although her influence was huge her body of work in comparison is small. Her two most defining releases are; *An Electric Storm (1969)* under the name **White Noise** (released on Island Records, the worlds first all electronic group) and *BBC Radiophonic Music* (1971). Delia sadly passed away in Northampton 2001 aged 64. Her legacy lives on.

REG DIXON

(Not to be confused with the Blackpool Tower organist Reginald Dixon), was born in Coventry in 1914. Although known mainly as a comic and a pantomime dame, he could also 'sing a bit', as was the way of the entertainer in the 40's. Many believed he was from 'up north', because of his stylised accent, but he was a Coventry Kid through and through. He even wrote a song called *Send me to Coventry (My Home Town)* and never lost touch with his roots.

Famous for his catchphrase, "I'm not well, I'm proper poorly" and his tiny trilby hat. He had great success on radio in 40's and 50's. His theme tune was *Confidentially*, which he wrote himself and in 1949 was a number 2 hit in the sheet music charts of the time, the song was also recorded by the likes of the Beverley Sisters, Max Bygraves, Geraldo his Orchestra and the legendary Danny Kaye! In 1951 when George Formby suffered a heart attack, Reg took over from him in the stage Musical *Zip Goes a Million*. Bringing it to *The Coventry Hippodrome* in September 1951 (SEE VENUES) for a two week run. He was to have more hit parade success with "Ordinary People" a song that featured in the musical. He also featured in the films; *No Smoking* (1955), *Channel Nine* (1955) and *Love In Pawn* (1953). In 1976 he appeared in the TV sitcom *Are You Being served*? (In the episode *No Sale*) No doubt from the recommendation of another well know pantomime Dame, John Inman. Reg retired to his Coleshill farm in the 70's, he died of Kidney failure in 1983.

Send Me to Coventry by Reg Dixon

You can send me to Coventry My Home Town
Send me where the spires One two three
Seem to ring a welcome Just for me.
You can send me to Coventry And I won't frown
For there's a lady there to greet me Named Godiva
Down in my home town.

GODIVAROCKS@YAHOO.CO.UK

DOC MUSTARD

Doc Mustard or (Roland Oliver or 'Ollie') original a bass player from the Cov outfit **The Machine** who featured on the *Sent From Coventry* Compilation album with the song *Character Change* (they included former **Specials** drummer Silverton in their ranks) *(SEE THE SPECIALS)*. 1982 they became **Hot Snax,** and secured a support slot with Bad Manners. A recording deal looked to be on the cards, but as you will see many times in this book, it never happened. Ollie joined the new band **The Ring** and later became **Doc Mustard and the Colbart Kids** and began recording his weird and wonderful brand of quirky peace songs like the single *Nuclear Boogie*. He was a fixture around the scene for many years, with his bizarre glasses and outfits .
He was also a fixture around Coventry City centre busking with his penny whistle (and his dog Paxo), much to the annoyance of the nearby shop workers. He now lives in Penzance under the new name of **Chilli Dog Slim** and still releasing his peace ballads. As a point of interest he's the only Coventry musician who has bothered to donate any of his stuff to Coventry's archives, maybe other bands old and new should do the same. Check out his great website at http://freespace.virgin.net/chilli.dog_slim/

DRAGSTER

Dragster where Kitsch 50's Americana meets trailer park trash-rock head on. Coventry has (I'm glad to say) a large pot of contenders to be the next chart act from the City. These lots are definitely one of them. Subtle they aren't, if a bottle of *'Jack'* could sing it would probably sound something like this band. There new line-up looks like this; mainman Diesel (guitar), Bettie Page look- alike Fi (vocals), Wendy X (bass), Jamie (drums) and Heather Mars (guitar).

Already they have the kind of friends most newish bands could only dream of. They were co-managed for a year by former P.I.L man Jah Wobble (with Simon Mattock), produced by Rat Scabies of the mighty Dammed (who told them they were the best band he had heard in 15 years!). Their debut single *Redneck* was to further increase interest in the band. To the extent that when local lad Martin Atkins (of P.I.L, Killing Joke and **Pigface**) (SEE NUNEATON) heard the song he included it in the **Pigface** set. Topping that he insisted that Fi come over to the States and join them on their US tour. It was a huge success and Fi spent 5 weeks living the Rock 'n' roll lifestyle. The five song CD *Trailer Trash* was released to further extend their popularity, it received rave reviews from *Kerrang* and *The NME*. On June 13th 2004 they re-launched themselves with a new (hilarious and well-designed) website and a new single *Narcotic Zombie*. **Dragster** look set for huge things the only question is how far can too far go?

T.E. DUNVILLE

A long time before Coventry became known for **Pete Waterman, The Specials** or even **Frank Ifield,** there was a very famous singing son. A certain **T.E Dunville** to be exact, Coventry's first (and probably biggest ever) star. He was born Thomas Edward Wallen in Coventry 29th July 1867 at 32 New St, moving to 15 Lower Ford Street then to 13 New Street (now demolished, just to the rear of the Cathedral ruins where *Cov University* now stands) and educated at *Bablake School*. The son of a tailor whose father had plans for his son to follow his chosen occupation. Teddie had other ideas and ran away from home to find fame in London with 2 other boys (calling themselves **The Three Spires**). They got as far as Northampton, he came back to Coventry penniless and hungry. He settled down in a job at *Rudge Whitworth* for a while. Until he was sacked *at 16* when a foreman slipped on a floor Teddie had been oiling up to practice his splits. He then formed a dancing comedy troupe **The Merry Men,** eventually going solo changing his name to **T E Dunville** (TE as in 'tee-hee' and **Dunville** from a Whiskey firm) they also happen to be his real initials.

By 1890 he was a huge music hall star famous for his long lanky haired wig, tight trousers and big boots (Max Wall and Billy Dainty were to 'borrow' his style many years later). Billed as An *'Eccentric Comedian and Contortionist'*, his song *Lively On, Lively Off* became his theme tune, other favourites were *Little Boy-Pair Of skates, Then The Band Played* and *Dinky Doo 22*. He was way ahead of his time in turning news items of the day into comedy. He was earning an amazing £100 a week (that would equate to around £6,000 a week nowadays) an absolute fortune. Such was his mastery that despite having a slightly withered arm he was able to do his act with little attention to it, despite his often-acrobatic antics. He was in great demand from American promoters, he however was booked solid for four years ahead, so breaking The US was never to happen. He published his autobiography in 1912 entitled *The Autobiography of an Eccentric Comedian.* He was also mentioned in PG Wodehouse's short novel *The Swoop*.

His style of humour however became somewhat 'passé' by the turn of the Century and by 1913 he was struggling for work. His last appearance was at *The Grand* in Clapham on March 20th 1924. Two days later he was dead. He had overheard someone declare he was 'past it' and he had slit his throat and thrown himself into the Thames at Caversham Lock near Reading. The simple words *Jesus Wept* adorn his grave.

He made five commercial Edison Cylinder recordings through his career (*Enquire Within, Nine Gallant Highlanders, Scoot, The Volunteer Fireman* and *The 3 Stages of Women*) It's so sad that all recordings of his voice are now believed to be lost for ever. There is talk as I write this book about a lasting tribute to 2Tone in Coventry. Much as I agree with that, I can't help thinking that this man has been forgotten almost completely by his own town (apart from the Telegraph and John Ashby, even by the City Archive and The Museum have no mention of him). How about something for him? Surely this Coventry legend deserves that at least. I aim to try and lift this man's status in Coventry, please get in touch if you want to help, let's get a blue plaque for him or something in The Museum at least. I also intend to write a short book about him entitled **The Star A City Forgot** again let me know if you would like to buy a copy when it's available.

THE D.T.'s

The D.T's from Leamington's and the areas prime RnB band. Hard gigging and hard playing they delighted audiences all over, especially noted for front man's Simon Hicklings amazing blues harp virtuoso. Steve Walwyn and Chess Chaplin were former members of rock band **Chevy** (SEE CHEVY). The **DT's** album releases include *Shakin' and Stirred* and the powerful *Live at the JB's*. They supporting Steve Marriott (Ex-Small Faces, Humble Pie) and he became such a fan that he asked them to be his backing band. So Messrs Steve Walwyn (Guitar), Greg Rhind (Bass), Simon Hickling (Harp, Vocals) and Chaz Chaplin (Drums) Became **Steve Marriott and The DT's.** They toured extensively and released the album. *Sing the Blues Live*. Steve Walwyn left to become part of the legendary Dr.Feelgood, he is now their longest serving guitarist,(he also occasionally front's his own band). When Steve Marriott tragically died by fire in 1991, Chaz Chaplin joined The Razors and Simon Hickling went on to record with the likes of Bo Diddley and Paul Rodgers. Currently he still blows a mean harp and he still fronts **The D.T.'s** on their *Never Ending Tour*.

SIMON HICKLING

PAGE 24 GODIVAROCKS@YAHOO.CO.UK PAGE 24

EUROPEAN SUN

European Sun came out of the remains of Leamington Spa punk band **Flack Off**. Rod Goodwin (bass & Vocals), Arthur Jackson (Guitar) and Rick Collet (drums) were **Flack Off's** original line-up. Rod a kingpin on Leamington music scene had been organising concerts in the area, generally shouting at people to halt the apathy and do something about the lack of gigs. By 1980 livewire vocalist Clare Ellice had joined the band and turned the whole sound and image around. They released the single *Cocktails at Six* on Sofa records, produced by who else but Johnny Rivers at Woodbine (SEE STUDIOS). After many a chaotic concert the band finally split. Clare went off and opened the *Nerve Boutique* in Coventry, later marrying Horace Panter of the Specials, (SEE HORACE PANTER, SEE THE SPECIAL). Rod went on to form **European Sun.**

E. Sun was a more sedate affair compared to the anarchy of **Flack Off**. John Beaufoy and 'Chrissie' along with Rod made up the band. Chrissie always reminded me of her namesake Chrissie Hynde. She too was dark and sultry and had a great rock voice. Plus she was the kind of woman that you didn't mess with. They released a great single *Answer Me*, on Iguana Records in 1983. Iguana was part of the Horizon Studios group (SEE STUDIOS), overseen by producer Dave Lester. At one point **E.Sun** looked like they were on the verge of big success, but when Rod Goodwin their driving force and founder member left the band in 1985. The split was inevitable, when they went supernova however Coventry lost a great little rock band.

EYELESS IN GAZA

What's the best thing to come out of Nuneaton? George Elliot, Larry Grayson, errr-no. In my opinion it's **Eyeless in Gaza**. No question. When Martyn Bates and Peter Becker came together they created something unique.

Martyn had been the vocalist with the mark 1 **Reluctant Stereotypes** (SEE THE RELUCTANT STEREOTYPES). When their quirky jazzy sound began to be replaced with the Coventry Ska sound, a rather unchuffed Martyn left and a rather happy **Paul King** joined (SEE KING). Martyn who had been experimenting with industrial sounds teamed up with the like-minded Peter in 1980. **Eyeless In Gaza** were named after a novel by Aldous Huxley, and were to make many an inroad on the indie charts. Their coming together was a dynamic that would create a range of breathtakingly original music. Always with one foot in the ambient bucket, but never afraid to test the water of other genres. What set them apart was Martyn's unique voice, used as an instrument rather than just a vocal, it melded perfectly with the searing atmospheric keyboards and Becker's pumping bass-lines.

From the first brilliant and very collectable single, *Kodak Ghosts run Amok,* they set out their store in splendid fashion. The classic album *Photographs As Memories* (Cherry Red Records) followed. Surely one of the finest debut albums ever! It contains the changeling song *From A to B,* a tangled mass of pure melancholy. This in my opinion is the finest song EVER committed to vinyl. Closely followed by the spine tingling *Seven Years* and *Speech Rapid Fire.* The pleasure continued on the albums *Caught In Flux* in 1981, the stunning *Pale Hands I loved So well* 1982 and *Drumming The Beating Heart* in 1982. In 1986 they released the album *Back from the Rains,* the following year feeling that Gaza' had run a full course, they disbanded. Becker joined **In Embrace** (who would include local drummer **Joby Palmer**) and Bates went head to head with a solo career. His output was prolific to say the least, but *Letters To A scattered Family and Chamber Music 1* both deserve a mention here.

Bates formed the low-key band **Cry Acetylene Angel** (including ex-**Bron-Area**'s Martin Packwood on Bass). Then onto a rather more serious venture **Hungry i**. With a line-up including John O'Sullivan (guitar & Vocals) and Simon O'Grady (bass & vocals) both from the Cov band **20 Days** . Also in the line-up was Steve Dullaghan (former **Primitives** guitarist) (SEE THE PRIMITIVES) as joint 'mainman' with Bates who took over the vocal duties. They released 2 EP's in 1991, *Falling Orchard* & *Second Step,* and recorded an album at Cabin Studios, (SEE STUDIOS), but it never saw the light of day. In 1992 Bates and Becker collaborated together with poet **Anne Clark**, bringing around a reunion of Gaza' in 1993 with the album *Fabulous Library* (one of the bands more commercial works). More albums have followed, and the dynamic that is Becker & Bates continues to turn out a unique brand of stunning sounds, be it as E.I.G, as solo projects, collaborations or as producers in their own Ambivalent Scale Recordings based in Nuneaton (SEE STUDIOS). Eyeless in Gaza, never hit the mainstream, but that's part of their appeal, their creativity was never caged by record company 'suits'. They have always been a 'secret garden' outfit, often stumbled upon by accident, delighting the listener with something original and unmatched, Nuneaton should be proud of them.

GODIVA ROCKS SOUND BYTE WITH-Martyn Bates, (Reluctant Stereotypes & Eyeless In Gaza) some kinda wonderful: early events / first outings –shooting spiderwebs into the ether. Eyeless in Gaza, & a first ever gig : The Climax … not THE climax at all, no of course - not just a first kiss, but an apt setting and irony. it felt like love, and it WAS love: Eyeless in Gaza, ranting, raving, righteous and religious, rampant and petulant, pleasured and penetrating - fervour, a forever affair. Nuneaton & Coventry & Eyeless never mixed much – too left of centre and wilful for most of the time, but … nevertheless! Right here was where mesmerising, electrifying gigs were had – several at The General Wolfe (a sardonic "have you started yet?" one poor soundguy-sap's bemused beer guzzling question while Eyeless were half thru the set's opening improvisation) / some sheer shining poetry one moon struck night at the Lanch, doing a CND benefit that we set up with the divine and celestial THIS HEAT (enigma Charles Bullen being a fellow Nuneatonian of renown and mystery) – where the bar staff shut up shop and refused to serve any drinks because Eyeless were "too bloody loud" / and then at the The Zodiac with the absolute audacity and monstrous originality, violence and tenderness and sheer nascent strangeness and flair of Nuneaton's Bron Area (the audience comprised God's Toys I seem to remember) / the Queens Head - can't remember a bloody thing about it / also, a series of nights at The Nag's Head in Nuneaton, focussing around the record label that I started in the post-punk euphoria of independence(an impetus which was REAL and pragmatically a genuine route for a brief moment there – innovate! mobilise! Do it yourself! ...all good watchwords STILL).

Prior to all this came the unsung impetus – the motivator –the twenty-second century sci-fi thrash 'n trash of the strung out URGE … this band were IT: intelligent dirty noise, the crazed b-movie to die for, beaming transistor radios at the audience in a two chord garage frenzy of sonic ecstasy and ugly – and yes: they were all beautiful punk style, content & essence: all vapour trails and evacuation, all seeds and stooges with a cheap home-made chemist and mad scientist kits. Magnetic revolving boys throwing shapes in the shadows, they signed to Arista, and promptly found themselves left to die … its MORE than a sad story, this ...it was, and still is, a tragedy for all true believers in the creed of music head****.

Eyeless in Gaza were always a plaintive hymn to paranoia: even when they were trying be 'approachable' and 'cheerful pop' ..and, somewhere, in the twisted shapes we threw, we never invited audiences in, as it were . However, I believe that Coventry and Nuneaton audiences, then as now, only wanted prescribed peer group approved rock musics –and that's hard for new and original stuff. C'mon! Combat apathy, and lethargy, and insularity ! Do It! C'mon all you new bands! Let's see YOUR ideas! DON'T just copy what's popular, & what's "in." C'mon : Energy! Focus! Creativity! Now! Ok! I confess ! For me, all those years ago, Coventry and Nuneaton did indeed provide a (meagre, but nevertheless extant) platform for initial investigation / rush of adrenalin – usually shared with small, curious audiences of like minded creative people – who were instigators – 'caus , to me, THAT'S really what the heart and soul of Coventry & Nuneaton lie. And you know, that's STILL some kinda wonderful…

PAGE 26   **GODIVAROCKS@YAHOO.CO.UK**   **PAGE 26**

DON FARDON

Don Maughn first hit the charts in 1965 as a member of Coventry's premier band at the time **The Sorrows** (SEE THE SORROWS). He left the Sorrows in late1966. Now using the name Fardon, he created **Don Fardon and the Soul Machine**. Although they became a popular stage act they never had the impact to hit the big time. Don split the band and in 1968 recorded the John D. Loudermilk song *Indian Reservation* Fardon remained under the direction of **Sorrows** producer Miki Dallon, on Dallons own YoungBlood record label. It's pumping bass-line and atmospheric brass fills gave the song (ostensibly a protest song) a perfect sense of foreboding, not a million miles from the sound that had been achieved on **The Sorrows** hit *Take a Heart* (SEE THE SORROWS). It failed to chart in the UK, but got to an amazing number 20 in America in September 1968. Using the Scottish backing band **A Touch of Raspberry** he continued to tour the club circuit, performing cover versions, intermingled with his own songs.

In 1970 he was approached to write a song for a TV documentary about George (mines a large one, liver that is) Best, called funny enough *The World of George Best*. The song was *Belfast Boy* and it reached 32 in the UK charts in 1970. Feeling that *Indian Reservation* was a good song, and that Don was now a chart star in his own right, the song was hastily re-issued. It paid off big time when it went to number 3 in the UK charts. He continued to release singles and the occasional album (*Indian Reservation, I'm Alive* and *I've paid My Dues*) without chart success. He moved into the Pub trade managing the Alhambra pub in Coventry (now of course gone) and the Plough Inn at Eathorpe. Of late he has switched over to the country & western side of things, even releasing a Line dancing CD (including among others, *Achy breaky heart* and *Hello Mary Lou goodbye heart*) from the *Line Dance Fever* show. He is currently producing music in South Africa.

FESTIVALS

GODIVA ROCKS SOUND BYTE WITH- Don Fardon, (Sorrows and as a Solo artist). The Sorrows got their break when we did a Battle of the Bands at *Coventry Theatre*. There were local bands there like Tony Martin's Echo Four, The Matadors, the Mighty Avengers and The Sabres, plus us the Sorrows. Tony Hatch was in the audience that night and invited us down to London. We actually ended up with 'Sounds Orchestral' producer John Schroeder. As for Coventry, well I left because I hated the concrete jungle it had become. Currently I'm producing music in South Africa and still involved in management.

Cov' has had a succession of festivasl through the years. Starting in 1966 with *The Technical College Arts Balls*, that included the Move as headliners and The Moody Blues in 1967. Then there were the famous *Lanchester Arts Festivals*, **Indian Summer** (SEE INDIAN SUMMER) played in 1971 along side African rockers Osibisa. In 1972 we had Pink Floyd here, and Chuck Berry (SEE CHUCK BERRY), this was to be the most celebrated of all the Lanch Festival concerts, just for one song alone, My Ding A-Ling. There was Memorial Park concerts where **The Flys** known then as **Midnight Circus** (SEE THE FLYS) played as did the great **Peppermint Kreem** (SEE THE PLAGUE). *The Rainsbrook, Rugby Rag's Blues Festival* in 1969, saw a great line-up that included The Nice, Pink Floyd, Taste and Free! The Belgrade Festivals were always pretty good, I used to look forward to my press pack to see who was lined up that year. Bands who have appeared include, **The DT's** (SEE THE DT's), **King, European Sun, Jimmy Jimmy**, (SEE KING, SEE EUROPEAN SUN, SEE JIMMY JIMMY).

COVA(R) 85
STARRING   FOR EAST AFRICA
COLOURFIELD
WITH
DESTINY — EUROPEAN SUN
INTIMATE OBSESSIONS — JIMMY JIMMY — JUMPIN' BAD
MAJOR 5 — RED ON RED — SHEER PRIDE
SPIDER MURPHY — STILL LIFE — THIS HEAT
TERMINAL TEARS — 20 DAYS — SUPERNATURALS
WITH LOCAL SPORTING AND POLITICAL CELEBRITIES
AT THE
LANCHESTER POLYTECHNIC
STUDENT UNION PRIORY ST COVENTRY CV1 3FJ
SATURDAY OCTOBER 19th 1985
DOORS OPEN 5.30 p.m. TICKETS — £1 FOR
ADMISSION PLUS £4 DONATION
TICKETS AVAILABLE FROM COV. POLY STUDENTS
UNION. COVENTRY EVENING TELEGRAPH OFFICES,
COVENTRY INFORMATION AND MERCIA SOUND.
TELEPHONE ENQUIRIES COV. 618961 and 442607
(12.00 to 2.00 p.m.)
IN CONJUNCTION WITH MERCIA SOUND, BRUM BEAT,
COVENTRY EVENING TELEGRAPH, COV POLY S.U.
AND COVENTRY CABLE TV.
R.O.A.R.

HAZEL & NEIL O'CONNOR AT THE BUTTS

In 1981 when racial tension in Britain was at a high, a Festival against Racism was organised by Jerry Dammers (SEE THE SPECIALS) on June 20th 1981, (Dammers had been primarily motivated after seeing an Asian doctor stabbed to death at his local fish and chip shop in Albany Road). It was to be an all day charity concert held at the Butts Stadium, Allesley Old Road. The line up was **The People, The Bureau, The Reluctant Stereotypes, Hazel O'Connor** and **The Specials**. (SEE THE RELUCTANT STEREOTYPES, SEE HAZEL O"ONNOR). My personal stand out moment was towards the end of Hazel O'Connor's set, she came and sat down at the front of the stage with her legs dangling over the front of it. The opening bars of *Will You* began and the words Spine and shivers spring to mind. A beautiful song, a beautiful moment and the end to a terrific day .It was just one of those magical moments you never forget. **The Specials** and **The Stereotypes** were on top form too, I'm just glad I was there.

In 1985, we were all too well aware of the nightmare that was occurring in East Africa, taking a lead from the 'big boys' of Live Aid. Local soul guru **Ray King** (SEE RAY KING) had initiated the idea got myself and Telegraph scribe Jim Taylor (SEE MEDIA) Dave Howarth the Poly entertainment officer Paul and Tony Smith of **This Heat** (SEE RAY KING) and Greg Paprocki assistant manager of **Terminal Tears** (SEE TERMINAL TEARS) together as the organising committee. **Mercia Sound** and **Coventry Cable** (SEE MEDIA) came on board too, and we had 10 weeks to finalise everything. The weeks leading up to the event had seen the national tabloid papers fill loads of column space about the fact that local page three 'stunner' (sorry I couldn't resist that) Debee Ashby was to turn up as a guest. The papers were busting a gut on hearing that feminist students at the Lanch led by Fiona Pryor were calling Debee degrading to women, and threatening to picket the show. Well it's some19 years on and the truth can now be said, it was ALL a set up to promote the concert. We concocted the whole thing up. God bless Fiona Pryor, the students and Debee for making the 'ultimate' sacrifice for charity, and going along with it all and god bless the tabloids for being so gullible.

Main Pic- From The Sun Above- Covaid Stagepass

The whole concert went down pretty well (for the full line up see the poster previous page), no major upsets (apart from the BBC who were recording a Ted Heath concert over at the Cathedral, and were worried about sound levels). No one was really standout, good or bad. As for the headliners **Colourfield** (SEE COLOURFIELD), well Terry Hall's family were present, his poor Mum Joan had to witness her son being heckled by some of the audience for previous remarks he had made about *Coventry City FC* (he supports the red team from Manchester). Highlight was Echo and The Bunnyman's Ian McCulloch joining the **Colourfield** for a version of the Doors LA Woman. A total of £4,425 was raised by the concert for East Africa. Finally don't forget the *Phoenix festival* (SEE STRATFORD),*the Coventry Jazz festival* (SEE JAZZ) *The Leamington Peace Festival (SEE LEAMINGTON)* and *The Leamington Classical Music Festival* (SEE CLASSICAL MUSIC).

PAGE 28   GODIVAROCKS@YAHOO.CO.UK   PAGE 28

THE FLYS

Whenever I hear the name **The Flys**, the first thing that comes into my head is the Song *Sixteen Down*, a perfect piece of power pop punk if ever there was one. That's the sad thing about this Coventry outfit. They could write some terrifically powerful songs, but failed to make an impact on the charts. They always had the drive and determination to be bigger than they were, they just couldn't seem to cut the mustard when it mattered. Originally called **Midnight Circus** (who had once played at The Memorial Park), they changed their name to The Flys in late 76. They comprised of Neil O'Connor (vocals & guitar), David Freeman (guitar & Vocals), Joe Hughes (bass & Vocals) and Pete King (drums).

They released an EP on their own Lama label in 1977, entitled *A Bunch of Fives* the lead track was *I Can Crash here*. It was the last track however *Love and a Molotov Cocktail*. That (and the fact they were supporting The Buzzcocks) was to help persuade EMI sign them, indeed within a year *Love and a Molotov Cocktail* was out on the EMI records. Although it didn't chart, it did their reputation no harm whatsoever. The singles *Oh Beverly* and *Fun City* followed, as did their debut album *Waikiki Beach Refugees in 1978*. A single also entitled *Waikiki Beach Refugees* was released from the album this was probably to become their best known song. 1979 saw the release of the EP *Four from the square* with the brilliant lead track *Sixteen Down*. The singles *Name Dropping*, *We Are the Lucky Ones* and *What Will Mother Say* were released in 1979/80 along with their second and last album (not counting greatest hits packages) *Own*. Graham Deakin (from John Entwistle's Ox) had by this time replaced Pete King on drums. King was to go on and join Christian rockers **After the Fire** chalking up a top 5 hit in the USA with *Der Kommissar* and later joining **Zip Codes** in 1983.He tragically died of cancer in 1987 aged just 26. (The original drummer in **Midnight Circus** Paul Angelopoulis, also died aged 24 from a drug overdose). After much touring over the years supporting the likes of The Ruts, The Buzzcocks and John Otaway. The rot had set in and with much in fighting in 1980 they split. Neil was to join his sister's band **Hazel O'Connor's Megahype** (SEE HAZEL O'CONNOR) and progress as a producer/arranger. Dave Freeman and Joe Hughes became members of **Roddy Radiation and the Tearjerkers** (SEE RODDY RADIATION), they both went on to form **The Lover Speaks** (SEE THE LOVER SPEAKS). Freeman had also released a solo single, *Stop in The Name of Love*, took a degree, issued poetry and co produced and performed on *The Raindancing* album for Alison Moyet.

GODIVA ROCKS SOUND BYTE WITH- Neil O'Connor (The Flys & Megahype).
One of the clubs, downtown in the Precinct, was a place called "Mr George" and was usually considered to be "the sophisticated nightspot for the over 23's" especially on the weekends....if you know what I mean. Though, occasionally, "Mr George" did have their adventurous side and during those heady days in 1977, would promote some punk evenings even going so far as to give up their Saturday night disco evenings and would have live punk /new wave bands, like us.
Hey the Sex pistols played there so we were in good company. Well, the first 2 times we played at this place we were hated. Too local? did they think that we thought we were better than anybody else? I still don't know but we received the whole shabang of glasses and bottles being thrown in our direction of the stage and crashing around us as well as the fashion of gobbing (appreciation?), we learned fast how to dodge these various projectiles, but 2 times in your home town is not a lot of fun.
But..we did have a small fan base, and one of these people, Adrian, was instrumental in changing all of our lives forever. At the time he was a young kid of 16 years who would sit in at our practices, he was a lovely person though very critical, he should have been our manager, precocious, opinionated, a real character. He was also a very good friend of Pete Shelley from the "Buzzcocks" or so he claimed, of course we took that information with a pinch of salt except....On a Saturday morning, two weeks after our last debacle at the famous "Mr George", David and I received a phone call from Adrian to ask us if "The Flys" would be interested to open for The Buzzcocks that very same evening at "Mr George".
Continued over....

Contunued from last page -Oh ****, not more glasses and gob...........please no!!!!! I called Pete, our drummer, "hey we have a gig tonight if we want" "where?" "Mr George" "Absolutely no way on this earth(or words to that effect)" "Pete, it's opening for the Buzzcocks" "OK, but if the glasses and the gob starts that's it I'm quitting the band"

So, in trepidation, we accepted and with trepidation we crashed the first chord of our first song in the set........and we went down a storm, not one glass crashed around our heads, yeah some gob but, if it can be said, friendly gob. We played the same songs that we'd been playing since a few months, nothing had really changed except, perhaps, we had now become acceptable because of our association, for that night, opening for these new stars of the scene , "The Buzzcocks".

And they were great. We had such a good time together and after that evening we opened for them for the rest of their tour, EMI saw us and we had our first record contract. Thanks Adrian and thanks Pete Shelley. Well, Pete, I hope this little anecdote, is OK for you.
Like I said at the beginning it's a very pleasant memory especially as without that particular Saturday The Flys may not have found a record contract and therefore Dave and Joe may not have met and worked with Dave Stewart and Annie Lennox and I would not be still doing what I love to do (since many years I'm a record producer though I prefer the French expression, as I live in the French speaking province of Quebec, "Réalisateur")

FOLK

PETE WILLOW

Folk music in the area is not as popular as it was, truth is pure folk has been so diluted with rock music for some 40 years now, that 'real' folk has been lost to all but the most ardent folkies. Of course it could be argued that is exactly what folk music is about, music of the people soaking up outside influences, metamorphosing into a slightly new genre. Whatever your view the place to go for all kinds of folk is **The Wurzel Bush Folk Club**, held at the British Legion Club in Brinklow. Local folk bands old and new include, **Newbold** (resident band at the Wurzel), **the Peeping Tom Big Band**, **Willows Folk**, **Colin Squire**, **Time After Time**, **Shkayla**, **Rod Felton**, **Isambarde**, **Whippersnapper**, **Gilly Darbey**, **Four Myters**, **Folklore**, **Sneaks Noise** (who would court controversy with their song about *Aberfan*), **The Gaels** (included. Sean Cannon now with Dubliners), **Pete Willow** king-pin of local folk, organiser of *The Brinklow Folk Festival* and member of the bands **the Oddsods** and **Amaranth** and *Cov Telegraph* folk correspondent. Moving on to the mighty **Meet on the Ledge** (named after the classic Fairport Convention track), now up to their fifth album. Then we have folk rock outfit **Godivaride** (who are actually 50% of local harmony rockers **Bait** (SEE BAIT). Not forgetting the great **Polly Bolton** (SEE POLLY BOLTON), **Kevin Dempsey**, **Dando Shaft** (SEE DANDO SHAFT) Nuneaton's **Fresh Maggots** (SEE NUNEATON), **Beverley Martyn** (SEE BEVERLY MARTYN) and **June Tabor** (SEE JUNE TABOR)

Waterfall folk trio consisting of Keith Donnelly, top fiddler Martyn Oram and Cov lass Gilly Darbey Formed In 1974, Keith and Martyn although not from the area roomed together at Warwick University, released two albums *Three Birds* and *Beneath The Stars*. Gilly went on to enjoy a successful solo career. (SEE WARWICK). Leamington born **John Edgar** is best know for his *Breton Tales After Dark* LP, he has also contributed to *The Palers Project* Procol Harum.a tribute album *From Shadow To Shadow* .

Other folk stuff includes *The City Arms Folk Club*, *Warwick University Folk Club*, The Coventry Traditional Music club held at The Malt Shovel Spon End, *The Warwick Folk Festival,* music at Coombe Abbey (including medieval banquets, **Paul King** used to be a player there). (SEE KING). The **Aardvark** and the **Peeping Tom Ceilidh bands**. Cov's finest bluesman **Mick Stewart**. **The Earlsdon Morris Men**, **The Coventry Mummers**,**The Armpit Jug Band**   (SEE JAZZ). Top fiddle player **Dave Swarbrick** lives in Coventry (SEE DAVE SWARBRICK), so does Guitar Maker **Rob Armstrong** (SEE ROB ARMSTRONG). It was nice to see on Radio 2's Folk Music awards that locals **June Tabor** and **Dave Swarbrick** both picked up top awards. Sadly Dave couldn't be there due to seriously bad health. For folk info click **www.wurzelbush.co.uk**

PAGE 30   GODIVAROCKS@YAHOO.CO.UK   PAGE 30

FOUR KINGS

A current 'one to watch' band, part of the Coventry rock pack. Formed in 2000, the band consists of Andy Beglin (vocals), Paul Hartry (guitar), Leigh Urquhart (bass), Dave Medforth (keyboards) and Chris Hartry (drums). The band have been compared to various rock giants, I would prefer to ignore such remarks and rejoice in the fact that they have a pretty original sound not obviously akin to anyone in particular. It's great to hear the keyboards and guitar working closely together with some superb bass/drum lines topped off with Andy's great vocals. They have supported the likes of **The Darkness** and **The Cooper Temple Clause,** and in 2003 became the first British band to play the *Athfest* musical festival in Athens Georgia USA and a return looks on the cards. The band have a self-produced CD available entitled *Life Through The Bottom Of A Glass.* Their website is at www.fourkings.net

FUN BOY THREE

As things started to deteriorate in the Specials (SEE THE SPECIALS), plans were already a foot by Messrs **Hall,Staples** and **Golding** (SEE TERRY HALL,SEE THE COLOURFIELD,SEE NEVILLE STAPLES) to start their own band. Indeed they seem to have their first single out before The Specials were cold as they say. Jerry Dammers had this to say at the time, "I'm disappointed that they have left, but I'm glad they stayed in the band long enough to record *Ghost Town*". That first single *The Lunatics (have taken over the asylum)* on Chrysalis Records. Was a masterful piece of understatement, Halls deadpan voice combined with lyrics of nuclear holocausts, was effective juxtaposition at it's finest. It only managed a chart placing of 20 (it's interesting to note that their other 'serious' single, *The More I See*, also did badly, maybe the record buying public were only interested in the FUN in Fun Boy Three, rather than any serious issues). The following year 1982, we saw a whole new side of the boys. As they teamed up with the female trio **Bananarama** on a cover of the Jimmy Lunceford song, *It Ain't What You Do it's The Way That You Do It*. Hall claimed he had teamed up with **Bananarama** because they were as talentless as them. Whatever the case the single shot to number 4, and got the girls careers off to a flying start. They reciprocated later in the year and released *Really Saying Something* (5) billed as **Bananarama** and the **Fun Boy Three**. **Bananarama** were to go on a clock up 24 more hit singles through the next 11 years, not bad for a talentless band!

Meanwhile back at the farm, the 'Funsters' were working hard touring and promoting their first album entitled *The Fun Boy Three* or *FB3* to be trendy. Produced by David Jordan, and clocking in at 7 on the album charts in 82. It was an adequate debut, if a little predictable, it did the job. It was at this time that Lynval was attacked by 3 white youths tooled-up with a knife, spanner and a claw hammer. He was left for dead outside *Shades NightClub, The Burgess* in Coventry City Centre. Despite having 29 stitches in his face and neck Lynval would thankfully make a full recovery. The next single The *Telephone Always Rings* (17), now minus **Bananarama**, it seemed the fun was a little less evident, not a bad single, just a little uninteresting. Getting one place higher at 16, was their next *Summertime*. Traditionally a powerful ballad, here Hall's understated monotone voice turns this classic Gershwin song into basically a dirge. Things were about to get better though when their second album *Waiting* (14) was released in 1983. This was more like it, produced by the legendary Talking Head David Byrne. It contained their next three singles (plus the wonderful *We're Having All the Fun* and my favourite FB3 song *Farmyard Connection*). The guys also cameoed as hitch hikers (holding up a Coventry placard) in the madness video *Driving In my Car*.

Next release was *The More I See (The Less I Believe)*, as I mention above, it only made the lower end of the charts (68). It was however a brave, brilliantly written attack at the sad/mad situation in the North of Ireland. That was being played out on British TV every night. This was the FB3 at their sardonic best. Relationship problems were addressed once again in the *Tunnel of Love* (10) followed a month later in February 1983. Relationships in the band too were beginning to show signs of fracture, Terry was coming into his own as a songwriter, and while Neville and Lynval were keen to crack America, Hall wasn't. Their final single was to be Terry Hall's pension song, *Our Lips Are Sealed*. Co written with Go-Go's Jane Wiedlin back in 1981, it had been a hit (20) in the US for the Go-Go's. It was a perfect choice for the Funsters swansong. As with **The Specials**, Mr Hall was already planning his next move. It was to be another trio The Colourfield (SEE THE COLOUFIELD). Lynval and Neville went off to join with Pauline Black to form **Sunday Best** (SEE PAULINE BLACK). Neville and Lynval would both go on to work behind the music scenes, with Seattle based Lynval managing the band **After Tonight** later producing Swedish ska band The Skalatones. Californian based Neville also moved into band management and appearing at *The Ben Sherman 40th Birthday Party* (with Jerry Dammers as DJ). He continues to release albums like *Special Skank Au Go Go* and promote his record label *Rude Boy Records* he also promotes his own designer-wear. So in 1983 we bid farewell to the Fun Boy Three, and more importantly, those dreadful haircuts!

FURIOUS APPLES

Coventry indie band based around the enigmatic Greg Crabb a mainstay of the Cov music scene in the mid 80's, (he also ran the Pilgrim Club disco). Along with his brother Michael on guitar they were heavy giggers and they knew how to promote themselves (including super 8 promo films). Members came and went including Nick Farrington, Martin Wilson, Steve Fardon, Mike Moore, John Wright, Raphael Moore, Clive Leyton and Whippet. They featured on a couple of local compilation albums. Released a single *Engineering* in 83 on Cabin Studios own Sonar record label (SEE STUDIOS) it plodded along fairly well with a vocal not unlike that of Gary Numan, though I doubt if Greg would thank me for saying that. Received considerable interest from CBS, but despite the best efforts of Manager Wayne Morris, and a name change to **The Pilgrims,** it sadly wasn't to be. Wayne Morris went on to manage **The Primitives**. (SEE THE PRIMITIVES). Greg Crab went on to form **The Mudsliders** with Clive Layton, Baz Eardly, and Ted Duggan (SEE HEAVY ROCK).

THE GIRAFFES

When The **Pink Umbrella's** who had become the **Attic Dressers** finally split up, Paul Sampson (SEE PAUL SAMPSON, THE PINK UMBRELLAS, SEE THE RELUCTANT STEREOTYPES) concentrated on his production work at Cabin Studios (SEE STUDIOS). While clarinettist Steve Edgson and drummer Rob Hill (SEE RELUCTANT STEREOTYPES, SEE THE PINK UMBRELLAS) formed **The Giraffes** with Sam McNulty ex-Squad & (SEE SQUAD) on vocals and guitar. With Richard Priest, AKA Larry Lupin of **Gods Toys** (SEE I) on bass and Nigel Williams on Guitar (who ran the long gone Left wing bookshop/caf☐ The Wedge). They were the bee's knees around the Cov music scene in the late 1980's. Headlining gigs at The Rose and Crown (The Giraffe House) and at The Belgrade Theatre Studio. Their pedigree was unsurpassed. They released a single (produced by Paul Sampson) in 1988 entitled *Pass Me By* (a catchy little number let down by sub-standard vocals). Followed by the second single *One Step*. Despite being the 'darlings' of the time, they went out with somewhat of a whimper.

TERRY HALL

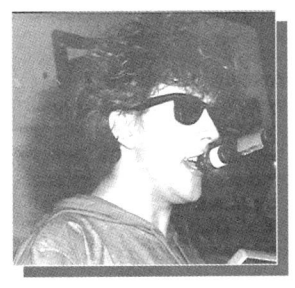

Born in Red Lane march 19th 1959. Worked by day for The David Fletcher Coin Shop in Station Square. He relieved his boredom by becoming a punk rocker at night in the band **Squad** (SEE SQUAD). Although Hall remains the bands most famous member he is not featured on either of their singles and although he spent most of his time jumping into the audience and spitting at people. By all accounts he never cut it as a punk. Help was at hand though, and despite his lack of cred' in the punk department, he was being head hunted by the **Coventry Automatics** (SEE THE SPECIALS). He joined on the spot and Terry Hall would shine in his own demonic way with **The Specials** for the next three years. Clocking up seven top ten hits including two number ones. Before moving on to more success with **The Fun Boy Three** and **Colourfield** (SEE THE FUN BOY THREE, SEE THE COLOURFIELD).

On leaving **Colourfield** he set about fulfilling his obligations to record label *Chrysalis*. He recruited two American ladies *Blair Booth* and *Anouchka Groce* to form **Terry, Blair and Anouchka**. They released the single *Missing(75) IN 1990*, a classic piece of Terry Hall 'matter of fact everyday gloom'. Followed by in my opinion the classic album *Ultra Modern Nursery Rhyme*. This included the single of the same name that must rank of one of Hall's finest moments. After a lay off from the music business, Hall was persuaded in 1992 by master muso and former Eurythmic Dave Stewart to join him in his contractual obligation album under the banner **Vegas**. The first single was *Possessed* (32), followed by *She* (43) (a Charles Aznavour song, who also appeared in the video). *Walk Into The Wind* (65) was the last Vegas single (this track featured the vocals of Terry's old singing partner and then Mrs Stewart *Siobhan Fahey* of Shakespeare's Sister and formerly **Bananarama**). They released the one album also called *Vegas* on RCA Records.

He then finally decided to go it alone a release his first true solo album in 1995 (that's excluding the endless stream of Chrysalis *Best of Terry Hall* compilations of course). *Home* released on Dave Stewart's Anxious record label. With collaborations from XTC's Andy Partridge, Nick Heywood and The Lightening Seeds Ian Broudie (who produced the album). The first single would be *Forever J* (67) written about Terry's then wife Jeanette. The album showed a mature Terry, but the sarcasm was still in evidence, well it wouldn't be Terry without that. The second single *Sense* in released in1994 did a little better a made 54 in the charts, it was co written with Ian Broudie and was a hit (31) for The Lightening Seeds in 1992. Terry also co-wrote *Lucky You*. This would chart twice for the Lightening Seeds at 43 in 1994 then at 15 in 1995. His next single would be *The Rainbows EP* (62) in collaboration with The Blur's Damon Albarn, the lead track was *Chasing A Rainbow*. For the rest of 1995 Terry worked with the likes of Marijine from the band *Salad* on the charity album *Help the War Child* album, and with alternative Hip Hopper *Tricky*. 1997 saw a new record label (South Sea Bubble Company) and a new single the wonderful and highly emotive *Ballad of a Landlord,* a real return to form, shame it only ranked at 50. It was followed with a cover of the great Todd Rundgren's song *I saw The Light*. The inevitable album followed entitled *Laugh* (50), full of angst, hurting and marriage break-up stuff. Sort of Terry Hall's answer to Dylan's Blood on the Tracks. Terry moved back to his native Coventry, though he had been living in Leamington Spa since leaving Manchester. Apart from a duet of *All Kind's of Everything* (the Dana song) with Sinead O'Connor for a Eurovision covers album, it became all quite on the Terry Hall front. Until he resurfaced with a real surprise a collaboration with Middle Eastern musician *Mushtaq*, entitled *The Hour of Two Lights*. Calling it eclectic is an understatement. Rock and Middle Eastern styles are woven with a veritable United Nations of musicians including a Tunisian singer, a Syrian flautist, a blind Algerian rapper from Paris, Polish gypsies and a 12-year-old Lebanese girl! It sounds like a nightmare but this potpourri of sounds really works and how. Halls understated vocals are the perfect foil for the elaborate back drop of swirling strings and drums that sound like they have as much character as the people playing them .It really is worth a listen.

What's next for Terry who knows, one thing is for sure Whether you consider him a laconic genius or a depressing waste of time, you have to admit Terry Hall is unique among the plastic, formulated pap that we often have to describe as music. Terry seems to be getting happier of late, and you may find this site interesting, Terry asks *The Ever Wondered* Open University site why his quality of life is better living in the country away from Coventry find it here http://www.open2.net/everwondered1/env/topic3.htm

HEAVY ROCK

Probably Chevy (SEE THE B LIST) were always the 'heavy' darlings of the area. Of course we have had our fair share of hard rockers. Cov trio **Chainsaw** were doing leather jacket business for some four years. Ian Heys, (vocals, guitar) Brian Evans (bass)(replaced by Martin Orum) and Mark Biddiscombe (drums)(replaced by Rich Carroll) always knew how to play the audience. They put three singles out in the 1980's, the brilliant *Police and Politicians Down, Down* and *Devils Daughter* in 1984. **Paris** could also do the business, with the great Pat Millar on vocals, they released the single *You Are The One* in 1989. Their drummer was Ted Duggan who also played in **Chevy** and **Drops of Brandy** and currently plays for **Banco De Gaia** (SEE BANCO DE GAIA). Gavin Ward (ex-Varukers)(SEE LEAMINGTON) of **Bolt Thrower** is from Leamington, their fan club is based in Leamington and they record in Coventry. Although this death metal unit with many albums to their credit claim to be a Brummie band, go figure.

Lee Dorrian is a big name in the world of 'metal'. The former vocalist with **Napalm Death** was born in Woodend in 1968. He describes it like this, "I grew up on a council estate, the hardest part of town there's no surf boards or beach buggies there! There might be a few burnt-out cars and glue bags on the floor, but there's no palm trees". Lee once let metal legend Dave Grohl (then with Scream now with the Foo Fighters) crash at his Coventry home after a gig, apparently spending most of the night discussing the finer points of Celtic Frost. Lee was with Napalm Death from 1987 to 1989. Playing 'grindcore', infamous for their abrasive screaming vocal style and ten-second songs. Lee screamed his way through 2 albums *Scum* and *From Enslavement to Obliteration*. Leaving Napalm Death 1989 and forming **Cathedral**. Musically they are far more accessible than N.D. leaning towards the doomier side of Black Sabbath, so far they have released some 11 albums, the latest being *The VIIth Coming*. Nicholas Charles Dingley was born in Leamington and was adopted and grew up in Cov'. He took the name **Razzle** and joined Finnish Glam rockers Hanoi Rocks as their drummer, they charted in 1984 with a re-make of the Credence Clearwater Revival song *Up Around The Bend* (61) and the album *Two Steps From The Move* (28). He sadly was also to die in 1984, killed in a car that was being driven by Mötley Crüe's very drunk Vince Neil.

RAZZLE

Other heavy boys of the area include **Mithras** (spot the Alister Crowley connection there) and **Arbitrator** a Warwick based thrash metal outfit from mid eighties released two albums *Balance of Power* in 1991 & *Darkened Reality* in 1994. Hardcore US band **Brutal Truth** teamed up with Coventry Techno rockers **Larceny** for the single *Perpetual Conversion* in 1995. Then we have the new wave of Local rock bands like the mighty **Four Kings** (SEE THE FOUR KINGS), the black metallers **Siren Fall, Sandstone** (their debut self produced CD is worth checking out). Then there is the much talked about **Dragster** (SEE DRAGSTER) **Fume** and Kenilworth's **Cepheus** (lead vocalist Izzy Ackerly has a great voice) the very very brilliant **Thoria** (SEE THORIA).

A GODIVA ROCKS TRIVIA BOX

The Satanist/author and teacher of the dark Aleister Crowley was born in Leamington Spa on 12th October 1875. He referred to himself as *The Beast* (popularising the phrase 666, The number of The Beast) His influence is far and wide none more so in the world of rock music (especially with the 'Goth' movement and Marilyn & Charles Manson). Led Zeppelin (and in particular) Jimmy Page had a deep interest in him. Page actually owned Crowley's former house *Bolskine* on the banks of Loch Ness. Those reverse speech 'freaks' who play records backward claim Stairway To Heaven is riddled with Crowley inspired satanic messages. Ozzy Osbourne wrote and recorded the song *Mr Crowley*. Iron Maiden sang *The Number of the Beast*. The Beatles included Crowley on their Sgt Pepper cover (he's the second one in from the Left top row). Australian weirdo Duffo mentions Crowley in his song *Give Me Back me Brain* and local metal band **Mithras** is a name inspired by Crowley's teachings.

VINCE HILL

Always a local favourite always synonymous with Coventry. Having had the pleasure to talk to Vince whilst researching this book, I can say he's a very down to earth human being with no pretence. Indeed his whole family seems to be just the same, all genuine people. Vince was born in Holbrooks on April 24th 1937. He was a baker and a coal miner, but singing professionally was where his life was leading. His first public performance was at the Prospect Public house in Margate at 15. He and his brother Jack would begin singing in local pubs like the *Bantam and Stag* and various clubs around Coventry. He continued his craft in the Royal Signals band during his national service and as part of the cast of the musical *Floradora*, later joining **The Teddy Foster Band** in 1958. His first real taste of fame however came when he became part of Len Beadle's singing group **The Raindrops**. (its line-up included Jackie Lee who would go onto to chart with the songs *White Horses* and *Rupert The Bear*, and songwriter Johnny Worth who would write *What Do You Want* for Adam Faith). They featured on the BBC radio show *parade of the pops* basically singing the current songs of the day.

He left the Raindrops in 1961 to go solo, although he continued to appear on *parade of the pops* and appeared on other shows such as TV's *Stars and Garters*. This was to help him launch his solo career. Indeed in 1963 he gained his first chart entry (49 and a re-entry at 41) with *The Rivers Run Dry* on Pye records. He moved to Columbia Records and more hits followed like *Take Me to Your Heart Again* (13), *Heartaches* (28) and *Merci Cheri* (36). It was his next hit however that would prove life changing for Vince. After much persuasion Vince convinced Columbia Records that a song that had originally been sung by Julie Andrews would be 'hit' material for him. The song was of course *Edelweiss*, and Vince was right, it was a hit, a huge hit getting to number two (although many say it got to number one, not in the main BBC chart it didn't). It was to become his signature tune for the rest of his career, a career that saw him top the bill at the Palladium and Talk of the Town. Plus starring in his own successful shows *They Sold a Million, Musical Time Machine* and *Gas Street*, a show that would highlight his presenting and interviewing talents. He still found time to make more hits singles like the *popular Roses of Picardy* (13), *Love Letters in the Sand* (23) and *The Importance of Your Love (*32). As well as charting with the albums *Edelweiss* (23) and *That Loving Feeling* (51).

Vince is such an unassuming man that I bet you weren't aware he composed songs as well as sang them. He and his musical Director Ernie Dunstall wrote a song for Brendan Dougan that went to number one in the New Zealand charts. Such is his global popularity, his records sell not only in the UK, but in the likes of Canada (where he has also had his own TV series) and Australia. In 1976 he was the subject of honour on *This Is Your Life*. By 1983 he had added acting to his CV, first in the radio drama *Tolpuddle* (he also wrote this) and playing Ivor Novello in the stage play *My Dearest Ivor* he also managed to find time to write the stage musical *Zodiac*. His last big hit was to be (well so far) *Look Around (and Find Me There)*(12). He still continues to release albums and tour all over the country, his current *I'm still Standing Show*, is so named because of his recent battle with cancer In his spare time he likes to encourage his son Athol in his musical career. Plus spending time with his wife Annie on their boat, and he still looks out for the Cov City results, good man!

GODIVA ROCKS SOUND BYTE WITH-Vine Hill (Solo star) When I was asked by Pete Chambers to write something about myself I thought – Where do I begin. Some people say I am a Coventry lad who made good. I suppose – but I never really know whether I have made good or not – As I always say – mostly I feel as if I am still trying – to make good that is!

I lot of you will know, I guess that I was born at 24 Hen Lane, Holbrooks and although I was born in Coventry and went to Hen Lane School- as it was then – my first tentative notes in front of an audience were in a pub in Margate, of all places. It was aptly called The Prospect. It's just a car park now I understand .My mother cajoled me into entering a Talent Contest which I won – the first prize was a week's holiday at the pub – the second prize was 2 weeks! – as they say.   **Continued over**

PAGE 35   GODIVAROCKS@YAHOO.CO.UK   PAGE 35

> **Continued from last page.** Having got the taste for this singing lark I took it quite seriously and had lessons with Ivy Fitton and soon started singing around the local pubs and clubs. Hen Lane Club – The Bantam – especially The Bantam, The Unicorn Club and Rowleys Green are still vivid memories for me. I soon started to stretch my wings though – Cox Street Club – Radford Club, all round the Midlands and up as far as Sheffield in Yorkshire.
>
> I've lived away from Coventry now for well over 40 years and I know there have been many changes – some for the better – some for the worse. I doubt that I could find my way round the old place now and I certainly could not go and stand where the old theatre was. The fact that a great historic town like Coventry now does not have a proper theatre that can take big shows of international standing beggers belief. We all wrote, we all spoke nobody listened. I well remember as a lad going to the Hippodrome with my Mum. Perhaps that after all was where I first got the bug – ah well – Happy Days .Come on the Blues – they are always the first result I look for on a Saturday.

"I"

After the revolution that was punk, many bands were heading away from 'new wave' looking for something that had the ethos and strength of punk, but harnessed in a far more creative 'arty' way (or *Arty-Natty* as the band first ever song puts it). **Gods Toys** were such an animal. Fronted by *Dill*, who was forever the devine frontman, one of those guys that was always a star, despite if success would come his way or not, he was *it*. They played their first gig at Warwick University supporting **The Specials** and **Squad** (SEE VENUES, SEE THE SPECIALS, SEE SQUAD). They once described themselves as a 'fun show band', and that pretty much summed them up. With Dill leaping around the stage in bizarre clothes, and Larry Lupin (in even more bizzare clothes and full make-up) the demented axe victim playing his guitar like it really hurts. With John Hobley on drums, Nick Kavaz on keyboards and Chris, Dickie on bass (who also happened to share a flat with Jerry Dammers of **The Specials**, who helped in the toys' conception). Their original rock and reggae sound made them fleeting darlings of the national music press, they released two singles, the staggeringly good *All the Born Losers* in 1980 and *Everybody's Got A Mother* in 1981. Despite all the interest and the constant rumours that they were about to break and a support slot with Adam and the Ants it was not to transpire. Chris Dickie left to become a recording engineer at RAK with Mickie Most. Larry joined **The Giraffes** (SEE THE GIRAFFES). For Dill it was back to the drawing board.

Dill soon began work on his next project and formed the enigmatic **I**. Based around the concept of something approaching a quasi-religion (including face painting ceremonies on stage and their very original I-Society fan club). Although a large dab of doubt would always be applied to any seriousness on Dill's behalf, as just a few months earlier **Gods Toys** were saying things quite the opposite things about God and religion. Dressed in white robes (basically formed out of the band **The X-Certs**) Dill and drummer Rick Medlock, Guitarist Chris Hull, Dave Pepper (SEE DAVE PEPPER) and Rex Brough on bass and Cello. Would on stage run through a hymn sheet of delights, such as *Sanctus, Life Is For Living, The Birth, Iconoclast* and their first and only single *I*. The single was as powerful as anything I have ever heard, with it's opening lines of, *I am glorious, I am wise I am I, and I for the eyes*. Great stuff. The great Paul Johnston replaced Rick Medlock (and later Rob Hill), while Dave Pepper left to be replaced by Colin Kiddy. Dill in his pursuit of perfection was to turn I into some mis-fit of a disco combo (much to my annoyance at the time). Singing live to backing tapes, giving the religious theme the heave-ho replacing it with percussive African-based rhythms. Creating something lifeless and sterile, never two words I thought I would ever apply to Dill. Not long after the inevitable happened and the band split, with Paul Johnston going on to become a record producer at **Rythmn Recording** studios (SEE STUDIOS) in Leamington. Rex became a member of **The Pookah Makes Three** and later a record producer (as well as creating a website that includes a fab Coventry bands section). Chris went on to form the band **The Ring**.

FRANK IFIELD

Although he actually only spent a short time in Coventry, Frank is king of the heap, and it doesn't matter that the Australians claim, he will always be 'Our Frank'! (Frank himself considers himself as an English born Australian, having allegiance to both countries). Francis Edward Ifield was born in Coventry November 30th 1937, he lived in Evenlode Cresent, Coundon for 9 years. Until his Australian parents returned to their homeland, Dural near Sydney to be exact. Frank's singing career began at the tender age of 13 singing mainly on the radio. By the time he was nineteen he had released over forty records, including the huge antipodean hit *There's a Loveknot in My Lariat* He was a huge star in the Australian continent, but Frank was keen to crack his native Britain. So doing the unthinkable he left the safety of his Australian stardom to start all over again in the UK.

Evenlode Cresent, Coundon

Frank and his manager Peter Gormley arrived in London and their first port of call was to Norrie Paramor's office. Paramor was recording director of the UK EMI Columbia label, and had a lot to do with the success of the likes of Cliff Richard, Billy Fury, and Helen Shapiro. He liked Frank straight away and signed him for Columbia. *Lucky Devil* was the first UK offering in 1960 charting at 22. Followed by *Gotta Get A Date*, only charting at a lowly 49, Norrie started to look for other ways 'his' star could achieve some of the success he had enjoyed in Oz. He even had a shot at *the Song for Europe*, he came second with *Alone Too Long* to Ronnie Carrol who was chosen to represent Britain with *Ring-A-ding-Girl* in 1962. (He missed out again in 1976 with the song *Ain't Gonna Take No For An Answer*, Brotherhood of Man won the heat and of course the contest that year with *Save Your Kisses For Me).*

It wasn't until Frank tried out some songs for Norrie that his place in musical history began to take shape. With guitar in hand frank started to sing and then suddenly go off into a yodel. Norrie was amazed and loved it, although Frank wasn't entirely certain that the UK was ready for such a thing. Studio time was booked at Abbey Road, and a defining moment in Frank's career began to unfold. *I Remember You* was born. It was an immediate success, selling some 102,500 copies in one day alone! It hit the number one spot in the UK in 1962 and got to number 5 in the States. it became the first record to sell a million in UK. (The song was originally performed by Jimmy Dorsey from the film *The Fleets In.* Harry Pitch played the distinctive harmonica. He also played harmonica on the 1970 hit *Groovin' with Mr Bloe).* In August of 62 he was back in Coventry playing *the Coventry Theatre* (SEE VENUES). Three months later *Lovesick Blues* was released, again it hit number one in Britain (number 44 in the States), there was no looking back for our Frank. What happened next was to make history. When his next release *The Wayward Wind* also made it to the top Frank became the first artist in UK history to achieve a hat trick of number ones (and 3 gold discs) in one year. He was at number one with the three number ones for a total of 17 weeks. (not including his number one EP, *Frank's Greatest Hits).* It was a marvellous achievement, sadly his next single never made the top, *Nobody's Darling But Mine* was to peak at number four. However *Confessing That I Love You* was to take him back to up there one last time. Such was his stardom, in 1962 he had **the Beatles** (SEE THE BEATLES) as a support act, the audience were not interested in these lads from Liverpool, they came to see Frank. Indeed a very collectable US album featuring both Frank and the Beatles was released by Vee-Jay Records in 1964.

All was well in the Ifield camp, not just content having a quartet of number ones. He was also enjoying performances at the likes of *The Royal Variety Show, Sunday Night at the London Palladium* as well as appearing on *the Ed Sullivan show* stateside. More hits followed, *Mule Train* (22), *Don't Blame Me* (8) By 1964 however Beat Boom had well and truly taken hold, and The tables were turned for Frank as far as The

Beatles were concerned. None of his remaining 7 releases would rise above the number 24 position (Incidentally despite *Waltzing Matilda* virtually becoming his signature tune, he has never actually charted in the UK with it).

Mr Ifield, of course was always more than just a hit single (or 6 hit EP's and 4 hit LP's) Frank would concentrate on TV appearances, and become an all round entertainer and actor, producer and set up his own record label. He visited Coventry again 1967 to appear at the *Coventry Theatre* 30th Birthday Show. During his run he celebrated his own 30th Birthday and the birth of his child Mark, who is also a Coventry kid. In the mid 60's Frank played at the prestigious *Grand Ole Opry* and was made an honorary citizen of the State of Tennessee. He would come synonymous with Country and Western music in America and in Australia, where his status is almost unsurpassed. Inducted as he was to *the Country Music Roll of Renown*. A mini Frank Ifield revival hit the UK in 1991 when *The Yodelling Song* (originally called *She Taught Me How To Yodel* and the B-side of *Lovesick Blues*) was sampled and re-mixed by The Backroom Boys and charted at number 40. He still continues to release albums and his autobiography will hit the shelves soon. Now that will be worth reading. He was and remains an inspiration to all Coventry people.

GODIVA ROCKS SOUND BYTE FROM-FRANK IFIELD (Solo star) In 1935, Richard Joseph Ifield, his wife Muriel and their first born son Jim, left their homeland in Sydney Australia bound for England in order to further his career as an inventor. He made a bee-line to Coventry in the Midlands being the centre of the British motorcar industry. He quicky secured a job with Riley motorcars and lived in a rented property at 98 Evenlode Crescent Coundon, where in May 1936 his second son John was born. This meant working harder to keep his growing breed...Then on 30th November 1937, yours truly, Frank Ifield was born. My memory of those early years in Coventry is fairly sketchy as I was only a toddler when the Riley Company went into liquidation in May 1938. As luck would have it my dad was snapped up in June of that same year by 'Bendix Brakes' a subsiduary company of Joseph Lucas Ltd and we moved to No.1 Wherrettswell Lane in Sollihull. However, I still wear the title of 'Coventry Kid' with great pride. Most of my youth was spent during the war in the Midlands and dad was a prominent inventor working for Lucas on secret war time projects and invented the fuel systems for jet aircraft. In 1947, war was over and Dad decided to return to Australia with the family that had grown by this time to 6 boys, proving he was not only a prolific inventor.

By now, I had turned 10 years old, and having to put down roots in a newly adopted homeland was an exciting challenge. Living out in the countryside of Sydney and hearing the unfamiliar sounds of country music around me, filled me with the desire to be in Showbiz. I did my first professional show in 1950 aged 13, where for nearly a decade after, I gained as much as I could learn of stagecraft, television, radio and recording before summoning the courage to try my luck by returning to England as my father had done more than 20 years before. My main dream was to play the mecca of showbiz "The London Palladium".

In November 1959, I caught the Inaugural Comet flight, 'bearing my fathers fuel systems' to London in order to reach my goal and in a matter of two years I found myself playing before Her Majesty at ...you've guessed it - The Palladium. Throughout my entire career the generous people of Coventry and the Midlands have been my great support and I have played there countless times. Yet one show in particular stands out: It was in 1967 when I played the Coventry Theatre. This was the "Birthday Show" which ran from October to November. Significant for several reasons: It was the 30th birthday of the actual Theatre which, I was informed, opened on the very day and date that I was born. Then, during the finale of the opening night on the 6th October, Ted Rogers announced to me that my son Mark was born. To cap it off our closing night on November 30 was also a celebration of my own 30th birthday. Today, although I live back in Australia, my mind is filled with the many fond memories of my life in England and the close friendships I have made and I make it my business to return as often as possible. A fellow Coventarian Frank Ifield

INDIAN SUMMER

Progressive rock band from Coventry. It's line-up included former **ACME Patent Electric Band** members Rob Jackson (keyboards and vocals)(SEE ROB JACKSON) and Malc Harker (bass). Paul Hooper (drums), & Col Williams (guitar)(who was in the band **From the Sun**) completed the band. Spotted by Jim Simpson who then managed Black Sabbath (and later to be my editor at *Brum Beat*) they released an album also called *Indian Summer* on RCA Neon records in 1971. The album wasn't as successful as it deserved to be. It did showcase the bands talents, especially Robs keyboard playing and amazing vocals. The album became very collectable and was eventually released in CD format. Sound-wise they were akin to the Steve Winwoods band *Traffic* although maybe a little more progressive in flavour, indeed Rob's vocals could be compared favourably to Winwood's. As the album was released Malcom Harker left the band, he was replaced by Wez Price formerly of **The Sorrows** (SEE THE SORROWS). In 1972 after a tour, four very disillusioned musicians returned to Coventry, penniless a decided to call it a day. Rob joined the band Ross, Colin Williams left the music business and Paul Hooper would team up with Rob again in **The Dodgers** and **The Fortunes** (SEE THE B LIST) he also had a stint with club band Smackee (SEE CLUB BANDS).

JAZZ

OK I'll come clean here, I enjoy all types of music (as this book hopefully shows). The only musical form I have never been able to 'get' into or understand is modern jazz. I have tried, I remember my editor at The Coventry Weekly news, a jazz freak himself. Thought it would be good for me to review a modern jazz gig. So off I went to the Bulls Head, Binley Road in Cov and took in all the info the guys from Warwick Uni had to 'teach' me about the noble art. Despite my attempt to understand it, it still turned out to be a mass of unfocused wailing and cymbal crashes…..Mmmm Nice. Well no, not nice modern jazz is and will always be the Shakespeare of the music world. The snob brigade pretending to enjoy it because it supposed to be cool. Don't get me wrong, I'm talking about the 'real' weird stuff here. I enjoy fringe Jazz. like Dave Brubeck. I also enjoy trad jazz, and big band jazz, but not this nonsense.

OK, with that off my chest, I will move onto my thumbnail of Coventry Jazz. Well when it comes to Jazz and dance bands in Coventry there is two sites to check out The main men with all the answers are **John Wright**, from Coventry who runs the ultimate site for jazz enthusiasts and collectors, check his informative site out at http://www.jabw.demon.co.uk/. And **Ron Simmonds** (one of the City's top Trumpet players) a walking encyclopaedia on the subject his site is at http://www.jazzprofessional.com/ronspages/index.html

Leamington's **Jack Payne** is probably the most celebrated of the dance bandleaders in the area. Born in 1899, he moved from the midlands and became the leader of the Hotel Cecil band in London. Broadcasting from the hotel, and releasing countless records he took over the BBC dance band Orchestra. Broadcasting daily at 5.15. He made two films in the 1930's, eventually becoming a theatrical agent and disc jockey at the BBC. He died in 1969. Other local bands were **The Bob Wilson Orchestra, The Leon Orchestra, Len Pepper Orchestra, The Bill Monks Band, The Dud Clews Orchestra** and **The Jack Owens Orchestra**. They would play at places likes, Neal's Ballroom, Centre Ballroom on the Holyhead Road, The Rialto, Coutaulds, Arden Ballroom in Bedwoth and the Matrix (SEE VENUES).

Later we had **The Tierra Buena New Orleans Jazz band,** Duke Ellington played at The Cathedral in 1966 (the next jazz band to do it were John Surman & The Salisbury Festival Chorus)(SEE COVENTRY CATHEDRAL). The Mercers Arms and The Hotel Leofric were great places for jazz (SEE VENUES), as is Warwick University probably the Spiritual home of local Jazz. They once had their own Jazz in house radio station and even gave Humphrie Lyttelton an honorary degree in 1987. The Anthony Braxton Quartet recorded a live album in 1985 at the Arts Centre, entitled funny enough *Coventry*. Don't forget the mighty *Coventry Jazz festivals*, that have included the likes of jazz guitarist Martin Taylor, **The Phoenix Collective** (comprising of young jazz musicians from all over the City) and Stan Tracey, Courtney Pine, Jacqui Dankworth, Nguyên Lê, Man,Caravan and Kenny Ball. The great John Spencer and his band **The Nostalgics,** have entertained many a mature (and not so mature) audience in regular *Blitz Balls* and sing-a-longs since 1980.

Brass bands in the area include **The Rolls Royce Brass Band Coventry,** who have released a couple of CD's. **The Coventry C.P.A Band, The Coventry Festival Band. The Dunchurch Band, The Bulkington Silver Band, The Bilton Silver (Rugby) Band,The Daw Mill Colliery band** and **The University of Warwick Brass Band.**

The fantastic **Armpit Jug Band** were formed while they guys were students in Coventry. They changed their name to **Wang Dang Doodle** in the 90's, but soon went back to their original name when the bookings started to dry up. Their style of humorous jug band, delta blues and foot stompin' music has always guaranteed any audience a splendid night out. *Sweet Sue* and *Ukulele Lady* are my personal favourites. **The Sound Of Three Spire's** are part of *The Barbershop Harmony Club,* being a massed chorus who sing in this distinctive close-harmony style (I wonder if they sing *What Would You Say*, the Hurricane Smith song this sounds great in barbershop style). Better not forget **The Avon Jazz Band** from Stratford Upon Avon. **The Richard Pryor Jazz Players** (now defunct) from Coventry released one CD EP entitled *Live At Kelly's* on the *Take Your Hands Records label* based in Coventry. Last but by no means least, we have **The Coventry Semi-Automatics,** a tongue in cheek name for Horace Panter's **Coventry Ska-Jazz Orchestra** (a play on **The Specials** original name **The Coventry Automatics**). The former **Specials** Bassman pulled this 10 piece together for the *Cov Jazz Festival*, it includes his son Laurence Panter on Keyboards. (SEE THE SPECIALS, SEE HORACE PANTER).

ROB JACKSON

Rob a legend in Coventry music. He began as an apprentice at Morris Engines (a place where I also worked). His first band was the **Rochester Beaks.** He later became a member of the Psychedelic unit the **ACME Patent Electric Band** (complete with it's own lightshow and strange smoke effects). It also included Malc Haker in it's ranks both later joined the Coventry's progressive rock outfit **Indian Summer** (SEE INDIAN SUMMER). **Indian Summer** released one very good album, but never got the attention they deserved. A somewhat disillusioned Indian Summer split in 1972 Rob joined local soul and blues band **Monster Magnet** then heavy band **Ross,** originally a backing band for the Who's John Entwhistle they released two albums. Then moving to **Moon** (SEE THE B LIST) (a London based pub rock band that included many Cov members in it's ranks) releasing the *Too Close For Comfort* and *Turning The Tide* LP's in 70's and then onto big boys **Badfinger.** Replacing Pete Ham, Rob contributing not just his keyboard skills, but his song writing skills to boot. After three good years with Badfinger he formed **The Dodgers.** Who included in their ranks Paul Hooper (ex-**Indian Summer**) and **Roger Lomas** formerly of **the Sorrows** (SEE ROGER LOMAS, SEE THE SORROWS). Despite releasing two singles (*Love on The Rebound* & *Anyti*me) and an album (*Love on The Rebound*) for Polydor in 1978 they split somewhat acrimoniously in 79. Bob then had stints with playing with the likes of David Byron (ex Uriah Heep) Jack Bruce and The Searchers. Rob and Paul Hooper are now members of the Fortunes (SEE THE B LIST). The Jackson legacy continues with Rob's 22-year-old daughter Emily Jackson who is studying music at The Liverpool Institute of Performing arts. She has been hand picked to join playwrights Willy Russell and Tim Firth on tour in their show *In Other Words*.

GODIVAROCKS@YAHOO.CO.UK

TIM JAMES

Local blues man, and Cov's prime blues harpist.. Played in the **Bo-Wevils** with Kev Dempsey later of **Dando Shaft** (SEE DANDO SHAFT). He was also in **The Soul Sect** and later authentic blues band **3am,** it was here his blues harp playing came to the fore. In the early 70's he joined the Progressive rock band **ACME Patent Electric Band** (who included Rob Jackson and Malc Haker and famed for their use of mole smoke on stage). When Jackson and Malc Haker left to form Indian Summer (SEE INDIAN SUMMER, SEE ROB JACKSON). Tim hooked up with **Ra Ho Tap** and **The Band With No Name** and **Last Fair Deal** (this included guitar ace John Alderson who had previously been with **Wandering John** and **The Travelling Riverside Blues Band**). Finally going solo as **Tim James The One-Man Blues Band.** He has become something of a musical legend around the local blues scene and creator of a great website located here at http://www.timjamesblues.com/lists.htm#top

JB's ALLSTARS

Just before the break-up of the **Special AKA** (SEE THE SPECIALS), drummer John 'Brad' Bradbury a huge reggae and Northern soul fan (much in evidence on The Specials track *Sock It To 'Em J.B* and his own record label *Race Records.*) formed the Soul unit **JB's Allstars.** With himself on drums, Dee Sharp on vocals, augmented by the likes of Robert Awahi on guitar, Jason Votier on trumpet and (Elvis Costello's keyboard king) Steve Nieve. Recording on the legendary RCA Victor label the first release was *Backfield In Motion,* originally a hit in the States for Mel Harden and Tim McPherson. Brad got it to number 48 in 1984. A great powerful first offering with some terrific brass and vocal interchanges. I remember interviewing Brad at the time, he seemed the happiest he had been for a long while, he had great hopes for his new venture and his enthusiasm was at a high. Other singles in the same power-soul tradition followed like *One-Minute Ever Hour, Sign On the Dotted Line* and *Ready Willing and Able.* Their swan song was to be the last Two Tone single of all time *Alphabet Army* (SEE TWO TONE). John left the music business and got into computers, he was last seen on TV taking part in Changing Rooms with Carol Smillie from his home in Belsize Park London.

JIGSAW

Formed in Rugby in 1966, although Bernard and Scott were Coventry kids. They were a veritable local 'super group' comprising of Clive Scott (who was then a resident of Radford) on vocals and keyboards (from the **Atlantics** and the **Transatlantics**), Barry Bernard on bass (from **Pickertons Colours** (SEE PICKERTONS COLOURS). Kevin Mahon on tenor sax and Tony Campbell guitar (both from **The Mighty Avengers** (SEE THE MIGHTY AVENGERS) Tony Britnel (from **The Fortunes**) and Des Dyer on drums.

They played regularly in Coventry at Mr George's (SEE VENUES), It would take some 2 years before they released their debut single *One Way street.* Their vocal harmonies and imaginative lyrics saw them release classic song after classic song, none unfortunately heading chartwards. Indeed their 1972 single *That's What It's all About* Is probably as good as any song Paul McCartney has ever penned, again, no hit. Just to compound things in 1974 the bands writing machine Scott & Dyer were to have a massive hit on their hands, but ironically it wasn't for **Jigsaw**. The song was *Who Do You Think You Are,* an infectious slice of commercial pop that gave the band **Candlewick Green** a number 21 hit with it in the UK and Europe. While Claude Francoise charted with it in France as did Bo Donaldson who reached number 12 in the States. To make matters even worse, two years previously their outstanding arrangement of the Bach composition *Jesu Joy Of Mans Desiring* had earned the US combo Apollo 100 a number 6 hit entitled *Joy*.

Their own chart success was to continue to elude them. However when the guys joined Splash Records (their sixth label), the final piece of the puzzle clicked into place. Their big break came when an Australian film company was looking for a theme tune for the movie *Man From Hong Kong*. David Essex and The Four Tops were approached, but turned it down due to their work commitments. Jigsaw took it on despite the fact that they had just completed an album, and only had three days to come up with something brand new. The song was handed over with little enthusiasm on the part of the writers Des Dyer and Clive Scott. Pretty soon though they had an Australian number one on their hands with the hugely successful *Sky High* it also flew to number 9 in the UK and 3 in the USA. Jigsaw fever was well and truly kicking off around the globe. Clive and Des won the most performed song in 1975 award, then later an Ivor Novello certificate of honour award. They began a lengthy world tour, fitting in TV appearances in Spain, America, UK and Japan In 1976 Sky High became a Japanese number one, it would stay in the Nippon charts for two years thanks to a Sumo wrestler using it as his entrance music. Their Japanese tour was reminiscent of Beatlemania, with the guys being mobbed every night. World-wide Sky High sold in excess of 3 Million. It took 8 years, but it paid of in the end.

The UK follow up was *If I Have To go away,* good but not in the same league as S*ky High*, it charted at number 36 in the UK. While it's US counterpart *Love Fire* made 30 in the Billboard charts, their album *Jigsaw* also made a small dent on the US album charts. Although the hits ceased to the most part, athough they did make the Brazilian hit parade with the song *Who's Taking You Home* in 1978. They continued to work in production and contribute to film soundtracks. In 1994 we had a triple 'local' connection when Mike Stock and Matt Aitken (*sans* Coventry's Pete Waterman) produced a cover version of **Jigsaw's** *Sky High* for an artist called Newton whose real name was Billy Myers. Not the same Cov artist **Billie Myers** (SEE BILLIE MYERS) (wrong sex for a start) but an interesting coincidence. It would reach number 56 on it's second release.

Nowadays Tony Campbell is working in the optical lens industry. Barry Bernard is a D.J./children's entertainer and conjurer. While Des. is still singing in the clubs in a Duo with Steve Fern called "Fingers & Thumbs". He is also now teaching Drums at various different schools. Clive Scott is still working full time in the music industry, as a writer and producer and has a recording studio called *Racetrack Studios*. He writes for the likes of Boyzone and Blue. He is currently working with Denise Van Outen writing songs for her first album with BMG.

GODIVA ROCKS SOUND BYTE FROM- Clive Scott (Jigsaw) At the beginning, when we were a six piece with Tony Britnell on sax, every Gig was an adventure, as he was so unpredictable. I remember one venue, I think in the Birmingham area, which had a very low stage ceiling. While throwing his sax in the air Tony (accidentally initially) managed to break one of the fancy glass lights above the stage. When this got a great response from the crowd, Tone proceeded to systematically work his way across from left to right, until the stage was awash with smashed light fittings. On our next return to the venue, now fitted with new replacement lights, he 'accidentally' did the same again. On our next few visits the management were prepared and removed all breakable lights before our arrival: Until Jigsaw got the job of being the unnamed backing band for Arthur (Sweet Soul Music) Connelly. As the band took the stage and started the sort of Blues Brothers style intro music for the entrance of the big star, the look of horror could be seen on the Manager's face, as he recognised the demented sax player preparing to toss his lethal saxophone into the air. I also remember the bewildered look on Arthur's face as he crunched onto the stage through the carpet of broken glass.

PAGE 42   GODIVAROCKS@YAHOO.CO.UK   PAGE 42

JIMMY JIMMY

Formed out of a buskers Jimmy Kemp and James O'Neill. Who's close two part harmonies of Beatles songs and cute little hats seemed to be a permanent fixture on Hertford Street outside what was Habitat/Index now the 99p shop. So the story goes **The Jimmmy's** were 'discovered' playing there and Epic records signed them up for a deal. They released an album and a bunch of singles including, *I Met Her In Paris, Silence* and the obligatory Beatles cover *All You Need Is Love*. What sounded good at a busking level never really cut the ice at gigs, they always appeared to be still □ busking. Although because of their recording contract they made second on the bill at Covaid (SEE FESTIVALS). Thing improved slightly when they employed a full band. Although it wasn't till **Out Of The Blue** were formed that the whole sound took off, albeit without Jimmy Kemp. **Out Of The Blue** were a stylish six piece unit comprising of James O'Neill (Vocals & guitar), Howie Price Sax), Rob Arnall (keyboards), Miles Woodroffe (bass),Ray Jenkins (guitar) and Steve Kenny (drums). I had a lot of time for this band, I remember I once got a call from an excited Sean O'Sullivan he was the A&R guy at A & M Records asking me all about them. He had become interested in them when the news broke they would be supporting Wet,Wet,Wet. Despite such interest they finally split-up and probably went back to their day jobs in Hertford Street.

BEVERLY JONES

Beverly is often sited as Coventry's answer to Brenda Lee, she began singing in Coventry at the age of 14, and entered a talent contest at the Ritz cinema in Coventry singing strangely enough a Brenda Lee song *Let's Jump The Broomstick*. She was to win it and got the singing bug with a capital 'B'. She formed her own band hand picking her favourite local musicians and went under the name **Jackie Laine and the Three Jays**. Beverley was singing in the *Craftsman pub* in Radford, when a man who liked her sound approached her, and promised he would contact her shortly. To her surprise he did and London beckoned.

She was successful in another talent competition and won herself a 5-year recording contract with the famous *EMI* label. She changed her name to Beverley Jones releasing the singles, *The Boy I saw with you*', '*Wait Till My Bobby Gets Home*' and '*Why Do lovers Break Each Others Heart*'. Although none of them charted, it's testament to her success, when a certain Dusty Springfield was once in Beverley's dressing room and was told to leave because It belonged to Miss Jones! She had an incredibly powerful voice, and recorded some strong material, in a fairer world she would be in the record books several times, but it wasn't to be. Although she was 'known' enough to have her life story depicted in a comic strip in the *Judy* comic. Things were going well for the teenage Beverly Jones, but the records she was making were using big bands as backing. She desperately wanted to return to using a beat band, so in '63' she teamed up with Coventry band **The Millionaires** for a while, (Ricky Dawson, their lead singer, was known as "The Duke"). Later joining up with the band **The Prestons** and switched labels to Polydor and recorded the powerful single '*Heatwave*' (a perfect pop record, complete with a dynamic organ solo). Eventually leaving **The Prestons** she fronted new band **Mad Classix**, she would marry the lead singer (also from Coventry) **Johnny Wells**. She spent the rest of the decade being a mum but continued singing whenever she could, including a stint in the band **Hells Angels**. In 1976 she had joined four guys and the group **Formula 5** were born, even getting themselves on the talent show of the time New Faces. Despite the lack of chart success Beverly's great voice did herself and Coventry proud and she got to mix with the likes of the Beatles and Freddie and The Dreamers in the bargain. For more information log onto Beverley's website at *http://beverleyjones.4t.com/index.html*

JOHNNY B GREAT

Johnny Goodison a big man, with a big voice. Originally an apprentice toolmaker in the City went under the name **Johnny B.Great** along with the band **The Goodmen** consisting of Don Kerr (guitar) Olly Warner (bass), Al King (sax) and Nigel Lomas (drums). Nigel (who was also in **The Zodiacs**) is the older brother of Roger Lomas (SEE ROGER LOMAS). They were managed by Larry Page based at The Orchid Ballroom in Coventry (SEE VENUES). Their first vinyl outing was the 1963 Decca single *School Is In* with backing vocals supplied by the Coventry school girl trio **The Orchids** (SEE THE ORCHIDS), who were also managed by Larry Page. Although not a hit it did make history by becoming the first single released by a Coventry pop group. They were to return the favour and play on the Orchids first single *Gonna Make Him Mine*.

The mighty *Acapulco 1922* followed. It's plain to see why Mr Goodison was to go on to become a successful session singer when you hear his dynamic vocals on this truly classic record. The fact it never charted remains one of those sad little mysteries. It did become a hit however for the likes of Kenny Ball and Herb Albert. The B-Side *You'll Never Leave Him*, was also covered by Lulu (with the obvious gender change).

The music world is littered with tales of "If only" and "So near, yet so far". **Johnny B.Great and the Goodmen** have such a story to tell. Just after the release of *School Is In, Decca* were looking for a band to record a sure-fire hit that had done well in the States for the band The Contours. The Goodmen were a gnat's whisker in securing the session, but because they had just had a single out, the song *Do You Love Me* was given to Brian Poole and The Tremeloes instead. Frustratingly for Johnny and the boys it went straight to number one. Unabated they continued to release more records included *If I Had A Hammer* (Johnny performed this for the film *Just For You*, a movie that also featured **The Orchids**). Rather bizarrely Johnny and co appear on the B-side of the original *Doctor Who theme song*. This rather strange unrelated pairing was billed as **Brenda and Johnny** singing the Rogers and Hart song *This Can't Be Love*. Even more curious is that there is a connection. The A-side is performed by **The Radiophonic Workshop**, featuring Coventry's Delia Derbyshire! (SEE DELIA DERBYSHIRE). So a Coventry connection there after all, more by luck than judgement of course. For a while they went under the name of **The Quotations,** backing the likes of The Walker Brothers and Little Richard. From then on Johnny became a name on the session circuit. In 1970 he reverted back to his real name of Johnny Goodison and released the single *One Mistake*. While drummer Nigel Lomas joined his brother Roger Lomas in the group **Clouds** and later **The Eggy** (SEE ROGER LOMAS). Meanwhile Olly Warner joined **The Autocrats.**

In the mid seventies producer and composer Tony Hiller put together The **Brotherhood Of Man**, (this was the mark one model, not to be confused with the mark 2 version that went on to win Eurovision with *Save Your Kisses For Me* all completely different members). They were Johnny Goodison with Roger Greenaway, Tony Burrows, Sunny Leslie and Sue Glover. Each member already had an impressive history, Roger Greenway lead singer with The Fortunes and writer of *You've Got Your Troubles*. Sunny Leslie and Sue Glover were much in demand backing singers. Sunny achieved a solo hit with *Doctors Orders* and Tony Burrows would later dominated the charts (and appear on one *Top of The Pops* 3 times in the same night with 3 different songs). He was the 'voice' of The Pipkins with *Gimme Dat Ding*, White Plains *My Baby Loves Lovin* and Edison Lighthouse with

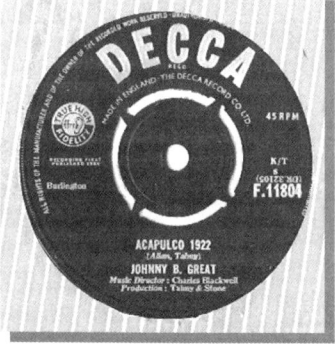

Love Grows (Where My Rosemary Goes) and much later First Class and *Beach Baby*. **Brotherhood Of man's** first single *Love One Another* failed to set the charts alight but their second outing *United We Stand* (co written by Johnny under the alias Peter Simons) clocked in at number 10 In the UK (and 13 in the US). It was adopted as a Gay anthem in America. *Where Are You Going To My Love?* Saw them at 22 in the British charts, it was also co written by Johnny. On leaving **The Brotherhood of Man** he joined the James Last Orchestra along with Sunny Leslie as a backing singer, but still persued his own career with **Big John's Rock'n Roll Circus** putting out singles *Lady* and *When Will You Be Mine* and the album *On the Road*. He also wrote the hit song *Give A Little Love* for the Bay City Rollers and produced the hit single *Race With The Devil* for the heavy band Gun. He continued releasing singles under his own name (*One Mistake, Summertime Blues*) and as **Johnny Goodison and the Second Time Around** (*Get It Together*) throughout the seventies, his last single was to be *I'm Going Down*. On September 3rd 1988 Coventry was sadly robbed of a unique talent when Johnny died from a heart attack.

JOHNNY, JIMMY AND NIGEL AS IT 'APPENS.

THE BROTHERHOOD OF MAN

GODIVA ROCKS SOUND BYTE WITH- Nigel Lomas (Johnny B Great, The Zodiacs, Clouds, The Eggy) We were the Resident Band at The Wolfe and The Freeman, Thursday Friday and Saturday nights. One Sunday we were asked to play at the Irish 32 Club at Orchid Ballroom, after The Wolfe gig. The Manager LARRY PAGE liked what he saw and asked us if he could manage us, we agreed and went for a record test at Holick and Taylor Studios Birmingham. The Songs were Dancing Party (Chubby Checker), My Mothers Eyes. Dick Rowe chief A&R at Decca came to see us and signed us to Decca.

Larry Page employed us to play resident at the Orchid Ballroom for a short period. In between times he ran talent competitions with a view to building his own stable of artists, such as The Orchids, Shel Naylor, Little Lenny Davis and The Chimes, and on some of our records we were augmented by session men known as Decca sound. Big Jim Sullivan (guitar), Jimmy Page, John Paul; Jones (bass) Eric Ford (bass) Arthur Greenslade (keyboards), Red Price (sax) Benny Green (sax) Kenny Lord Baker (trumpet) Bobby Graham dummer (ex JoeBrown) Ronnie Stevenson Drummer – Johnny Dankworth). Vocal backing ex Vernon Girls The Breakaways, Musical Director Mike Leander (Gilitter Band) Producers Shel Talmy and Mike Stone of Hermans Hermits, Kinks, Stones, Dave Berry and P.J. Proby.fame.

In July 63, Johny B Great passed an audition for Nottingham. The band increased from 4 Johny Goodison (piano and vox.) Nigel Lomas – (drums) Dick Morden (Lead guitar – deceased) Colin Warner (bass) to Morden Don Fern (Bass guitar)- Rockin Ronnie (Tenor Saxophone) and Mel Thorp (alto sax) .This was brought to an abrupt end in October 1963 after outstanding success, because the Mecca Organisation would not allow Recording Groups to be part of their set up, so we chose to leave to carry on touring. We often meeting up with the Stones at the Knutsford Services, getting banned from the services with the sugar lump raids. We continued touring 1964. We were also set to appear in a film, but once again fate was not kind and our transport broke down, Johnny went on ahead while we waited for the van to be fixed , by the time we made it to the studio Johnny had performed If I had A Hammer on his own. Our moment of glory had gone.

PAGE 45   GODIVAROCKS@YAHOO.CO.UK   PAGE 45

KENILWORTH

Sleepy little Kenilworth, small but had/has a lot of bands to offer. **Los Cimmarons** who consisted of Dave Smith (vocals), Ray Dutton (lead guitar), Mark Gilks (rhythm guitar), Dick Scott (bass) and Des Kendrick (drums) Were a young beat band circa 1965 from the town, they recorded a demo at *Panthos Studios, Balsall Common*. Songs included *You Called Me, That's Why I Can't Sleep At Night, If I Were you* and *All Of The Day*. Also in the 60's beat band **The Mustangs** (SEE THE MUSTANGS) were based in the town. In the 70's new wavers **The Tory Party** ruled the roost.

The Ak band, were probably the nearest thing Kenilworth ever had to a hit band. Playing ska music very much in the mould of Bad Manners, their song *Pink Slippers* has graced many a Best of Ska album (like *100% British Ska*). They released the singles *8 3 12* and *Over You* as well as the aforementioned *Pink Slipper* in the early 80's. They also released the album *Manhole Kids* on RCA in 1981. Lead vocalist and Bass Player Neville went on to join the band **Coma Cou,** who featured on the *Rhythm Method* (SEE STUDIOS) album along with Kenilworth poet **Mike Starkey.** Not forgetting the gloriously named **Desperate Dan Cowpie Blues Band** who actually supported the mighty INXS once in Leicester. **St Vitus Dance** were also based in the town, joined *Lenchest Ltd* an agency that handled Bronski Beat, there was talk of a video for their song *Strange Head*, heaven knows if it was ever released. **Lament** are the current contenders of the Town. A six-piece band armed with the kind of chill music that Sade could only dream of. Kath Kimber has an naturally amazing voice. Combine this with the musicianship of Yael, Anthony, Ben, Rob and Dave and you have a perfect blend of jazz/folk/blues. Already they have a huge fan base, if you want to know why check out their fine albums *lament* and *In The Dark Hours.*

Katharine Brown (guitar and vocals), James Gardiner (drums) and Catherine Preston (bass) are collectively known as **Little Girl With Cherries.** A young rock band with an attitude, they describe their hometown as a multicultural melting pot of OAP's. As you can see they have a refreshingly humorous take to their music. **The Way** were formed in 2001, they consist of Chris Clarke, Kit Thrippleton, Marcus D and Nicky Ellis-Ryder. Very much a pop band, with some great harmonies going on *Make Me Rich* is a splendid track. They have taken part in *The Coventry Youth Festival* along side the likes of Liberty X and Blazin' Squad. Heavy rock band **Cepheus** are also from the town (SEE HEAVY ROCK). Not forgetting **Silversand** and **Usual Suspects.** Lastly we have *MDM Music* in The Square, a guitar shop run by Mick Dolby. For Bluegrass music the Mecca is *Kenilworth Sports and Social Club* every Friday . Then there's the coversband **The Poptarts.**

KING

Get your boots on, here's our favourite 80's band **King.** When the death bell finally peeled for **The Reluctant Stereotypes** (SEE THE RELUCTANT STEREOTYPES), Winston Smith miraculously transformed into Paul King and brought along fellow Stereotypes bass man Tony Wall and drummer Colin Heanes. Enter one Perry Haines, founder and editor of the iconic fashion *ID-Magazine*, and Duran Duran video director. He became the bands manager. Taking over stylistic and financial control completely. **Kings** success was all part of a charted campaign for Haines. This is evident in the bands primal name **The Raw Screens,** the raw talent hidden under a screen, their name was always going to be King. This was Perry's way of keeping his brainchild hidden until they were ready for full national consumption. Gigs at the *Sportsman's Arms* and *The Hope and Anchor* gave them the time to gel, and how.

When King were finally unleashed the package was complete, In Paul King they had a front man of the highest order, theatrical, good looking, charismatic with a perfect 80's voice (but a product of the 70's). Add the musically gifted Jim 'The Jackel' Landsbury from soul band **Team 23** (SEE DAVE PEPPER) doing his best axe hero dynamics on guitar. Not forgetting the workmanlike Tony Wall on Bass, the keyboard wizardry of Mick Roberts (a former member of local band **The M.P's,** who released the single *Life On The Dole)*. and the fine drumming of Colin Heanes. They just couldn't fail, but first the package had to be wrapped in something, with a fashion icon as a manager you always knew it would be something a bit special. The imagatron was on full power with Max Miller suits multi coloured sprayed Doc Marten boots with matching leather jackets for the boys in the band. Paul insisted they were not a fashion band, preferring to be in the Melody Maker than The Face, but the reality was clear. As Perry told me at the time, he had the Pride he was now after the love. Their image was given a finally tweak and in the *Pete Best fate for drummers style* Colin Heanes first then John Hewitt a little later were dismissed. Hewitt was from the Cov punk band The **The Pseuds,** that also included Dexy's man Mick Gallic. He also drummed on Love and Pride, replaced by permanent live stand-in the former Members drummer Adrian Lillywhite and brother of producer Steve Lillywhite.

OK, got the music, got the look (and a deal with Doc Martens boots) now for the hit, *Love and Pride,* a sure fire winner, straight in your face, vocals coming in the first few seconds, it couldn't fail, it did. Originally released in 1984 it got to number 84. It was put on the back burner, while *Soul on My Boots* was released, again the British public was not following the game plan. Haines then secured a support slot for the band on the Culture Club tour. No longer playing the likes of **The Wolfe** and **The Lanch**, this was big time arena's like the 11,000 seater NEC. This time *Love and Pride* did the business and shot to number 2 in January 1985. Kingmania had hit. Paul King always dedicated the song (and eventual single) *Torture* to Barbara Dixon and Elaine Page who would hold the top spot that January effectively robbing King of a number one hit. I remember walking down St Michael's Road in Stoke and saw Paul King through his window sat at the piano working at his craft, I wondered what was to come. The answer was the debut album *Steps in Time (6)* (produced *by* Richard James Burgess of Landscape fame, who also drummed on the album). It was a clear indication that King had done their homework, if ever a groups very ethos was captured in a time capsule of an album then this was it. *Steps In Time* was the perfect title and a near perfect debut, from the first doom laden beats of *Fish* to the echoes of confusion in *Trouble,* you just knew that Paul Kings life had been building up to this.. *I Kissed the Spikey Fridge* was probably the Day in The Life of the album. Dynamic and unflinching, when Paul sang ,"Come on and do the la la la", you knew you just had to join in. *Won't You Hold My Hand Now* was released and proved a minor blip at 24, before *Alone Without You* pulled them back to number 8. Along came the second album *Bitter sweet.* OK it's own up time here, while researching this book I went through my old Brum Beat cuttings, where I was aghast to find that I had absolutely panned this album. I love it now, and see no distinction between the first LP and this one, it's all King to me. So sorry lads I got it wrong. On a personal note, at the time of the first album I was on track to be Kings fan club secretary, I went down to 'Kingbase' in London to meet Perry. Sadly it had to be all self-financing and I wasn't about to take that risk, a year later they had split, so I probably made the right decision after all.

Anyway back to King, *Bitter Sweet* attained a healthy number 16 in the charts, it spawned the singles The Taste of Your Tears (11) and the aforementioned Torture (23). After the hype, and countless TV interview (where the lads would always mention Coventry), they split, or rather Paul went solo leaving the other 3 permanent members, behind. Whether this was pre-planned by Mr Haines or just an escape policy we will probably never know. What we do know is this all round complete band that was impressive live (and I for one saw them countless times) was sadly no more. King died young, too young. Paul went off to record the solo LP *Joy* (produced by Dan 'Instant Replay' Hartman). A sort of Paul king's salute to Atlantic Records. The lone single

I Know hit the lower reaches of the charts at 59. Paul also appeared on the Ferry Aid single *Let It Be (1)* produced by Pete Waterman *(SEE PETE WATERMAN).* When the playing of music was over, Paul became a VJ at MTV then with VH1, he's now a senior producer. Perry Haines went on to manager Neneh Cherry, Portishead and Massive Attack, he now works bizarrely as a conservationist with the RSPB. Mick Roberts spent many years as a session musician and studio technician. He was part of the band **The Walnut Conspiracy** with Anthony Harty, they both now play in **The Flying Tortellinis** (SEE THE B LIST)**.** He is also part of the brilliantly funny, though vastly underrated Cov' comedy troop **The Cheeky Chappies.** Jim Landsbury was to work as a sound engineer with Bhangra artists notably **Stereo Nation** (SEE STEREO NATION).

GODIVA ROCKS SOUND BYTE WITH- Paul King (Reluctant Stereotypes & King) My earliest musical memories of Coventry were the Monday night disco at Tiffany's, formerly the Locarno, now a library in the lower precinct. DJ Pete Waterman 'yes he of Pop Idol fame' used to spin reggae & soul tunes alongside mimed performances from the likes of Desmond Decker & Gloria Jones. This weekly event was attended by what seemed to be every under 14 year old in the city & was my first experience of the sexual & violent tensions that always accompanied the Coventry gig & also my introduction to great music, heavy petting & running the gauntlet of the various gangs & thugs between Tiffany's & Pool Meadow bus station.

Alongside the Saturday night reggae youth club at Queen Road Baptist church. Monday night at Tiffany's was the beginning of life long love affair with the sounds of Jamaica that more obviously showed its influence on bands such as the Coventry Automatics whose weekly residency at Mr Georges was always a good night to attend & which laid the foundations of the cities 2-Tone scene as they metamorphosed into The Specials quickly joined by The Selecter.

Both bands recorded at Horizon Studios that used to stand next to the railway station now demolished & was run by Barry Thomas. The studio became identified as the 2-Tone studio & home of ska with the likes of Bad Manners flying up from London to record there with Selector producer Roger Lomax himself a one time member of Coventry pop rockers 'The Dodgers'. Horizon Studios house band was the Reluctant Stereotypes, which is where my music career began. Always a fan of the local live scene I had witnessed great acts such as The Flys 'Love & a Molotov Cocktail'- The Radiators - The End & instrumental jazz ska'ers the Reluctant Stereotypes whose electrified clarinettist Steve Edgson & guitarist later producer of 'Crash' by The Primitives ☐Paul Sampson asked me to add some vocals to their off the wall approach to pop in 1979. The Stereotypes toured the nations clubs; pubs & universities for two years non-stop finally claiming a performance in the Old Grey Whistle Test alongside Adam & the Ants as they banged Ant mania onto the pop charts. As the Stereotypes went our separate ways Ken Brown owner of the General Wolfe in the Foleshill Road offered a life line with free rehearsal space above his pub & live venue. Ken played a big part in supporting & bringing live music into the city I saw a brilliant early Eurythmics show at the Wolfe along with many others.

King came into official being around 1982 playing the General Wolfe ☐ Dog & Trumpet ☐ the Hope & Anchor & the Belgrade studio theatre as we crafted our sound & style. Locally the one Coventry show that will always top my list had to be the bands Apollo gig in March 1985. The first rock show I had ever been to was David Bowie's performance at the theatre in 1973 in full Ziggy mode. Without wishing to sound clich☐d it really did 'change my life' & so Kings show at the height of our chart activity was a full circle in life terms & one I will always remember with affection. PAUL KING

DENNIS KING

Born in Coventry in 1897, stated out as a Shakespearian actor but with a superb baritones voice, good looks and six foot stature, it was inevitable he would eventually leave Britain behind for Broadway. By 1920 he was Stateside making a name for himself. He would soon become Broadways top leading man in the likes of *Showboat, My Fair Lady* and *The Three Musketeers*. It was however in the role of Francois Villion in *The Vagabond King* that he is most remembered. Literally stopping shows with is breathtaking rendition of *Song of the Vagabonds* night after night. He also appeared with Laurel & Hardy in the film *The Devil's Brother (Fra Diavols)* in 1933. He died in New York in 1971.

GODIVAROCKS@YAHOO.CO.UK

RAY KING

Inspirational soul musician that has never really had the recognition he deserves either as a musician or as all-round good guy and as a central figure in the creation of The Specials (SEE THE SPECIALS). Started out as **King Size Kings** in 1965, making the semi-final of *The Melody Maker Beat Contest*. They then became **The Ray King Soul Band** with the line-up that looked like this, Ray King (vocals), Jim Lang (tenor sax), Ken Horton (baritone sax), Terry Leeman (organ), Paul Williams (guitar), Paul Slade (bass) and Malcom Jenkins (drums who had been with **The Pickwicks** (SEE THE PICKWICKS).

Having signed in 1967 to *Pye's Piccadilly* record label they released their first single *Behold* overseen by John Schroeder. They took up residency at the famous *Playboy Club* in London (that played host to the likes of Sinatra, Sammy Davis and George Harrison). They recorded a live album there for Direction Records in 1968. Other singles included *Baby I need You, Now That You're Gone* and *What You Gonna Do*. They eventually changed their name to **The Ray King Soul Pact**, and Terry Howells replaced Terry Leeman on keyboards. Embarking on a tour of UK and Europe that lasted some 18 months non-stop. They played with the likes of Ike & Tina Turner, Marvin Gaye, Otis Redding, Jimi Hendrix and Stevie Wonder! When he got back to Coventry Ray was appalled at the amount of drugs present at clubs in the City (this was the mid-sixties remember), because of it he became close to never playing Coventry again.

Whatever the reason they called it a day in 1968, Leeman joined **The Peeps** later **The Rainbows** and **Still Life** (SEE THE PEEPS, SEE STILL LIFE). While Ray King fronted the following bands **Pharaoh's Kingdom** (that also included Lynval Golding and Silverton Hutchinson later of **The Specials**), (SEE THE SPECIALS) then **Boss**. Ray later took on band management, notably Coventry's **Close To Tears** that he renamed **This Heat** (complete with a new leather jacketed image). They played **Covaid** (SEE FESTIVALS), not surprisingly, for Ray who was one of the first came up with the idea to have a relief concert for Africa in Cov. Straight after *Covaid* **This Heat** got a new manager Mike Henry (he managed **Jimmy Jimmy** (SEE JIMMY JIMMY)), and a new name **The Glory Boys**. that was the last I heard of them. As for Ray, well he went on to set up the agency *JCT* with Cabin Studios boss John Lord (SEE STUDIOS) they were looking for a soul band, the circle was complete!

L'HOMME DE TERRE

Local Cov unit (with a awful joke name, a play on the French for potato, literally meaning 'Man of the ground' as opposed to 'Apple of the ground'). They consisted of guitarist Ady Dix (formerly with **The Targets**), Cary Lord on bass and Caron Joyce on vocals.. A throughput of guitarists including Tony White (from **The Editors**) and Johnny Thompson from **The Wild Boys** (SEE THE WILD BOYS). With keyboard player Toby Lyons (Former **Swinging Cat**, and would be **Colourfield** Member) and Billy Gough on drums (also ex-**Swinging Cats**) (SEE THE SWINGING CATS, SEE THE COLOURFIELD). They came second in the battle of the bands at The Lanch (SEE VENUES). In 1980 they were one of 6 local bands to feature on the *Boys and Girls Come Out To Play* EP (other bands included **The Human Cabbages, The Clique, Profile, Famous Five and First Offence**). Their track (in my view the strongest of the 6) was the ska based *Get A Grip*, thus track boasts some powerful vocals from Caron Joyce. In 1984 Caron, Cary and Ady formed the power pop outfit **Aramalite,** releasing the double A-side single *Living on the Edge/Breakaway* on Cabins Studio's own Sonar Records (SEE STUDIOS). Adrian Dix along with his partner Angie Williams are currently campaigning for there to be a local song writing contest in Coventry as a possible feeder for *Eurovision*.

GODIVAROCKS@YAHOO.CO.UK

LEAMINGTON SPA

Apparently the town has the highest per capita musicians of any UK town. The Leamington Spa Theatre Royal was hosting shows and plays in the 1920's It wasn't until the early 1930's however that Leamington's popular music legacy had a false start. When Leamington born bandleader **Jack Payne** (SEE JAZZ) had put the spa town on the map musically. The town would have to wait many years before any real 'scene' was to happen. Enter **The Challengers** in 1957, formed during the skiffle boom, they were to last until 1965. Lead vocalist Woody Allen joined **The Three Johns.** Other Leamington 60's beat bands included **The Trojans** and **The Sons of Sin. Johnny Clifford and The Presidents** recorded at Cov's *Pathos Studios* (SEE STUDIOS). Soul band **Jalopy Ride** were formed in 1967, their line-up included the famous local producer Johnny Rivers (SEE STUDIOS) on organ and Paul Shanahan who would later join chart act **Cupids Inspiration** on guitar. (This would be a mark 2 **Cupid's inspiration**, without any of the original members that performed on the number 2 hit, Yesterday *Has Gone.* They would become the nucleus of the Leamington rock band **Chevy** (SEE CHEVY)).

The seventies saw local progressive rockers **Barnabus** win the *Melody Maker* National folk/rock contest of 1972. I remember seeing them play at The Walsgrave Hotel in Coventry, I was so impressed because they had a mixing desk! Local unit **The Incas** came third on *The New Faces* TV talent show in the early 70's (SEE TALENT SHOWS). In the early 70's, they had an album out entitled *X-Certificate* on *Tank Records,* it was a bit naughty. Local lady Polly Bolton was singing with **Dando Shaft** (SEE DANDO SHAFT, SEE FOLK). Punk rock was to have an impact on the town, **The Swell Maps** lead by Harbury based Nikki Mattress (later Nikki Sudden) released a few good singles including *Read About Seymour* and *Dresden Style.* In 2002 ex Rolling Stone Mick Taylor played guitar on a Nikki Sudden's album *Treasure Island* recorded at WSRS in Leamington. **The School Meals** were loved by the NME, they released the single *Headmasters* (on Edible Records*)* John Peel played it. They changed their name to **The Defendants** and faded away. **The Shapes** (line up included Seymour Bybuss and bassist Brian Helicopter) always did the business, a great live band had a four track EP put out the 70's on Sofa Records, tracks were *Batman in the Laundrette, Chatterbox, College Girls* and *What's for Lunch Mum?* The eventually signed to Good Vibrations Records and released the single *Disaster.* They also recorded an album *Songs For Sensible People* that would take years to see the light of day. Also on Sofa Records were the mighty **Flack Off** (SEE EUROPEAN SUN), with *Cocktails at Six,* Rod Goodwin was a major mover in the Lemmy' scene. **The Varukers** were an all out punk band in the style of Discharge, *Protest and Survive* was an early single from them, Gavin Ward left to form the Brum based heavy metal band **Bolt Thrower** and Garry Maloney joined Discharge. Other early 70's bands included **Why Not** and **Peppermint Rainbow.**

Radical punkies **The Joyce McKinney Experience** appeared a few times in the nation's indie charts, (Mark Bailey of The KLF used to be their roadie). In the late eighties Leamington became a sort of equivalent of Madchester as NME did a 2 page spread on entitled 'Thrash City.' Bands included **Joyce McKinney Experience, Bad Beach, Slab** (jazzy punk fusion, had the album *Dissension,* and a couple of singles *People Pie* and *Mars on Ice).* **Bad Beach** released an album *Pornocopia.* **Jackdaw with Crowbar** (formerly **Small Town Thunderers**) released an album, *Crossing the Great Divide.* John Peel's words before he played their session was, 'this band are from Leamington Spa, everybody seems to be from Leamington Spa these days.' **Mummy Calls** (SEE MUMMY CALLS), really had it all and should have been huuuuuuuugggggeeee,the weren't. Leamington's Woodbine Studios or WSRS (SEE STUDIOS), became a mecca for local and not so local bands. There were a number of albums released in the 90's entitled *The Sound of Leamington Spa,* to showcase Woodbine and Johnny Rivers, none of the mainly britpop acts were from the town, (and even stranger, none of the tracks on Volume one were recorded in Leamington, subsequent volumes were). The Jazz Butchers were probably the most well know act on the album. Other 80's bands included **Depraved** they had an albums entitled *Stupidity Maketh the Man* and *Come On down* and **Victorian Parents** managed to get themselves on the TV. **The Church, Sharks In Italy,**

(were rumoured to have released an album on *Warner Brothers* in Canada), **The Hop** (who got into the last 8 in *Brum Beats* Battle of the Bands competition) **Cardboard Cutouts** and **The Renegades** also hailed from the Spa town in the 80's. **Banco De Gaia** made Lemmy his base in the 90's (SEE BANCO DE GAIA). Rumours abound that Adamski (now Adam Sky, who's biggest hit, was *Killer* featuring Seal) hails from Leamington, I can't confirm this either way. **Superfly Blue** were a six-piece band playing funkrock/jazz and dance. **Firedaze** (who used to be **Dawn After Dark**) had a pretty good CD released on *Dead Music Records* in 1999. The lead track *End of the Light* could probably be described as medieval folk rock, they also released 3 other singles and a compilation album. **Go Ask Alice** were active in the 80's, as were heavy band **Hell?s Bells** as were blues boys **The Howlin? Wolves. 4 Forty** and **Red Hat, No Knickers** are 2 Lemmy based club bands with a great names.

Penfold are a current Leamington band setting the local scene alight, this power pop unit have a 6 track CD available entitled *Green*. **Mawda** are a pretty interesting punky combo too, quirky and unrefined, but we like that. **Gemma Morgan** has a great voice and deserves some press. The outstanding **The Broken Dolls** are the local band of the moment (SEE THE BROKEN DOLLS). **Souler Rhythm** from Lemmy and Warwick, are a hard working soul/jazz/funk seven piece, not to be missed. **Genius Breed** have a fine vocalist in Paul Walton, their 3 track demo was well impressive, sadly things have seemed to have gone quite of late. **Bridges** are another hard gigging Leamington trio that showed a lot of promise. **Nizlopi** a bright duo who kinda' play their own original music, borrowing from many styles (I get Van The Man and The great Rory McLeod). They already have one quite brilliant album out *Half These Songs Are About you*, and another one following soon, wonderful stuff. Others include **Bovaflux**, indie bands **Budapest, The Great Blind Degree** and **Franksound**. Plus **Cyanide Smyle, Genius Breed, Le Cod Afrique, Llease, The Old No7 Band, Incept, Invention 5, 28 Stitches, The Stolen, Breathing Ether** and **Subject To Change**.

PENFOLD

As for Leamington in song, well you have *Oo La la Lemmy Spa* from **The Joyce McKinney Experience**, *Leamington* from **The Shapes**, and *Flowers From Leamington* from **J-Pac?s** *Heart's and Flowers EP*. Another Lemmy' song occurrence that springs to mind is in the comedy song *Twenty-Four Hours in Tunbridge Wells*. Coming from the 1970's TV show *Rutland Weekend Television*. It's a sort of Gene Kelly pastiche, sailors on spa town shore-leave. Inevitably Eric Idle and Neil Innes sing, "We've Been to Leamington, we've been to Malvern, and we've been to Cheltenham with all of the swells. But the place we dig the most in the world is Tunbridge Wells". **Trinity Street Direct** are based in the town, and provide a database fan-club info on many bands from their HQ at 3 Alverston Place in Leamington. They represent such diverse acts as, S Club Seven, Catatonia, Gabrielle, Lush, Darius,U2, Oasis, A1 and our own **Billie Myers** (SEE BILLIE MYERS). Now over 20 years old the company sent out reply-cards with CD's nowadays it's all done by e-mail. The Company has had some 'strange' visits from fans over the years with fans thinking their idols actually live at that address. Like the guy who came all the way from Italy with a model he had made of Liam Gallagher insisting he must hand deliver it to him

On the live stuff front, well Black Sabbath played *Jephson Gardens Pavillion* on May 17th 1970 *The Leamington Peace Festival* takes place in *The Pump Room* gardens every years. In the late 70's the *Crown hotel* in the High Street used to have live bands on, like **School Meals, The Shapes** and **Chevy** played there. **Mummy Calls** played downstairs at *Winston's* where they used to have bands on regularly on a Saturday night. Elvis Costello, The Photos & Alien Sex Fiend played at the *Spa*. **Mummy Calls** once played at the *Pump Rooms* when they were on the verge of stardom. Mick Jagger filmed part of a promo video at the *Pump Rooms* (SEE THE ROLLING STONES). *Bath Street Community Venture* was a good place in the 80's/90's. Leatherface & Nomeansno were two of the better-known bands. *Kelly's* of Court street were hosts to Half man/ Biscuit, Levellers, and Vibrators, Eddie & the Hot Rods... On 29th January 2002 the Mighty Jethro Tull played and indeed recorded three tracks there for their 2002 reunion DVD *Living With The Past*. The tracks were, *A Song For Jeffery My Sunday Feeling* and *Some Day the Sun Won't Shine For You* (the last track also made it to the album version of the project). Their line-up included old favourites Glenn Cornick, Mick Abrahams and Clive Bunker. These days the Lounge on the Parade is the place to be. Lastly Tachbrook Park, Leamington is a main Sales & Distribution centre for EMI (and *Virgin*) Records.

LIEUTENANT PIGEON

Before we start let's get one thing clear, despite being labelled ' a one hit wonder', **Lieutenant Pigeon** have enjoyed a career path that is festooned with great songs and a body of work that would put many a band to shame. Above all that the 'One hit wonder' epithet is factually inaccurate. Lieutenant Pigeon was a perfect case of the 'best-laid plans of mice and men'. For three years the nucleus that would form Lieutenant Pigeon were members of the Coventry unit Stavely Makepeace (SEE STAVELY MAKEPEACE). That was meant to be the 'serious' project, Lieutenant Pigeon was merely an off-shoot novelty act designed to run alongside Stavely Makepeace the main priority. It of course it never worked out like that.

Without a real hit record to their name, the creative force behind **Stavely Makepeace,** namely Rob Woodward (vocals, piano) and Nigel Fletcher (drums) liked the idea of an off-shoot band based around two pianos, drums and bass. (**Stavely** was far more experimental, with a violinist in their ranks). To give it an even quirkier edge Rob recruited his piano teaching mother Hilda Woodward on second piano (no not Mrs Mills as TV's Eamon Holmes keeps insisting), Steven Johnson **Stavely Makepeace's** bassman completed the line-up. So they began recording a bunch of new songs in their own studio, the front room of Rob's mums at Kingsway, Stoke Coventry. Decca had been interested in **Stavely** so they used this contact to cajole a recording contract for **Pigeon** with the mighty Decca (a label Rob had been associated with some 10 years previously as **Shel Naylor** (SEE SHEL NAYLOR)). The deal was done and the first single was to be *Mouldy Old Dough*. (Rob would say the title was a reference to decimalization that had occurred in the UK a year earlier, in fact the title had just came into his head for no reason and meant nothing in particular). Say what you like about this song, the fact remains it's unforgettable! It's also pretty unique, *Red River Rock* was probably the nearest I could compare it to when I first heard it. It had an off-key slightly unreal double piano sound, with a penny whistle bridge. Basically an instrumental except for Rob's growled vocals the title now and again, it would eventually strike a chord, but not yet.

ROB INSIDE THE KINGSWAY STUDIO

Mouldy Old Dough was dying a death, Radio One hadn't playlisted it. Even a TV interview showing their front room studio in Rob's mums house in Coventry on Central Television (with Chris Tarrant, who would become a close friend of Nigel Fletcher), failed to turn the tide. Well that news programme wasn't to help them, but one in Belgium was. You see unbeknown to them, *Mouldy Old Dough* was being used as a theme tune to a current affairs programme in Belgium, before long it was topping the Belgium charts! Decca began pushing it in the UK. On October 10th 1972 it hit the number one spot in Britain. The first number one from a Coventry group, the first instrumental chart-topper since Fleetwood Mac's *Albatross* and the best selling single of 1972.

It was to stay there for four weeks, putting them (Coventry) on the musical map. I remember hearing it first time at The Walsgrave, it was exciting times for me, a number one from my home city. I can only

PAGE 52   GODIVAROCKS@YAHOO.CO.UK   PAGE 52

Imagine what it must have been like for Rob, Nigel, Hilda and Steve. They were riding on a wave of publicity, the press loved the idea of Mother and son in the same band. Hilda at 60 became one of the oldest people to appear on *Top of the Pops,* because of this they were never a live band, (Their only live performance was on Jimmy Saville's Speakeasy radio programme 17th June 1973). I began this entry by saying **Pigeon** were not a one hit wonder, and it's very true. Their second release *Desperate Dan* (much in the same mould as *Mouldy Old Dough*) made it to number 17, and lets face it many a career has been made by bands not even getting into the top 20, it was to be their last UK hit. Meanwhile *Mouldy Old Dough* was charting in the likes of Canada, Japan, Spain, Holland and Australia. Rob and Nigel also received an *Ivor Novello* award for the song. Despite the hits stopping in the UK, they would still score a number two hit in Australia with *I'll Take You Home Again Kathleen* (plus the hits *The Blue Danube* and *The Grandfathers Clock)*. More singles (but no hits) followed in the UK, *The Fun Goes On, Oxford Bags,* the delightfully strange *Rockabilly Hot Pot* (I have a demo version, with a lyric sheet, a nice idea except the only lyrics are [Ooh-a ooh-a rockabilly hot pot] plus the odd bit of yodelling, brilliant). Its B-side is the Scott Joplin inspired *Gosford Street Rag* (SEE COVENTRY BY NAME). They also released the following LP's *Mouldy Old Music, Pigeon Pie, Pigeon Party* (I believe the cover for this was shot in the Old Ball Hotel) and *The World of Lieutenant Pigeon* was set for release in 1976, but never saw the light of day. Although there has been a few hits packages since. In 1981 they released the single *Bobbing Up and Down Like This* on Neville Staples Shack Record label (SEE NEVILLE STAPLES, SEE THE SPECIALS, SEE THE FUN BOY THREE).

That was pretty much the end of the **Pigeon** singles trail (although **Stavely Makepeace** was to continue a little longer). Rob & Nigel continued their studio work, recording jingles and the like, with Nigel joining bands **Tasty** (with Steve) and **Oakie**. While Rob released the solo single *Bogie* and formed **The Caretakers**. In the late 80's **Pigeon** was reformed and toured Scandinavia (albeit with only Steve being the original member). The last time I saw Rob on TV was in 1988 on *Never Mind The Buzzcocks* in the line up parade, they picked the wrong man! On 22nd February 1999 Hilda Woodward sadly passed away aged 85. In 2000 Nigel and Rob wrote the book *When Show Business is No Business*, it's an absolutely wonderful (and hilarious) read, I thoroughly recommend it, get it from www.billboswell.co.uk Also on the site is various new Lieutenant Pigeon items for sale. Including the CD of *Opus 400* their most ambitious song for many years. I also recently found a polyphonic Nokia ring tune of *Mouldy Old Dough* on the net, so people evidentially still want to hear it. There are a few who would smirk at their name, (Keith Chegwin had the cheek to put their number one on his worst songs ever album). Their brand of music was original and put a smile on everyone's face and to those who would mock them I would ask when was the last time you had a Number One record?

GODIVA ROCKS SOUND BYTE FROM- Rob Woodward (Lieutenant Pigeon & Stavely Makepeace). I think a lot of musicians, singers and bands have done the city proud over the years such as the Specials, Selecter, King and Hazel O'Connor -Even quite a few unsung heroes. In fact during the early 60's Larry Page who was at that time the manager of the Orchid Ballroom got together some local talent (Including myself) to try to match the sledgehammer impact of the 'Liverpool sound' - calling it The Coventry sound but needless to say -without success! Personally being a staunch Rock'n'roller I would have loved to have seen the emergence of a great Rocker such as Presley or Jerry Lee Lewis in the 50's period to match the likes of Cliff Richard and Marty Wilde. Without scoring points for myself, I would have loved to have fitted this particular slot myself (However, being only around 12 years of age at this time -hardly old enough for the young ladies of the day to throw their knickers at me!!!!)

Still, we were grateful for the Mouldy hit. With Decca records on our side at this time I felt we could muster a lower half of the top twenty with Mouldy, but when it hit the number one spot I was knocked sideways -to say the least! I must say that reality did kick in though as to follow up a number one hit with further success definitely had the cards stacked against it -as far as the UK was concerned, this of course proved to be the case (Desperate Dan reaching No 17). The classic double edged sword!

GODIVAROCKS@YAHOO.CO.UK

ROGER LOMAS

Roger David Lomas was born in Keresley Hospital on 8th October 1948, he grew up in Foleshill. Although he's probably better know nowadays as a top flight producer, he has an impressive history of performing. From local bands **George and the Dragons** and **The Clouds** (that also included Nigel Lomas, Rogers older brother on drums and Tony Martin from **Tony Martin and the Echo Four**). His big break came when he joined Coventry's first freakbeat combo **The Sorrows** (SEE THE SORROWS), apparently because he had the right guitar & amp. **The Sorrows** time had passed in the UK, but they were still just about hit makers in Italy. By 1967 however Roger had left them and returned to the UK (to see his new-born child amongst other things), and to begin a new project.

Roger formed a new band **The Eggy.** He tells me that it was just a 'joke' name, coming from the their lead singer who they used to call Bill 'Eggy' Bates. The **Eggy** line was Bill Bates (vocals) he had previously sang with The **Boll Weevils,** Nigel Lomas (drums) (from **Johnny B Great and The Goodmen** and **The Zodiacs**) (SEE JOHNY B GREAT). Roger on guitar and Billy Bates (bass). They

CLOUDS

released their one and only single on the newly formed Spark Record Label. Both songs had been previously demoed by Roger while he was with **The Sorrows**. They were *Hookey* and the A-side *You're Still Mine*. I have the pleasure of owning this track (twice in fact, by **The Eggy** and **The Sorrows** too). It's a fantastic piece of rockin' freakbeat, reminiscent of *Hi Ho Silver Lining*, but pretty damn good. When **Eggy** had an ouef 1971 (sorry about that), Roger teamed up with his old Sorrows pal Pip Whitcher to form **Rog & Pip** to do session work, Paul Hooper (later of **The Dodgers** and **Indian Summer**) (SEE INDIAN SUMMER)joined they became **The Zips** in 1973. Finally becoming slightly glam rock as **The Renegades** (the leather all-in-one suits they wore were all made by Roger himself) they consisted of Nigel Lomas (drums), Mick Eastbury (bass) with Pip and Roger both on guitar and vocals. They released one pretty awful single in 1973 on Parlophone entitled *Lovin' and Forgiving* (with *Never Let Me Go* on the B-side). Both sides featured singer Virginia Williams and were

THE EGGY

produced by Roger. He then went to **The Dodgers**. Who included in their ranks Rob Jackson and Paul Hooper (ex-Indian Summer) (SEE INDIAN SUMMER, SEE ROB JACKSON). They released two singles (*Love on The Rebound* & *Any*time) and an album (*Love on The Rebound*) for Polydor in 1978.

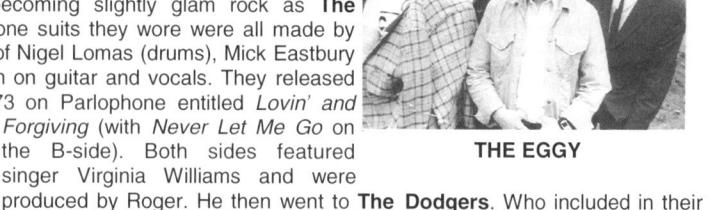

THE RENEGADES

It was around this time Roger had built a four-track studio in his Broad Street garden. He got a visit from a certain Neol Davies with an idea for a new song, it was duly recorded and the track would eventually be called *The Selecter* and grace the B-side of **The Specials** (and 2 Tone) first single *Gangsters*. It would also pave the way for Neol to form a band around the name **The Selecter**. (SEE THE SPECIALS, SEE THE SELECTER, SEE 2 TONE). From then on Roger became 'the man' when it came to producing 2Tone. He became the 'In-House' producer at Coventry's *Horizon Studios* (SEE STUDIOS). He produced Bad Manners, The Modettes, The Vetoes and **The Selecter.** In 1979 he had the honour to have three of his productions on the same Top of the Pops. He also got to be on *TISWAS* on a regular basis, appearing with his white roller' as the chauffeur. He has produced over 17 hit singles and over 10 LP's. He became Roy Wood's tour manager, and continued to produce acts like **The Specials,** Desmond Dekker and Roy Wood. He set up his own *Ro-Lo Studios* in Coventry where he famously recorded, engineered and produced dub reggae legend Lee 'Scratch' Perry's album *Jamacian ET*. Winning Roger a *Grammy* for the best reggae album in 2003. Rogers son Kevin is also in the business as part of The Subterraneans.

GODIVAROCKS@YAHOO.CO.UK

GODIVA ROCKS SOUND BYTE FROM- Roger Lomas (The Sorrows, The Eggy, record producer).
Which do you prefer producing or singing?
1. My career as a Producer has been very good to me... but, being totally honest, If I had to choose just one area in the music industry to earn a living from, then it would be standing on a stage strumming a guitar.

What was the most memorable thing about The Specials days?
2. The most memorable thing about The Specials days was how blind the record companies were at the time, in not spotting how huge the whole 2 TONE movement was to become. They totally blanked the Specials in 1979, as they did The Selecter two years earlier in 1977 when I recorded their first single in my home studio.

Whets your proudest moment?
3. I suppose my proudest moment music-wise in addition to producing 18 'hit' singles to date, was receiving a prestigious Grammy Award last year (2003) for producing an album entitled "Jamaican E.T." with legendary reggae artist Lee'Scratch'Perry'. It won the Best Reggae Album category for 2002 & again was recorded in my own studio.

Was there some kind of Coventry club at the TISWAS studio?
4. With regard to the Tiswas days .... I personally got to know all the production team & the presenters of the show at Central TV due to the fact that my business manager at the time, Mike Smith was, & still is, married to Sally James the show's main presenter at the time. As far as Nigel Fletcher is concerned I know he is a personal friend of Chris Tarrant, hence his connection there.... otherwise I am not aware of any Coventry club, as you put it.

Was it a bad experience in *The Dodgers?*
5. Playing in The Dodgers was certainly not a bad experience for me, on the contrary I loved almost every minute of it. All of the members of the band are still some of my best friends & always will be. We did a couple of good tours and made a couple of good records, who's failure I put down to rotten timing as the punk movement was taking off big-time, & anything musically credible at the time, seemed to fall by the wayside.

THE LOVER SPEAKS

When **The Flys** split up in 1980 (SEE THE FLYS), Dave Freeman and Joe Hughes became members of **Roddy Radiation and the Tearjerkers** (SEE RODDY RADIATION). Freeman also released a solo single, *Stop in The Name of Love*, took a degree, issued poetry and co produced and performed on *The Raindancing* album for Alison Moyet. In 1986 Freeman and Hughes formed **The Lover Speaks** (the name was taken from Roland Barthe's *A Lover's Discourse*). After getting their demo tape through to producer Jimmy Iovine (via Dave Stewart and Chrissy Hynde) they secured a deal with A&M Records. Releasing the eponymous LP in 1986. An album that boasted some carefully crafted atmospheric moments (a huge departure from **The Fly's** punky sound). The track (and I quote Freeman here). "That followed me like a slug". Was the single *No More I love You's*. Charting in the UK at 58, (more about that later). The band toured with The Eurythmics and had a second track from their album *Every Lovers's Sign (remix)* go to number 6 in the US hot dance music charts. A second album *The Big Lie*, never saw the light of day and A&M let them go as they say. That would be the end of the story if former Eurythmic Annie Lennox hadn't decided to cover *No More I love You's* on her 1995 *Medusa* album. Eventually releasing the song as a single, achieving a number 2 in The UK and number 23 in The US. Dave Freeman likened it to a Lottery win, claiming both himself and his accountant loved Annie's version of the song. Dave in the interim released countless low-key solo albums as well as enduring his Coventry home burning down.

THE LUDICROUS LOLLIPOPS

Student based Coventry outfit, **The Lollies'** released 2 singles and 2 E.P's between 1990-92. Played 'crazy pop' in a Ned's Atomic Dustbin style. Were well received especially by Steve Lamacq at radio One, even clipping the national charts (112) with the *Scrumdiddlyumptous* EP. Sadly in 92 it all went sour and the end was inevitable.

BEVERLY MARTYN

It's not a well-documented fact but folk singer Beverly Martyn was actually from Coventry. Born Beverly Kutner she attended *Broad Heath School*. She went on to The *Corona Academy of Theatre* where she became the front person for the jug band **The Levee Breakers**. She later released her first single on Parlophone *Babe I'm Leaving You*. She eventually signed for Decca's progressive label Deram in 1966. Known as simply 'Beverly' her first single was *Happy New Year* followed by a cover version of Donovan's *Museum* in 1967. She was taught to play guitar by the legendary Bert Jansch. She played at the famous Monterey Pop festival, introduced by none other than Paul Simon. Her voice can be heard saying "Good Morning Mr Leitch, have you had a busy day?" on the track *Fakin' It* from Simon and Garfunkel's *Bookends* LP, (the comment incidentally is reputedly a diatribe aimed at folk singer Donovan Leitch). She met John Martyn when he became her backing guitarist. They signed to *Warner Brothers* in America, and *Island Records* in the UK, releasing *Stormbringer* in November 1970, it featured Levon Helm from The Band. John and Beverley married in 1969. The couple would record one more album together *Road To Ruin* in 1970. Beverley gave up music to spend time to bring up the couple's children. Although she would make the occasional appearance on John's albums, the couple finally separated in 1978. Beverley released her first solo album *No Frills* in 1999, showcasing her pure and distinctive voice, (it also features her son Spencer). Meanwhile the quite brilliant John Martyn (a man with a voice like tortured velvet) continues to knock out classic records despite the setbacks of drink and drug dependency, marriage breakdowns and recently loosing a leg.

BRIAN MATTHEW

Brian was born in Coventry Sept 7th 1928, and is probably one of the best known DJ's of the early sixties, his voice was like that of a kind old uncle. He originally started out as an actor and studied at RADA and had much experience in rep. His broadcasting career began in 1948 in Germany. He joined the BBC in 1954 and presented classic shows such as *Saturday Club, Late Night Extra* and *Be My Guest*. He also hosted the seminal TV show *Thank Your Lucky Stars*. Though *Saturday Club* (originally *Saturday Skiffle Club* in 1957) remains his finest moment, with some 14 appearances by the Beatles (SEE THE BEATLES). They first appeared in January 1963, and pretty much made it their own. It became a perfect platform for their dry 'scouse' humour, especially at Christmas time. When the audience was treated to seasonal messages and the like. Brian even appeared on their *Live at the BBC* album, and his Beatle interviews have turned up on many bootleg LP's. Coventry's own Frank Ifield has also made appearances on his show.

In the mid sixties he presented and produced *The Easy Beat* radio show on Sunday mornings. While the 70's saw him present the film review show *Round Midnight* on Radio 2 and released the records *Goodness Gracious Me* (with Maureen Evans) and *What's It All about* (with Peter Murray).
In 1988 Brian was named *Music Media personality of the Year*. He still broadcasts on BBC Radio 2 on Saturday mornings on *Sound of the Sixties*, where he was recently heard played and talking about **The Orchids** (SEE THE ORCHIDS) and Stoke Park!

GODIVAROCKS@YAHOO.CO.UK

MEDIA

Every town and city needs some sort of kingpin foundation when it comes to representing urban culture, if it's lucky the local newspaper will fulfil the role. Coventry has been lucky to have the *Telegraph*, say what you will about them, but we all use it sometime or the other. Wonder kid (and former Henry VIII pupil) *Paul Connew* and his *City Beat* column came in circa 1965. Before then pop music reporting in Coventry seemed a little patchy. Paul ran an article in *The Coventry Express* in May 1965 on an *Express* poll of local bands. Winners were quite worryingly **The Matadors** who although played in the area a lot were in fact a Hinckley band. While **The Mighty Avengers** from Rugby came 6th and Coventry's own **Sorrows** came last at number seven! (SEE THE MIGHTY AVENGERS, SEE THE SORROWS). Paul himself raised the age-old question of *The Coventry Sound*, and suggested that because the scene was becoming more diverse such a sound could soon establish it's self. It could be argued however that the more diverse a sound the less chance there is to have a unified Coventry Sound? Paul also wrote *Teen Scene (*with *Heather Tayton)* for the *Coventry Standard*, he eventually went off to work at The Daily Mirror.

The Great *Coventry Evening Telegraph* has had many pop writers, but they didn't really appear until 1967 in the form of Ken Hillman. Other notable music scribes were Matthew Pearson, Simon Bradshaw, Chris Wilson, Tracey Harrison, Demetrious Matheou, Alastair Law and Jim Taylor. Jim was there when I was at Brum Beat. There was always a bit of friendly rivalry between us, until we both ended up on the Covaid committee (SEE FESTIVALS). That kind of put everything in perspective. I remember being paranoid about the fact I had become the manager of the band **Terminal Tears** and felt a little compromised as a scribe (SEE TERMINAL TEARS). I later found out Jim was also managing a band too, Jim moved on to the tabloids in London. Simon Kelly was another muso journalist around at the time, he had a lot of flair as a writer. Robert Plummer took over from Jim at *The Telegraph*. Although in my humble opinion the best music scribe *The Telegraph* have ever had is the current man, Dayle Crutchlow. His style of writing is superb, he also has his finger on the proverbial pulse. It can't be long before Canary Wharf beckons. Having said that Dayle has gone one better than managing a band, he's in one! Mr Crutchlow is in Nuneaton outfit **Lazy Eye**. So maybe he has a future there as well. Dayle also edited *The Telegraphs Go Magazine* shame it came to an end it was always a great read and boasted some great photography from Joe Kerrigan. Can I also mention Alan Poole here, another class act from *The Telegraph,* his style of writing is both compelling and incisive.

Other mags of note are *The Broadgate Gnome* an underground 'hippie' newspaper set up by Ian Green and Paul Leather, it ran from 1970-71. It also has a great retro website at http://www.broadgategnome.co.uk/. *Hobo* was similar publication, it included a soul page from Pete Waterman (SEE PETE WATERMAN). I must also mentioned my paper *Brum Beat* a midlands music freesheet. It was pretty good in my opinion, former Black Sabbath manager Jim Simpson was the Editor, I did the Coventry Column, *The Coventry Gazebo.* I also wrote the column *Surround Sounds* in the freesheet *The Coventry Weekly News,* oh happy days. *The Rugby Advertiser* too has a long tradition on mentioning local bands. *The Observers* (be it Cov, Rugby, Leamington or Nuneaton) all include some local scene column space as does *The Coventry Citizen*. Yeah we would always like a bit more, but Editors and Subbie's know best (no sarcasm intended there). During the 2 Tone revolution many magazines and music papers highlighted Coventry. Q Mag did a great " 2 Tone map and *Musicians Only in March 1980* did a info packed centre page spread on the city. Worth a mention was *The General Wolfe* great in-house mag called *The Wolfe* (SEE VENUES), then there's *Alternative Sounds* our finest fanzine followed *by Adventures In Reality* (SEE *ALTERNATIVE SOUNDS)*. These really did pull it off albeit in a very basic cut 'n' paste way, but at least we had at last a great (and enthusiastic) source of information on the local scene.

attenshun'
MUSIC FROM ROUND 'ERE

As for the web we have *IC Coventry* basically T*he Telegraph* on-line at http://iccoventry.icnetwork.co.uk/. Then there's CWN http://www.cwn.org.uk/ both have a fair amount of music news on their pages. By far the best local music site is *Attenshun* at http://www.attenshun.co.uk/ its full of local stuff it really is a must for area bands. As for local radio, well what can I say, there has been lapses into the local band arena, *Mercia (Sound or FM)* have been know to have a band contest. Incidentally *Mercia Sound* came on air at 6.58am on Friday 23rd May 1980, the first song played by Gordon Ashley was Dan Hartman's *This is it!*

GODIVAROCKS@YAHOO.CO.UK

Local BBC tends to be more community orientated than the commercial boys. so local music can get a little look-in. TV too has not been very local band friendly apart from *COLT*, on Coventry Cable as it was. They had a very wonderful regular round up of local talent, sadly all that died when the NTL took over. Central TV did run The show *Rock Legends*, where Noddy Holder would showcase midlands chart acts of the past, including **Hazel O'Connor** and **The Specials** (SEE HAZEL OCONNOR, SEE THE SPECIALS).

THE MIGHTY AVENGERS

We have a local first here. Rugby's **Mighty Avengers** were the first local band to make an impact on the charts with *So Much In Love* in 1964, but I'm speeding ahead here. OK let's go back a little to 1962 when Tony Campbell (lead guitar, vocals) Dave 'Biffo' Beech (drums and vocals), Mike Linnell (bass and lead vocal) and Kevin 'Bep' Mahon guitar and harmonica) came together from various low-key local bands to form **The Avengers**. Soon after that they became **Dean Law and The Avengers**, Dean was soon to leave and they eventually settled for the name **The Mighty Avengers** (mainly because a band in Birmingham was also using the name The Avengers). After much touring (and local 'Twang Dances') they signed with Decca Records and released the single *Hide Your Pride*, by all accounts it was a non-starter. Their luck was about to change when the then Rolling Stones manager the enigmatic Andrew Loog Oldham took the band under his wing. Their second single *So Much In love* was written by Mick Jagger and Keith Richard (it's easy to imagine Jagger singing this by the way), produced by Andrew Loog Oldham with musical direction by John Paul Johns (who would eventually be part of Led Zeppelin). This time they made the charts at number 46 (and became 79 in The Single of the Year for 64). Being in the same camp as The Stones meant they had the pick of any song the Glimmer twins decided they didn't want to use themselves. As was the case for their next 2 singles, the great *Blue Turns To Grey*, sadly not to be a hit for **The Mighty Avengers**, but a certain Cliff Richard would go to 15 with it a year later. Their last offering in 1965 was the quite magnificent *(Walkin' Thru the) Sleepy City*. This really should have done the business big time. It was a well crafted pop song; sad thing is it never charted at all. By 1966 they would move on, and Tony, Kevin and Dave would form the nucleus of Rugby's **Jigsaw** (SEE JIGSAW).

GODIVA ROCKS SOUND BYTE WITH-Tony Campbell (The Mighty Avengers & Jigsaw) We played many venues in Coventry and Rugby first, being part of the Coventry "Twang" scene including a regular once a week stint at the Walsgrave Hotel. Other regular nights were run by "Friars Agency" and other promoters in the City including the Pilot, Parkstone Club and many many others. In fact on a Friday and Saturday, there were two pages of adverts for venues in the Telegraph, I think I counted twenty eight pubs with live bands one night. We regularly supported name acts on the Reg Calvert circuit. Now you might have known Reg, and if you did please forgive me for mentioning him, but he lived just up the road at Clifton Hall, and was host to two resident bands (Danny Storm and the Strollers and Buddy Britten and the Regents) who lived in and formed the backbone of his promotions around the area. Later he was responsible for putting the Fortunes together and lost his life during the Radio Pirates (Radio Sutch/390) era. He used many headliners and also local bands like us in support. We worked regularly with Joe Brown, and played with the Beatles at Nuneaton Co-op hall on the night that Love Me Do was released. Denny Laine (of Moodys and Wings fame) was also on the bill fronting his band the Diplomats.

We managed to start working further a field, and managed to secure a management deal with Kennedy St Artistes in Manchester. They were also managing Herman`s Hermits, Freddie & The Dreamers, Wayne Fontana and others, Our Manager Danny Betesh negotiated a deal with Decca and we recorded our first record "Hide Your Pride" at Decca No1. This is best forgotten and luckily died without trace. Our second attempt was under the guiding hand of that well known nutter Andrew Loog Oldham, then the Rolling Stones Manager, hence the reason why we recorded two Jagger/Richard songs "So Much In Love" and "When Blue Turns To Grey" (Later done by Cliff Richards who had a hit with it). **Continued**

Continued from previous page. Mild success with So Much, nothing with When Blue. None of the Stones played on our tracks , but we augmented with John Paul Jones (on piano) and Jimmy Page, both pre-Zepplin, playing session at the time, (Jimmy did that lovely solo in Dave Berry`s Crying Game). Our last effort with Loog Oldham was a track called Walking Through the Sleepy City, which was when he had had pinched Phil Spector`s "wall of sound" head. We recorded it in one take with at least forty session musos and everything but the kitchen sink on it.

We did not have great success in the UK, but So Much. did well in Australia. Loog Oldham was visiting Oz and he was questioned by the press, not about the Stones who hadn't had a hit there then, but about us. Since he was only our Recording Manager and wasn't really interested in us other than a vehicle with which to make money, he didn't know much about us, and the question took him by surprise. There are many happy memories of the Mighty Avengers time, not least the great early days around Coventry, the midnight band bowling league, late night meals at Gregs on Ball Hill. The good friends we made in other bands like the Hinckley Matadors, Tony Martin, Pip Witcher, Don Fardon and a lot more. Happy times in Manchester with Jimmy Saville, Gerry & The Pacemakers, The Hollies, Fourmost, Blue Jeans, Freddie & Herman (affectionately referred to as Gap Gob) We came to the end of the Avenger road in 1966, but Biffo and Kevin joined me when I decided to start a six piece band called Jigsaw, but that is another story. Tony Campbell.

MUMMY CALLS

In 1980 something very magical began happening in Leamington four guys came together to form Leamington's finest band **Mummy Calls**. With a sound all their own, they could mesmerise an audience with just a few well chosen lights, such was the power of their atmospheric delivery. I don't flatter them they really were that good. By 1983 they had reached the line-up of David Jones (vocals & guitar), Andrew Johnson (bass), Paul Williams (drums), Alan Adair (keyboards) and Paul Soleman (sax). It was the year that saw the release of their first single the enigmatic *Mary I Swear*. Recorded of course at Woodbine Studios (SEE STUDIOS), as I said at the time it was an imaginative gem of a song. David Jones had the knack of being laid back and 'in your face' at the same time with his stunning vocal deliveries. Apart from the single other live favourites were *Sexual Desire* and a classic among classics *The Chestnut Tree*. Shivers down your spine stuff, it all worked so well. It could only be a matter of time before **Mummy Calls** would hit critical mass.

Then so it was, in 1986 they signed for the US based label Geffen Records. (I was pretty smug as I predicted in my column that "**Mummy Calls** would leave Radio One jocks open mouthed". Well a few months down the line and Radio One DJ Steve Wright said this in his *Daily Mirror* column, "Watch out for Mummy Calls, they are brilliant"!) The dream was looking good, I still have the demos of the original album tracks, I still remember what the tracks sounded like live. When Geffen took the boys on they had a list of producers to choose, they figured that Hugh Padgham (who had worked with The Police, XTC and Genesis) would do the job. Well he did a job, but what came out was in my mind was a luke warm interpretation of a group that should have been in it's glory. Most of it wasn't that bad (apart from a couple of tracks that ended up sounding suspiciously disco), but it was all so under produced. *Beauty has Her Way* was the first single, it probably came out of it better than any of the other album tracks. It would however have sunk without a trace if it wasn't for the soundtrack of *The Lost Boys* film where the song featured. *Let's Go* was the second single, again it failed to pick up much interest. It had all looked so good for them, they deserved better than this, but as so often happens, a perfect band had yet again slipped through the net.

THE MUSTANGS (Lynne Curtis and)

Originally formed in Kenilworth (SEE KENILWORTH) though only Pat Brook was from the town, the rest hailed from Leamington. Began practising by using homemade guitars and amps, before they started earning money for equipment from playing at parties and the like. Supported Shane Fenton (Alvin Stardust). The consisted of Martin Williams (lead guitar), Pat Brook (rhythm guitar), Chris Allen (bass), Tony Ferrell (drums) and Mike Burns (guitar & vocals). For a time they included Leamington-based Porthcawl born singer **Lynne Curtis.** She was discovered by one of **The Mustangs** singing in a Leamington coffeehouse where she was working. During this time they supported The Beatles (SEE THE BEATLES) at *The Matrix Ballroom* on *Fletchamstead Highway* on 17th November 1962. Whilst playing at *The Orchid Ballroom* (SEE VENUES) Larry Page approached her to sign for him, this she did and eventually released in 1965 the *Decca* single *House for Sale*.

BILLIE MYERS

Coventry lady Billie Myers was born on June 14th 1971, to an English mother and a Jamaican father. Early jobs included nursing and an insurance agent in London. Her break came when producer Peter Harris happened to spot her dancing in a London club, and inquired if she could sing as well as she danced. She signed to Universal Records, recording her debut album *Growing Pains* in Miami, Florida in 1997. The album showed Billie's unique vocal sound (her voice had a stark jazzy angst quality to it) over a backing that wouldn't have sounded out of place on a U2 album. Backed up with the creative writing talents of Desmond Child and former Hooters mainman Eric Brazilian. It was a brave and dynamic mix of sounds fused together to create an outstanding classic of a debut album. The first single from the album was to be the haunting *Kiss The Rain*. Based on one of Billie's poems, it was to transport her to the upper reaches of the American Charts to number 15. Tours followed, including a support slot with Bob Dylan and Savage Garden. *Kiss The Rain* came no 31 in top US 100 of 1998. (Such was her success that the single spawned a parody entitled *Clean the Drain*) She infuriated the press with her ambiguous lyrics, refusing to reveal her sexual orientation claiming she was 'non-gender specific'. This was compounded with her second single *Tell Me* and it's sexually explicit video. In 1998 she began to conquer her home country and K*iss the Rain* charted at number 4 in the UK. Followed by *Tell Me* at number 28, her album *Growing Pains* was also to reach 19 in Britain in May 1998.

At the onset of her US success her family were all-unaware of her star status, it was only when a surprised relative in Canada saw Billie on TV and phoned Billie's shocked and a little miffed father Danny in Coventry that they knew what their daughters success. The next time she saw him again at the family home in Coventry she was at number four in the UK with *Kiss the Rain*. Her father (like any good father) felt obliged to warn his 27-year-old daughter of the pitfalls of the drug-laden world of music.

Her second album *Vertigo,* was to continue with her introspective observations. *Should I Call You Jesus* is a masterful rationale of organised religion (Universal cancelled this as a single). While *Bitter Fruit's* powerful lyrics are enough to make all but the most jaded of listener squirm in their seats. Coventry should feel proud that we have an artist/poet and thinker of the calibre of Billie Myers. Of late the creative Mrs Myers has been keeping a low profile. Although It would seem she has added acting to her talents. She has also parted company with Universal Records, but has some new material written, one stand-out track is the infectious *Wrong Side of Strange* this really does deserves to see the light of day. Preferably soon.

SHEL NAYLOR

Shel who? you say, well just hang on a minute, let me give you this mans pedigree and be prepared to be impressed. He was backed by half of Rock Legends Led Zeppelin, He had a song written for him by Dave Davis of The Kinks. If you were to buy his two singles today you would have no change from ▢100, he also went on to have a number one for four weeks in the UK charts. Now do I have your interest? I bet I do. Make no bones about this **Shel Naylor** is an undiscovered gem, a forgotten legend of the early sixties. Shel's career started at *The Orchid Ballroom* in Primrose Hill St Coventry, where he had entered a talent contest. The prize was a recording deal with Decca. Larry Page who ran the *Orchid* (SEE VENUES) had persuaded American producers Shel Talmy and Mike Stone to attend. Shel (or Rob as he was then), went down a storm and ran away with the prize, despite the many other acts that had also come from the city. **The Orchids** (SEE THE ORCHIDS) also gained their contract that night. Larry Page became his manager giving the 17-year-old the name **Shel Naylor**. He was Rob Woodward one day **Shel Naylor** the next. Rob believes his name was a kind of tribute to his producer Shel Talmy, but like it or not that was the name Larry chose, so Shel it was. He was to spend a little time in London to get a 'feel' of the business. Then it was off to Decca's West Hampstead studios to record his first single, despite him not really liking the songs on offer he eventually chose the Irving Berlin song *How Deep Is the Ocean*. That day the session guitarist was Big Jim Sullivan a legend in the business who has played on over 1,000 chart hits. Shel's voice is spot-on, my only gripe is the female backing singers who seem to get in the way at times. The B-side is a terrific version of *La Bamba* with some great Trumpet and drum fills (thanks to session great's Benny Green, Kenny Baker, Red Price on brass and Bobby Graham on drums). Now if ever a record had a curse on it this was it. To start with it was released on November 22nd 1963, the day President Kennedy was assassinated! It then went on to be voted a 'miss' on TV's *Juke Box Jury* (this went out on the day of his 18th birthday). The single understandably failed to chart.

As 1964 arrived Shel would record his second single, this time he was even less pleased with the choice of songs, but he opted for *One Fine Day* (written by Dave Davis of *The Kinks* another of Mr. Pages Charges). Rob also managed to record one of his own compositions *Stopin Joe* needless to say it wasn't selected. Playing on the session was John Paul Jones and Jimmy Page, both would go onto be part of Led Zeppelin the world's greatest heavy rock band. Although Rob was still unhappy with his vocals, he was pleased with Jimmy Page's great guitar solo. Despite what Rob feels about his vocals, to my mind *One Fine Day* is a great piece of 60's pop. On a different day it could have been a hit, as perusal it wasn't and *One Fine Day* (and it's equally good B-side that could have easily been the A, *It's Gonna Happen Soon*), were mostly lost Decca nuggets. *One Fine Day* was never recorded by the Kinks, it's only other form was as an instrumental on the Larry Page Orchestra LP *Kinky Music*. Because of this and the Jimmy Page and Kinks connection the single is worth in the region of ▢75, so you may want to check your record collections.

Rob took Shel on the road as it were, playing a summer season in Great Yarmouth along with Larry Page's other act **Johnny B. Great and The Quotations** (SEE JOHNNY B. GREAT) supporting the likes of Brian Poole & The Tremeloes and The Searchers. At the end of the tour his Decca contract was not renewed and a pretty disconsolate Rob Woodward (as he had reverted back to) studied his options and joined the Coventry beat group **The Pretty Flamingos** as vocalist and keyboard player. They included Alan Payne and Murray Winters in their ranks. They were know for their hard gigging including a 6 weeks cabaret stint in Leeds. Disaster was to strike them when their van full of equipment was stolen from Dean Street. Whether they ever got their instruments back or not is not known. What is known that Rob's luck was to change as he formed the experimental band **Stavely Makepeace** (SEE STAVELY MAKEPEACE) and later go on to top the charts for four week with you must have guessed by now, **Lieutenant Pigeon** (SEE LIEUTENANT PIGEON)!

NOISE LIKE NOISE

In 1985 as **King** (SEE KING) had finally made an impact on the charts, there were many local Cov' acts who looked on green eyed dreaming of similar success. The more notables of the time who chose to go for an overall 'packaged' image were **This Heat, Terminal Tears** and **Still Life.** (SEE TERMINAL TEARS, SEE RAY KING). **Still life** (not to be confused with the 'other' **Still Life** of the 70's signed to Vertigo) (SEE THE PEEPS) were four guys Tony Lowther (vocals, guitar), Phil Solman (bass, vocals) John Oswin (rhythm guitar, vocals) and Paul Woolnough (drums). Tony Lowther was a brilliant guitarist whose fingerpicking style gave him a Mark Knopfler sound (although Tony would always site Hank Marvin as his guitar hero). To say he was 'driven' was something of an understatement, if ever an individual was booked to be a success then Tony was it. Their Guitar based sound was full and dynamic in the true sense of the word, songs like *Watch Them Trying* and *Still Life* positively roared energy. Regular giging on the circuit gave them top profile in the City. In 1985 the played Covaid (SEE FESTIVALS).

In 1986 however **Still Life** were to re-invent themselves as **Noise Like Noise.** Out went John Oswin, in came new management (I was once asked by **Still Life** to be their manager, I chose instead to manage **Terminal Tears**). They claimed the change was, "Because we have grown up" whatever the reason things seemed to be moving for the band. They played their first London gig at The Claredon Hammersmith and then began riding a wave of press that had them linked to Chrysalis Music. They did eventually demo for the label, but by March 1987 **Noise Like Noise** had called it a day. Phil Solman (who had left the previous year) took a degree course and became an engineer at *Mercia Sound* and Tony joined the band **Wonderland** who were formally **Déjà Vu** part of Roger Lomas's (SEE ROGER LOMAS) *Springboard Productions*

NUNEATON / BEDWORTH

Arden Ballroom in Bedwoth in the 1940's was home to the **Jack Owens Orchestra** and the place to be during that era. As for the 60's well there were bands like **The Reason** and the soul band **Orphan Clyde** who actually played at The Star Club in Hamburg. The great Co-op (Hall) Ballroom (another Reg Calvert run venue) (SEE RUGBY) saw it's fair share of excitement in the early sixties playing host to The Beatles (SEE THE BEATLES)(still with Pete Best) who were the support to Tanya Day and **The Vampires** (SEE THE VAMPIRES).(Although Sandy manager of Nuneaton's *Graziers Arms* reckons the Fab four never played Nuneaton)? The Rolling Stones also played the venue on 15th of November 1963. They played 2 shows that day, In his book *Stone Alone* Bill Wyman tells of the earlier junior session. It was full of six to ten years old, who were not interested in R & B and proceeded to throw their afternoon tea (cream cakes) at the Stones! Sticky Fingers or what! The Who played there in 1965 Speaking of the fab 4, apparently in the 60's a local Nuneaton firm *Wood Bros* were busting a gut to keep up on orders of Beatle Pullovers they were turning out, as many as 300 dozen a week! In one New years eve 1965 a crowded staircase collapsed at the Ballroom killing four people at the venue. The Hollies, The Troggs, John Lee Hooker and The Fortunes all played there.

A certain Billy Breen was performing his drag act in the 60's. He would become better known as **Larry Grayson,** who was actually born in Banbury as William White in 1923. Not known as a real singer he did in fact release a record entitled *The Pom Pom song.* He also recorded the song *Shut That Door* his famous Catch phrase TV's *The Generation Game* (It's amazing how many times Larry's memory is evoked by the simple request of closing the door). When Larry passed away in 1995 it was noted that the two most famous figures from Nuneaton had been George Eliot a woman who wrote under the name of a man. The other was a man who dressed up as a woman before dropping his drag act and becoming Larry Grayson! The other local showbiz entertainer (who also happened to live close to Larry on the Hinckley Rd) was Bedwoth born George Formby

ALAN RANDALL

impersonator **Alan Randall**. Alan who began his career as part of **The Hotel Leofric Orchestra**, is not only the number one Formby impersonator he is also owner of the greatest collection of Formby memorabilia. He was co-writer of the musical based on Formby's life entitled *Turned Out Nice Again*. He even appeared on the last Beatles video *Free As A Bird* taking a bow on stage as George Formby. His records include *I Remember George, Ee But It's A Grand and Healthy Life, Meditating Hindoo man, Chocolate Moon, Down the Old Coal Hole* and *The Coventry City Song* (SEE COVENTRY CITY FC).

The Joneses were a Beat group from the town circa 1966 who wore bizarre psychedelic stage clothes. **Brian' Liquorice' Locking** was born in Bedworth December 22nd 1940, he was most famous as the bass player with **The Shadows** (replacing Jet Harris). Although he previously had some success with Vince Taylor and The Playboys and Marty Wilde and the Wildcats. Apart from the bass guitar he also played the harmonica and clarinet (hence his nickname). He stayed with the Shads' for just 18 months leaving in 1963 to dedicate more time to his religious beliefs (he was/is a devout Jehovah's Witness). Many say it was Brian that first got Cliff Richard and Hank Marvin interested in religion.

In the late sixties Nuneaton gave birth to a duo that went by the mouth-watering name **Fresh Maggots**. Mick Burgoyne (vocals, guitar, violin, glockenspiel) and Leigh Dolphin (guitar) formed the band and got themselves a contract with RCA Records. Their style ranged from folk rock to electro-rock. They Played Warwick University Arts Festival in 1972 and The Windsor Free Festival in 1973. They released a single *Car Song* and an album *Fresh Maggots* both in 1971. Their album included the songs *Rosemary Hill, Dole Song* and *Everyone's Gone To War*, by all accounts it's a fine album and as original as their name. **African Grass** and **Flood** were also 70's band from Nuneaton.

Punk rock was well represented in the town in the 70's with the likes of **The Pot, Rabid, Eoka-B** and **The Pubes**. **Ikstop and Barbwire** were punks of the Atherstone kind, and **The Civil Servants** came from Bedworth. The famous *77 Club* being the venue of choice (even U2 played here in June 1980 as part of their *11 O'clock Tick Tock Tour*). Less punk and more new wave power-pop were the high-energy act **The Incredible Kidda Band**. They had a huge following, especially in Germany for some reason. I had the pleasure to see them several times, they never disappointed. I am a proud owner of their 1978 single *Everybody Knows*. They were also responsible for the song *Camphill Go Go*, probably the only time Camp Hill as ever been immortalised on vinyl! They often moonlighted as **The Kicks** (releasing 2 singles under this name *Get Off The Telephone* and *If Looks Could Kill*), just about all their material has been put out on the double CD *Too Much,Too little,Too Late*. They had another single *Fighting the way Back* released on Carrere Records 1979, some of them later became **The Guy Gibson Flyers. The Flashcubes** US powerpop outfit formed in the 70's includes Nuneaton born guitarist Paul Armstrong. Justin Welch drummer (and only male member) with **Elastica** (who's album *Elastica* went to number one in 1995) was born in Nuneaton on 4th December 1972 (he also had spells with Suede and Spitfire). **Sidewinder** and **Firebrand** were 2 heavy band of the time The latter's 1985 single *Never Felt This Way Before* got to number 12 on the Nuneaton hit parade, now there's a thing!. *The Dugdale Arms and The Crazy Horse (or the Bonking Donkey)* and the ever-popular *Nags Head* (**Pinkertons** (SEE PINKERTONS COLOURS) played here in the 60's) were places for the rock-minded to frequent. *The Crazy Horse* was owned by the sadly departed Brian Harkins, who was not a member of Showaddywaddy (but his business partner was), Brian was *The Phantom Flan Flinger* on *Tiswas*. Indeed just about all his family were on the show, including his son Julian who now runs *The Nags*. Ian Morgan of Jive Bunny also did a DJ spot there for many years. The venue has just come second in the prestigious *Best Entertainment Pub Award*.

In the 80's Nuneaton Oi band **Crux** released the 12inch single *Keep On Running*. The Editors of fanzines *Damn Latin* and *Adventures In Reality* Alan Rider and Phil Clarke got together and formed electro avant gard outfit **Stress,**. They managed to top the NME electronic charts with the song *The Big Wheel* in the mid eighties. In fact Nuneaton seemed to be the place for electro duos in the 80's. The brilliantly outstanding **Eyeless In Gaza** (SEE EYELESS IN GAZA) came from Nuneaton (and have their own *Ambivalent Scale*

Recordings (stable mates on *Ambivalent* were **Eyeless In Gaza** and the brilliantly original **Kevin Harrison's** with *Earth 2*). Also in The eighties the *Bermuda Working Men's Club* was the place to be for all types of Northern Soul and mod music.

The Civic hall in Bedworth or *The Beduth' Civic Hall*, Opened on 29th September 1973. It has become a showpiece for the midlands. This 763 seater theatre has played host to the likes of Ken Dodd, Dave Willetts (SEE DAVE WILLETTS), Stephan Grappelli, Morecambe & Wise, Cilla Black and the legendary Pavarotti with the City of Birmingham Symphony Orchestra to accompany him. Indeed the CBSO were so impressed with the hall's fine acoustics that they have recorded three albums altogether at the hall! **Stephen Waterhouse** was born in Nuneaton and brought up in Burbage, he is an accomplished pianist, appearing at The Audi Junior Musician of the Year competition and winning many prizes for his playing. Troubled ex-Libertines front man Pete Doherty went to *Nicholas Chamberlaine* school in Bedworth in the 90's. He has also played at the prestigious Ivy restaurant in London.

Carol Decker (SEE CAROL DECKER) of T'Pau was brought up in Nuneaton. **Martin Atkins** most known for being the drummer with John Lydon's PIL was born in the town. He has been **Brian Brain** and has also played with Killing Joke and the industrial darlings **Pigface** and **RX**. Martin wrote **RX** track *Exfoliate* giving it a working title of *Nuneaton #3,* he now chooses to live in Chicago. **Jason Reece** of the destructive US Texas band **And You Will Know Us by the Trail of Dead** was born in Nuneaton and brought up in Bedworth. Current treacle town delights are **Loophole** whose style of rock manages to be melodic and hard at the same time. Their debut album *Glass* released in 2001 featured the track *Stream of Consciousness* and outstanding piece of rock with chugging guitar licks and the sort of vocals Liam Gallagher would be proud of. They have released two singles to date *Just Like Penny Lane* and *Panic*. Other bands currently on the scene (or at least they were when I wrote this). **ACME Rejects** (rock), **Deathascension** (from Beduff), **Corruption** (metal), the much mooted **Fiori** (grunge), **E-Mission** (rock), **Malachai** (grunk), **Hands Like Feet** (indie), (**Mortimer** (Indie rock), **Figurehead** (rock), **Everescent** (punk) **Desperation Ended** (rock), **Scarlet Phere** (garage rock) and Dayle Cruthlow's **Lazy Eye**. So maybe the Co-op Hall now sadly sits neglected, but just up the road the Nags still rocks. They recently won silver in best live venues awards. They now host live band 7 nights a week. that's good for music and good for Nuneaton!

THE CO-OP BALLROOM

HAZEL O'CONNOR

Hazel O'Connor was born in Coventry on May 16th 1955, living in the Wyken area of the city. After finishing at Foxford Grange School in 1971, she made up her mind that art in some form was to be her calling in life. After enrolling for art school it took but a few months for her to realise that the confines of further education at a college were not for her. So leaving college she decided to travel craving for adventure. Her cravings took her to a variety of jobs and places. Including an au pair in Amsterdam, and a street actor in Paris, a dancer in Japan and a nude model in London. It was when she was travelling in France and Germany that music came into her life and after further short treks to Europe with various muso's she finally used her intrinsic pushiness to get herself signed with Albion Records in the summer of 1978.

She had to wait a year before her second and possibly biggest break was to come. After being approached at London's Nashville rock venue she was offered a chance to audition for the lead role in a film that finally emerged as *Breaking Glass*. After many more auditions and screen tests she eventually won the part. *Breaking Glass* was a huge success. Hazel had well and truly put herself on the music map, even winning the *Variety Film Actress of the Year Award* and being hailed by the public and press alike as 'the queen of punk'. It was ironic that the part she played in Breaking Glass was to be similar to what was to come for Hazel. But such harsh reality was far off at this point and Hazel was not only a Box-office success but a chart success with hit records such as *Eighth Day* (5), and *Give Me An Inch* (41), both tracks coming from her hit sound track album of Breaking Glass (5). Acting was forgotten for the time being and Hazel and her band Mega-hype began touring included in Megahype's line-up was Hazel's brother Neil a former member of **The Flys** (SEE THE FLYS).

The tour proved to be success (it was also a success for the support band Duran Duran). Hazel's record continued to sell and it seemed she was getting used to her star-status The singles *'D-Days'* (10) and the powerfully dramatic *Will You'* (8) both charting. During the 1980-81 period Hazel found time to finish her auto-biography "*Under Cover Plus*", but it was in 1983 just after she finished filming the rather mediocre TV show *Jangles* that things began to slip downhill. The hits stopped and so did the offers of acting work, gone was the Queen of Punk image, and the *Breaking Glass* role was sadly coming almost true. Hazel always a fighter pulled herself out of it and signed a new recording contract with *R.C.A. records*. Although her peak was without doubt set very much in the 80's. It would be unfair and indeed untrue to say that her career died back then. Her acting since the 1980's has seen her play such parts as Vivienne in the highly acclaimed *Fighting Back*. And theatre roles in One Flew over the Cuckoo's Nest and *Girlfriends*. More albums followed and she released an acoustic album of her hits in 2002 entitled *Acoustically Yours*. She currently lives happily practising her Krishna faith in Ireland.

GODIVA ROCKS SOUND BYTE WITH-Hazel O'Connor (Solo Star) Music and Coventry have always been synonymous to my mind from early childhood listening to my Dad singing in the Wyken Working Men's Choir, watching music and dancing parties at our house as a child and later by the age of 11 going religiously every week to Saturday afternoon dances at the Locarno Ballroom getting hooked on all the new Mowtown music, hearing my singing heroine Nina Simone single "I've Got Life" being played and "having" to buy it - my first single.

Watching my first live bands Geno Washington and Ram Jam Band at the Locarno. Local band made good "The Sorrows" and the Rolling Stones at the Coventry Theatre. In my middle teens I saw every new band that came to play the Lanchester Polytechnic like Marc Bolan when he still say on the edge of the stage playing bongos singing Debora. I watched a sound check of The Who at the Lanch I was mesmerised. In my late teens it was my brother Neil and the band he was in The Flys that inspired me to try to write songs and The Flys played on my first demos.

The biggest thrill for me as a performer was playing alongside The Specials at The Butts when in spite of threats from the misanthropic right - a wonderful concert took place and people came out to show solidarity against the racist climate of that time. Anyway Music in Coventry for me has gone full circle as I'm play Glastonbury this year 2004 with The Subterraneans including Kevin Lomas, son of Roger Lomas who was a member of that first band I ever saw - The Sorrows.

A GODIVA ROCKS TRIVIA BOX
Here is a top ten of the most collectable records from local artists. Source Record Collector.
1. Soul Kiss Glide Devine-test pressing-Spectrum £250
2. Floating In space-Blister pack LP-Spiritualized £120
3. Still Life LP-Still Life £110
4. Lantaloon (with poster) LP-Dando Shaft-£80
5. One Fine Day-single-Shel Naylor £75
6. Leatherslade Farm LP-Jigsaw £65
7. Aurora Borealis LP-Jigsaw £45
8. Indian Summer LP-Indian Summer £35
9. It's All Over now-single-Martin Cure & Peeps £35
10. Kodak Ghosts Run Amok-EP- Eyeless In Gaza £25

THE ORCHIDS

The UK never really had a female vocal trio to match the likes of The Crystals or The Shirelles, or did we. Well yes we did, Coventry's own **Orchids** fitted the bill perfectly, with a bit of luck they could have been chart regulars. The girls were all at *Stoke Park Grammar school* as it was then. Georgina Oliver, Pamela Jarman and Valerie Jones were all 15 years old when they won a talent competition at Coventry's *Orchid Ballroom* (SEE VENUES). The legendary Larry Page who was manager of the ballroom secured them a recording contract with *Decca Records* and christened them **The Orchids** after the ballroom. Their first time on vinyl was singing backing vocals on the **Johnny B. Great and The Goodmen** single *School Is In* (SEE JOHNNY B.GREAT). The first Orchids single was *Gonna Make Him Mine* (this time **Johnny B. Great and the Goodmen** *were the backing musicians).* Produced by the great Shel Talmy (famous for his work with The Kinks), it was picked up by top TV pop show Ready! Steady! Go! Playing as dancer Patrick Kerr demonstrated the Hitch-Hiker. Although it didn't chart it was enough to give these three teenage girls a huge amount of publicity. As you will read below, the girls hated the schoolgirl novelty image Larry had given them, but Larry knew best. Indeed he even got them featured in the film *Just For You* singing the song *Mr Scrooge*. **Johnny B.Great** was also featured in it, as was Peter & Gordon and Freddie and the Dreamers. The film was later Americanised and re-edited as *Disk-O-Tek Holiday*.

With all this publicity it was fair to assume that their next single *Love Hit Me* would do well for them. Producer Shel Talmy insists that he & Larry were not going for a Phil Spector wall of sound on this. Who am I to argue with Shel Talmy, my view is this is a perfect mix of US female vocal song with a very English slant to it. It wasn't over-produced, there was something very unique and English about the whole thing. The girls voices sound amazing the whole thing works so well and my copy rarely leaves my record deck (that's a phrase I haven't used for many years). The B-side *Don't Make me Mad* is also a little gem. This was their big hit, although it never was a hit (it was to become popular in America however). How it failed to chart I will never know, maybe some felt it sounded too much like *Da Do Ron Ron*, whatever the case **The Orchids** biggest chance of national fame sadly went-a-begging.

Larry Page (manager of the Kinks & later The Troggs) and Shel Talmy were never shy in using their stars to help their other talent, so the next single was a Ray Davies song *I've Got That Feeling*. Once again they failed to chart. So it was decided that they would try to monopolise on the American interest. So the US only release *Oo-Chang-A-Lang* (on *London Records*) saw them using the name **The Blue Orchids** (there was already a group called The Orchids in The US). In 1965 they changed their name once more to **The Exceptions** (The schoolgirl look that they so hated made way for a new 'mod' look, even Georginas glasses went) They released one last single *What more Do you want*. The B-side *Soldier Boy* was interesting because Georgina wrote it, quite a feat for a 17 year old girl, and it's probably the best song they ever did, she really had the knack! It was clearly aimed at the American market, many were surprised it was sung by three white girls! They never did an album and that was very much it recording-wise, although there are supposed to be some 'lost sessions'

PAGE 66   GODIVAROCKS@YAHOO.CO.UK   PAGE 66

THE AUTHOR AND GEORGINA JUNE 2004

they did for the legendary US songwriter Bert Berns and Andrew Loog Oldam (who managed **The Mighty Avengers** and The Rolling Stones) (SEE THE MIGHTY AVENGERS). One song *Society Girl* was renamed as *Just Like Mine* for the US girl group The Rag Dolls. Despite **The Orchids** lack of chart success their legacy is a powerful one. Their output is highly collectable and they remain responsible for popularising girl singing groups during the 60's in the UK. In 1999 a TV play about a singing group entitled *Sex, Chips & Rock 'N' Roll* was written by Debbie Horsefield, although not totally based on **The Orchids** story, Val and Georgina still became sort of technical advisers to the show. Georgina is now an artist living in Vancouver, Val a former schoolteacher living in Cornwall and Pam was last heard of in Scotland. I met up with Georgina in June 2004 when she was over in Coventry, she was a lovely person we had a great time looking at the video she bought and her fantastic scrap book. She was just very happy that **The Orchids** can still arouse interest.

GODIVA ROCKS SOUND BYTE WITH-Val Jones (The Orchids)

There are lots of Orchid memories but a few spring to mind which might interest you. We were incredibly naive and star struck when we were 14/15. We saw the Orchids as a way to meet our favourite pop stars often (although we all loved singing, soul and R and B) We referred to our manager as 'Mr Page' as we did to all other adults we met.

We were once taken out to lunch by Andrew Oldham (Stone's manager) We were so in awe of him I don't think we uttered a word to him the whole time we were out. He took us to a posh pavement cafe in Soho. We didn't know whether he was paying or not and as we didn't have any money (we were still on pocket money and saw virtually no money from our record sales) we said we weren't hungry (we were!) and had nothing to eat! He must have thought we were totally weird.

We hated being presented as school girls. Our tastes in music were quite advanced so presenting us in school uniform and making us sing silly songs like 'Don't be like Mr Scrooge' made us really cross. Once on Ready, Steady Go Larry Page had some really horrible dresses made for us (they had orchid petals round the collar)....so we refused to go on and Cathy McGowan had to come and persuade us to perform. It made us seem like brats when I think back now.........but we had very little control over how we were presented and I think that was probably the straw that broke the camel's,.........

GODIVA ROCKS SOUND BYTE WITH-Georgina Oliver (The Orchids)

I can't remember exactly the moment we got together as a singing group. I think it just evolved. We were friends in the same class and like any teenagers we enjoyed pop music. A bunch of us would sing the latest hits together as something to do on our lunch breaks at school and I guess after a while it just became the three of us that sang while the others listened. We also took cello lessons for a short time - a very short time! I guess you could say we just enjoyed making music together.

We used to go dancing at the Locarno Ballroom every Saturday afternoon then for some reason after a while we changed to the Orchid Ballroom. One weekend Val and I didn't go so Pam went to the Orchid by herself. On Monday morning at school she informed us that she had entered us in a talent contest. Needless to say we were horrified. Singing in the school yard in front of friends was one thing but singing on stage in front of strangers was another.

We liked Tamla Motown at the time so we I think we sang Da-Doo-Ron-Ron by the Crystals, Mr Postman and maybe Tears on My Pillow. We won the contest and shared the prize money - one pound! Larry Page, the manager of the Orchid had "connections" in the music biz and arranged for someone from London to come and listen to us sing. "And the rest is history" as they say. We never became extremely famous or made a lot of money but we got to meet some famous people, **Continued Over**

Continued. among them the Kinks, Gerry and the Pacemakers, Hollies and Cathy McGowan of Ready Steady Go! One occasion I remember we were riding around London with Andrew Oldham in his huge American convertible. The top was down, the sun was shining and Dionne Warwick was singing "Don't Make Me Over" on the record player in the dashboard - we were impressed! When we had recording sessions at Decca Studios we would go for late dinner at the Italian restaurant around the corner where I got my first taste of spaghetti bolognaise - we thought it was very exotic. Another time we were taken to a dance hall in London somewhere to present a huge cheque to someone. I think it was a Pool's win or something like that. We sat in on a Kink's session one day and we were absent-mindedly tapping on some metal ashtrays in time to the beat. The recording engineer liked it and told us to carry on. I can't remember which song it was but we're out there somewhere in the background on one of the Kink's early recordings.

It was fun while it lasted and on the whole our lives didn't change that much. We didn't miss much school and teachers and friends treated us much the same as they always had, although they were interested to hear about who we had met and where we'd been. Whenever I look back now it feels like it happened to someone else and when people find out about it they are so excited and interested to know more. I'm always a bit shy about it all and find it hard to believe the renewed interest and how our records have become collectible.

GODIVA ROCKS SOUND BYTE FROM-Shel Talmy (Decca record producer & songwriter) Thanks for the kind words about the records, I've always liked them and think they could have gone farther with a little luck .But in all honesty, the fact they came from Coventry never registered as I got all of them via my then current associations. The Orchids were offered to me probably by Larry Page and I certainly wasn't going for a Spector sound, just a great girl harmony sound, and I'm American so guess I can't claim an "English" slant. The fact that they all came from Coventry never registered. And please believe I'm not trying to be presumptuous when I say that my "agenda" was as simple as trying to make as many hit records as I could. It was that . uncomplicated in the sixties.

THE ORCHIDS GROWING UP

THE ORCHIDS—real names Pamela Jarman, Georgina Oliver and Valerie Jones—were all born in Coventry. Pam and Val are 15 and "George" is 16 and they all went to Stoke Park Secondary Grammar School for Girls.

PANJABI MC

It's with more than a little satisfaction to see that the most recent Coventry artist to chart (at this time of writing anyway) is a British-Asian a Covasian. Those who would deride Coventry Asian culture and dismiss it as an 'Indian thing' can be assured that Desi/ Bhangra (SEE BHANGRA) has gone mainstream big time. More to the point the current Coventry sound has a very very big Punjabi edge to it! **Panjabi MC** or Rajinder Rai as his parents know him, has been perfecting his Art for some ten years now. What we are now hearing in the mainstream has been slowly maturing until it was potent enough to knock the socks off anyone who had an ounce of rhythm in their bodies.

Rajinder grew up in Coventry often worked in the families sari fabric shop, but he soon realised that his first love was to be music. The pattern for his musical tastes was well and truly set with an interest of traditional Indian music that his parents had brought from the sub-continent mixed with the Hip Hop and R&B that he was hearing in Coventry. He began rapping in Panjabi over Bhangra beats, at that time rap was considered somewhat aggressive by his Bhangra contemporaries. Despite the indifference he was to persevere and eventually prove that there was a place in Bhangra for rap. His name **Panjabi MC** (this is the Panjabi spelling of the word by the way) came about whilst rapping some black rappers named him *Indian MC*, he changed it to Panjabi MC, after explaining to them that Indian is not a language. He was to continued MC-ing and DJ-ing and generally building on his already growing reputation.

GODIVAROCKS@YAHOO.CO.UK

Giving himself something to fall back on he took business and marketing at University. After that he signed to Ninder Johal's Nachural label releasing albums in the early nineties like *Souled Out*, *100% Proof*, *Grass Roots* and *Another Sell-out* (the single *Rootz* was banned on it's release, coincided blasphemous by the Muslim populous). It was his third album however that would bring him and Desi music to the forefront. *Legalised* was released in 1999 it contained the track *Mundian To Bach Ke* (basically it's about a father-figure talking to a girl coming of age and telling her to *Beware of the Boys* or *Mundian To Bach Ke)*. It was a track that throbbed along fusing Bhangra 'dhol' beats and the bass line of TV show *Knightrider* together. With the legendary Labh Janjua's Hindi vocals (recorded in India) it was an infectious mix that helped the album become the biggest selling Bhangra album of all time. Although at this point it was still very much part of the Bhangra/Desi music underground scene, it was some 4 years before *Mundian To Bach Ke* began being picked up (at first in Germany) then by the mainstream hip hop DJ's looking for something a little different.

When it hit at the start of 2003, it hit big, number 2 in Germany, 22 in The States (even the Specials couldn't achieve this), number 8 in the UK, number ones in Greece and Italy. It was of course much more than a hit record, **PMC** had globally mainstreamed Bhangra, a massive achievement not just for him but for Bhangra music in general, and British-Asians and of course Coventry in particular! He followed it with the album *Panjabi MC-The Album* and the single *Jogi* (complete with a clever little video) charting at number 12 in Germany and 30 in the UK. Awards of plenty have come his way (including one from the BBC), and *Mundian To Bach Ke* has sold millions to date. **Jay-Z** the US rapper (and love interest of Beyonce Knowles) has also collaborated him. His success of course can never be taken away, but he (and indeed the whole Bhangra scene) must now consolidate this success to insure that Bhangra remains in the mainstream and continues to be enjoyed by Asians and non-Asians alike.

HORACE PANTER

Born Stephen Graham Panter in Kettering, Northants 30th August 1953. Picked up the nickname 'Horace' at school (due to there being a teacher there called 'Horace Panter') Came to Coventry to study arts at The Lanchester Polytechnic. It was here that he got to know local punk keyboardist and fellow art student Jerry Dammers. Horace was at the time playing with a local soul club band **Breaker,** Jerry went along to check him out, his bass playing impressed (as did the fact that he was a van driver in his spare time). Jerry suggested he help with some demos. From there **The Coventry Automatics** and later **The Specials** were born (SEE THE SPECIALS).

Lynval Golding christened him *Sir Horace Gentleman* because of his 'posh' cultured accent. His superb bass style in **The Specials** earned him praise from many of his contemporaries. If you check out *The Old Grey Whistle Test* DVD Vol 1 you will see Mark Ellen positively glowing with praise for H's bass playing (and dancing) technique on *Message To You Rudy*. His days

HOZ ON STAGE WITH THE AUTHOR OF THIS BOOK WORRYINGLY CLOSE!

with **The Specials** saw him clock up some 8 hit singles, two of which achieved the number one position. It was during the recording of the 3rd Specials Album *In The Studio* a somewhat acrimonious split occurred and Horace would play only a small part in Dammer's re-vamped **Special AKA**. In 1981-82 he would open the *Nerve* fashion boutique with his new wife Clare (former *Flack Off* vocalist) (SEE EUROPEAN SUN). Musically H was also behind mythical yorkshire rapper **Barnsley Bill** and the singles *Barnsley Rap* & *Freewheeling Rap*. He also played with **The Mosquitoes** then later **The Mix** two pub bands that entertained the beer swiggers at Coventry's *Whitley Abbey* public House. The Former was a R & B unit that included Steve Walwyn who was with Chevy (SEE CHEVY) and later Dr Feelgood. They released the single *Something Out Of Nothing* later recorded by Dr Feelgood. While The latter was a re-hash of a late 70's ensemble, included former **Urge** and **The End** man Dave Gedney (SEE THE URGE, SEE DAVE PEPPER).

GODIVAROCKS@YAHOO.CO.UK

Plus super session (and **I & Smackee**) drummer Rick Medlock and violinist Martin Bell. Bell would go on to become a member of The Wondestuff (He and Rick Medlock also played in **The Mosquitoes**).

The latter part of 1983 saw Horace become part of the 'super-group' **General Public**. Formed from ex-Beat members Dave Wakeling and Ranking Roger, with Stoker (drums) Micky Billingham (ex-Dexy's Midnight Runners) (keyboards) and Kevin White (guitar). I had the pleasure to see their first gig at the *Crompton Arms* in Handsworth, Birmingham in December 1983. For a while there was talk that former Clash man Mick Jones would be a permanent member of The 'Public'. History tells us that never happened, but he did play this one and only gig with them that night, and I got the only photos, (see Left)! Their first UK single also called *General Public* hit the charts in 1984 at number 60. Followed by a stormer of a debut album *All the Rage* (featuring Mick Jones). It was in The US however that **General Public** were to gain a more solid fan-base (helped no doubt by the former reputation of Dave & Roger's (**English**) **Beat** connections). *Tenderness* chosen as the US debut single, with it's clever lyrics, catchy chorus and the imaginative use of a bassoon played by Bob Porter. It hit the US charts making number 27 (Horace remains the only ex-Special to chart Stateside). The album *All the Rage* also made 26 on the US Billboard 200 and the subsequent US single *Hot You Cool* although missing the mainstream charts did attain a top 20 placing in the *hot dance music* listings. With this the band had cemented a favourable enough reputation to see them release the second album *Hand To Mouth,* it also spawned the song *Taking the day Off* (from the feature film *Ferris Buellers Day Off*). However after 3 years disillusionment and apathy arrived and they went their separate ways.

A ONE OFF PHOTO SHOWING GENERAL PUBLIC WITH HORACE(SECOND ON THE RIGHT) AND MICK JONES FIRST ON LEFT.

Horace joined Roger on his remarkably good *Radical Departure* album, then onto **Special Beat** that included Ranking Roger, Neville Staples, Lynval Golding and John Bradbury. They did extensive tours that included USA, Europe and Japan. Horace would give up touring for a while to concentrate on his teaching career. However in 1993 he would play with various other former Specials on reggae legend Desmond Dekker's album *King Of Kings.* This led to a reunion of sorts for **The Specials,** (SEE THE SPECIALS) and the release of the covers album *Today's Specials*. Generally accused of being less than a joyful reunion and more of a blatant cash-in. Live shows followed as did the single *Hypocrite* (66) (a Bob Marley cover). Despite the criticism they released another album *Guilty' Til Proved innocent*, this was far better received than the former offering, with it's jazzy flavours and hidden bonus tracks of live reworkings of *Gangsters* and *Ratrace.* Once more H returned to teaching permanently, keeping his hand in musically with **Box Of Blues** with Neol Davis (SEE THE SELECTER) and Anthony Hearty (former member of The Style Council and **Beachmantango**). More recently Horace has fronted **The Coventry Ska-Jazz Orchestra** that includes His son Laurence on keyboards (SEE JAZZ). He can also be seen playing in local hostelries with 4-piece **Blues To Go.** Horace remains not just one of the best bass players around, but also one of the friendliest.

THE PEEPS

Formed for a charity concert for Cov & Warwick Hospital in March 1963 **The Sabres** consisted of "Q" Martin Cure (vocals), Steve Jones (guitar), Graham Amos (bass) Paul Wilkinson (drums) and former **Zodiacs** member Terry Wyatt (guitar). Managed by Frank Jones (father of their guitarist Steve). They made a name for themselves when they made an 8,000 mile trip to Eastern Europe and became one of the first British bands to play behind the iron curtain in Czechoslovakia (as it was then). Martin Cure still has a following in those countries. They were signed to *Philips Records* by influential bandleader Cyril Stapleton, even playing at London's famous *2 I's* coffee bar and appearing on the ATV TV show *For Teenagers Only.*

THE PEEPS

By 1965 they had become **The Peeps** (a nod of the hat to *Peeping Tom*). Guitarists Jones and Wyatt had both gone replaced by Roy Albrighton (Jones would go on to **The Flying Machine** (SEE PINKERTONS COLOURS)) They continued to tour Europe where they had their strongest fan-base. Terry Howells (from **The Ray King Soul band**) (SEE RAY KING) joined on organ in 1968. They recorded at Radio Luxembourg Studios with Albert Hammond (of *Free Electric Band* fame) producing (also on the session playing cornet was Dick Cuthell who would go on to augment The Specials) (SEE THE SPECIALS). During their time they were also known as **Martin Cure and The Peeps** (not the Penny Peeps though as sometimes mooted, that was a Birmingham based band that included Martin Barre later of Jethro Tull. Although Barre did study at The Lanch). They released the great freakbeat single *Now Is the Time* on *Philips Records*. I have this song and it chugs along very nicely thanks, good guitar licks and nice harmony vocals, very much a Merseys sound. Other singles were *Can I Say, Gotta Get A Move On, Tra la La* (as **Martin Cure and the Peeps**) and *I Can make The Rain Fall Up.*

After some three years as a beat group the times had changed and so did **The Pepys** (notice the new spelling), by 1968 they reinvented themselves as a progressive band in the mould of Traffic called **The Rainbows**. With sculptured hair, bizarre eye make-up and multi-coloured flowing robes they moved their base to London. Terry Leeman had replaced Terry Howells on keyboards and Gordon Reed did the same on drums with Paul Wilkinson. Their first single *Rainbows* in 1969 was on *CBS Records* followed by *New Day Dawning (*an old **Peeps** song*)* also 1969. By 1970 however it was over for **The Rainbows** (sorry). Wilkinson went on to join **The Flying machine** (SEE PINKERTONS COLOURS). While Roy Albrighton joined German based **Nektar** (SEE THE B LIST). Cure, Amos and old band member Terry Howells (along new drummer Alan Savage) formed the Progressive band **Still Life.**

RAINBOWS

Still Life were one of those bands that release an album (**Still Life** 1971) that never really sells, but because it's on a collectable label (in this case *Vertigo*), it becomes a mega obscure collectors item. It can now fetch something like £80, for that you get six keyboard infused prog' rock gems namely *People In Black, Don't Go, October, Love Song Number 6, Dreams* and *Time*. Or buy the CD re-release for £65 cheaper! **Still Life** actually signed to Vertigo to make six albums, yeah right. After the one album they went their separate ways, Cure joined Cupid's Inspiration then **Chevy** (SEE CHEVY), Graham Amos sadly died in 2003, the other guys left music altogether. For more info see the great fan sites at http://www.republika.pl/pearlsofrock/stilllifeE.html and http://still-life.34x.com/internal.htm

GODIVA ROCKS SOUND BYTE FROM-Martin Cure (Peeps,Rainbows, Chevy) SABRES - First proper Band(formed with friends from Keresley Youth > Club) went Pro in '62 with a 7 months tour of the UK with Sir Robert > Fossett's Circus.Central TV "For Teenagers Only", Loadsa Local Gigs. > PEEPS - c'64 (out of sabres) First Record Deal on Phillips Recods, 5 > Singles Released."Thank Your Lucky Stars" TV Show, "Juke Box Jury" TV > Lots of Tours of Scandanavia....Nice!!!! > RAINBOWS - c'68/9 (out of peeps) 2 Singles Released on CBS > Records,Silly Clothes & Make-up for photo Sessions,spent a lot of time > in Germany, at the "Star Club " in Hamburg in particular.Lots of great > nights with visiting English Bands,like the time Ozzy Osbourne(pre > Sabbath) > joined us on stage for a wild finale!! > STILL LIFE - c'70 (out of rainbows) Short lived Band,but made one > Album(STILL LIFE-still available Today!!!)Guitarist Roy Albrighton > stayed in > Germany when Rainbows came back to the UK,so we made the Album without > a guitarist,just Drums, Bass,Hammond Organ & me on Vocals. > CUPIDS INSPIRATION - Joined in 1970 (Retired 2003!!)Moved to > London,gradually recruiting local musicians as the original members > dropped out.Came "Home" to Leamington Spa in 1974,all Local Musicians > by then. > CHEVY -c'80/81 (out of cupids inspiration) After years of playing > Covers we decided we wanted to write our own music,so CHEVY was > formed, > with the addition of local guitarist Steve Walwyn (now Dr Feelgood). **Continued over page**

GODIVAROCKS@YAHOO.CO.UK

Continued We > released an Album("The Taker") and 2 Singles from the Album,Recorded > Two "In Concerts" for the BBC and toured constantly in the > UK.Excellent Band,Played some fantastic gigs but with Naff Management > it was bound to end in tears.That's Rock & Roll Folks. > Chas(drummer) left and we replaced him with Ted Duggan,and carried on > with CHEVY mkII for a while, but eventually ran out of steam and > turned into............... > RED ON RED - c85-87 (out of chevy) We recruited the excellent Bob Jackson on Keyboards & Vocals and set about writing a load of new songs. > With a new set of tunes we built up a good local following and entered > Central TV's Battle of the Bands.We made the Final at Derby Assembly > Rooms and came second!(we wuz robbed) :). > Undeterred , we carried on and recorded a couple of sessions for the > BBC Radio 1 "In Session" series but unfortunately we couldn't secure > that > elusive Record Deal,as most of the Teenage A & R Persons we came > across deemed us to be too "Experienced".So,no record deal.no Band. > We decided to call it a day and Steve is now Playing with > Dr.Feelgood, Bob Jackson with the Fortunes,Ted Duggan a Pro Freelance,Bob Poole, Playing with a couple of Bands in Germany,Paul > Shanahan,retired from music and Yours truly still doing the occasional > singing gig with a pick up band,but making my living as a Sound > Engineer with my own PA Hire Company.

DAVE PEPPER

THE X CERTS, DAVE IS THE ONE WITH THE CIRCLE BEHIND HIM

Of the entire Cov music scene the 80's there's one musician that endured the whole decade in a variety of guises. Some may say Dave Pepper was driven others that he was driven only by the bandwagon he had jumped on that particular week. Dave worked at *The Coventry Music centre* in Whitefriars Street, he began his musical career in the **X-Certs** a rock trio that included Dave on Guitar and vocals, Gray Smith on bass and Kev Smith drums. (Kev was to sadly die in a car crash). They were a major player of the time, though their lack of image would paint them probably blander than they actually were. Such criticism probably became the catalyst for Dave's future image conscious projects.

Speaking of which was **Team 23**, a good time soul band for the 80's, I believe they billed themselves. Led very much by Jerome Heisler an intense human being who had come from one of the late 70's scenes finest new wave groups **The End** (they had included Dave Gedney (SEE THE URGE) and Mark Harold). Performing such gems as *Insect life, Another Shore* and *Panic In the Night* (this track featured on the *Sent From Coventry* Compilation LP). **Team 23** had supported Dexy's Midnight Runners but despite the constant comparison they maintained that they were not on the same playing field as the Brummie boys. **Team 23** wore pretty dapper US baseball shirts and shoes. In 1981 they released their only (and pretty good) single *Move Into The Rhythm* on John Bradbury's *Race Records*. (also produced by him) (SEE JB's ALLSTARS). Eventually Dave Pepper fed up with being a right hand man reformed **The X-Certs** again (including drummer Rick Medlock & bass guitarist and former **Editors** man Rex Brough) and became a leader once more. He was replaced in **Team 23** by Jim Landsbury later of King (SEE KING). **The X-Certs** were joined by Dill (SEE I) and became **I**. Once again playing second fiddle did not suit, and Dave began his next project.

Having recorded the solo track *One is One* at Cabin Studios (SEE STUDIOS), he set about forming his most ambitious project in the shape of **The Courtiers Of Fashion**. This new band were tucked neatly into the new romantic mode, although their use of mellotron, recorder and tabor were novel. Their single was released in a hail of well-groomed publicity with a launch concert at *The General Wolfe* (SEE VENUES). Members Pepper, Neil McCalister, Paul Johnston and Tracy Starzynsta sounded pretty convincing on the record also entitled *Courtiers Of Fashion*. Whether they actually achieved the medieval/modern fusion they aimed for was up for question but the said single (based on 15th Century book *The Courtier and Shakespeare's sonnets*) was

BLITZ KREIG ZONE

refreshing if a little pretentious. Next up he joined the **Ramrods**, who soon became **Major 5.** Dave who called himself Pep at this point, had switched totally from guitar to keyboards. **The Five** were an out and out rock outfit with former **Squad** man Danny Cunnigham (or Dansk) on vocals and guitar. They secured a support slot with The Pogues 1985, and their success started to look secure. They also had a good bunch of songs like *What Does love Say, Gimme A Reason, God knows, Jimmy D* and *Your always on my mind.* Dave however began diversifying by releasing a solo cassette *Strangers* and producing the band **Terminus Est.** Inevitably by summer 1986 Dave had left Major 5, and was replaced by Mick Tedder and Mark Patrick, who later became **Gdansk.**

As Sigue Sigue Sputnik started to become regular front page fodder in the tabloids (including front man Degville having a bottle thrown at him at their Lanch concert). Dave formed a new band called **Blitz Kreig Zone 2020,** he would support an outrageous mohican haircut and their music would be futuristic power chord rock. Or as they put it *sci-fi adventure, colour, 3d action to sound, new songs, new heels*. With a tour that included Coventry, Surrey, Brum and Leicester arranged they set about promoting their 12" single *Gender Man* and *TARA* released on *Rose Records*. (the latter being a song about a defective genetically created woman) They supported the fab Zodiac Mindwarp and the Love Reaction, a second single *21 Boy* would get to number 2 in the alternative charts (complete with a video single). When the Sigue Sigue Sputnik hype began to fade away sadly **Blitz Kreig Zone 2020** did much the same. When all said and done though Dave Pepper's legacy on the local music scene is an extensive one bandwagon jumping or not! He now has a business building kit cars.

THE PICKWICKS

Were originally known as **Tony Martin and His Echo Four,** by March 1964 Larry Page (SEE VENUES) had signed them and changed their name to **The Pickwicks.** They consisted of John Miles (vocals and lead guitar), Alan Gee (rhythm guitar), Tony Martin (bass) and Malcolm Jenkins (drums). A sutable image was created to go with the name (as was the deal in the 60's). So the **Pickwicks** were dressed in *Pickwick Papers* style with frock coats, top hats and false whiskers. That wasn't to last too long, as they could never find a place to clean the coats fast enough, so the image was soon dropped. They were more than just an image though, anyone who has ever witnessed them will know what a top flight freakbeat unit they were. Witness their second single *You're Old Enough* with *Hello lady* on the flip. On hearing these two

TONY MARTIN AND HIS ECHO FOUR

tracks you kinda start looking for which is the A side and which the B. *You're Old Enough* is a good enough song sung well, but it's a ballad in the style of Freddie and The Dreamers *I Understand*. Now the B side, that's what **The Pickwicks** were all about. *Hello Lady* positively rocks along in a 12 bar boogie style (played by session man Jimmy Page). John Miles's lead vocals are spot on dirty and gritty, freakbeat at it's very best. I talked to John about the way the single was released, saying I couldn't understand why *Hello Lady* was consigned to a B side. I felt that had it been an A side then *the Guinness Book of Records* would have had another entry. Low and behold, he agreed and told me they argued the point till they were blue in the face, but Decca wanted *You're Old Enough* as the A. needless to say it failed (as had their first single *Apple Blossom Time*, also featuring Jimmy Page).

After much giging they switched labels to *Warner Brothers* releasing the now highly collectable single *Little By Little* (a Ray Davies/Kinks song) in 1965. Soon after they split up, with Malcolm Jenkins joining **The Ray King Band** (SEE RAY KING) and Tony Martin joining Roger Lomas in **The Clouds** (SEE ROGER LOMAS).

THE PICKWICKS

PINK UMBRELLAS

So it came to pass that in 1981 **The Reluctant Stereotypes** split up (SEE THE RELUCTANT STEREOTYPES). With Paul King, Colin Heanes and Tony Wall going off to form King (SEE KING), while Paul Sampson and Steve Edgson did the same with **The Pink Umbrellas**. Beginning as a duo the Umbrellas soon became more than just a figment of Paul's fertile and somewhat nouveau psychedelic mind. Based around a concept of a fantasyland full to the brim with strange character like the enigmatic Joseph Monk (he's very strange). Plus places like *The Toy Museum, Lucy's Room* and even *the Mind of a Child*. Their music throbbed along with Paul's quirky clipped vocals grooving alongside Steve's stunning electric clarinet fills. Creating some wildly colourful harmonics, in deed there's a clarinet fill on the track *Joseph Monk* that positively sends shivers down my spine on every hearing. Steve is a master of his instrument, as Paul is a superb songwriter. On top of that they also ran the *Groovy Garden* (a name still in use I believe) it being retro 60's disco at Corks Wine bar at that time.

I spent many an afternoon at *Cabin Studios* on the London road (SEE STUDIOS) watching the creative process of the **Pink Umbrellas** unfold in front of me, Paul was chief in-house producer and in between other clients he was able to fit in his own sessions for **The Umbrellas**. By 1982 the duo had become a quartet with the addition of the great Rob Hill on drums (of course) and Barry Jones on bass (both from **The Mix**). *Raspberry Rainbow* was chosen as a single, a good choice because it sort of sums up the whole concept. It got some great airplay including Record of the Week on David Hamilton's *Radio Two* show, not really the target market for the boys, but who cares! New songs were written and recorded like the hilarious *Oh No! The Insectman* and *Dancing Girls,* as a live band they always excelled, even as a duo they were great but as a full band they were an experience that I never missed. By 1984 they concept was starting to grow a little tired and Rob Hill and Barry Jones left Rob became a member of **I** (SEE I). Steve & Paul tried to re-invent themselves as **The Attic Dressers**, but eventually they realised they had taken things as far as they could. Steve was to join **The Giraffes** (SEE THE GIRAFFES) and Paul continued to produce and engineer at Cabin studios (and work on his **F.A.T.E.** project *Twelve Times The Moon)*. He was to become a successful producer in his own right. His credits include work for **The Primitives** (including a Japanese tour playing bass and producing the hit *Crash* among many others) (SEE THE PRIMITIVES) and producing Catatonia (he produced the hit *Sweet Catatonia* (61)). Has also produced Cov's **Thoria** (SEE THORIA) He was apparently asked by The Stone Roses to produce their first album, apparently his manager never told him, so he never got the gig! He has also worked with David McAlmont & Ultramarine on their single *Hymn*. While Norwich's Neutrinos are his latest production project.

GODIVA ROCKS SOUND BYTE WITH-Paul Sampson (Reluctant Stereotypes, Pink Umbrellas & producer) 1. *Performing or producing, which hat fits you best?* Producing. I get much more variation in style, there's always a number of recordings going on at the same time, it's very fresh and rewarding moving between different projects. Although I spent nearly the whole of the 80s & 90s in recording studios I got out a bit. I played lead guitar for Screaming Lord Such 1986 captain rainbow loony party toured Canada/USA playing mandolin/guitar for BHANGRA group Aawazz 1988 1989 played bass for the primitives Japan tour 1990 music director/guitarist for David McAlmonts touring band 1994
Guitar for ultramarine Glastonbury 1995 bass for catatonia Bernard Black sessions Paris 1996
Yes, i still write. I wrote from 1975-85 then nothing then loads 1995-2000 i play solo gtr/voc shows now and again, but they've only been in London I still play instruments in the studio, mostly Bhangra work nowadays; Mandolin, Guitar, bass, banjo, tumbi.
2. *I recently started playing my old Reluctant stereotypes stuff again, I always liked Plans For Today, I now tend to think it's a brilliant crafted song. The lyrics are so intense but really good. Do you still write? Do you have any good memories of the Stereotypes dazzze?*
TV and radio sessions whistle test. look here with Toya playing the Belgrade with people climbing in the windows 'cause all the tickets were sold out. 40 gigs with The Q-tips. A seaside tour with The Specials in summer 1980 and the butts stadium, The Specials headlined, Ghost Town was number one. **Continued**

GODIVAROCKS@YAHOO.CO.UK

Continued 40 gigs with The Q-tips. I'm sure we played more than most bands, we did a seaside tour with the Specials in summer 1980 Reading festival 1981 was an experience especially being a ska band at a rock occasion.

3. Paul King mentions that the stereotypes got on Whistle Test, how was that and what song(s) did you do? You had to have released an album to get on whistle test. We had a good agent ITB The Songs we did were Nightmares and M.O.D. I never saw the broadcast cause it went out live in those days and at the turn of the 80s very few homes had a VCR. We did the show with Adam and the Ants. Presented by Anne Nightingale That 10 minute slot made our audience and fee quadruple overnight.

4. In your opinion what's the best band you have been in? (Ens, R.S. P.Umbrellas)?? I put all these bands equal for satisfaction ENS were deliberately uncommercial inspired by Henry Cow / Robert Wyatt/Beefheart we played regular at The Dive, Golden Cross, Climax, Earlsdon cottage, the Walsgrave, the Market Tavern. We did the odd time signature jazz thing. if people started dancing, we'd scrap the piece and compose something more unstomachable. this must have been a way of rebelling, getting the tortured artist thing out of the system it's the music that's important not the money. Reluctant Stereotypes. A conscious attempt for commercial successes. Fed up with the people in the factory where I worked saying when you going to be on the telly then. Pink Umbrellas. Was a refreshing release from the cold stiff brittleness of the current early 80s sound. I'll always be a fan of microphones and musical instruments.

5. Are you always happy after producing a song? Or do you always feel you could have done it better/different, how is the production process for you, how do you approach each song? The most common problem I have after producing a band is by the time a track is finished everybody knows it so well the band will often go and play it so much better after they have a clear picture in there mind of how to perform it with the right spirit, dynamics and attitude. If the artist doesn't satisfy themselves first, there's a good chance you'll hear that in the recorded material. I'm happy with the spirit of most of the recordings I've produced. Since the beginning of 2000 I've done all my work on Sony laptops and MOTU, whether in a studio or on location. I have a good selection of microphones. So I start an album project at a bands rehearsal facility if needed.

THE PRIMITIVES

1985 the **Primitives** (or the **Prim's** as the groovy set called them, the name came from the pre-Velvets Lou Reed band.) began life under the management of local T-shirt designer Wayne Morris of the shop *European Son*. Originally with male vocalist known only as Kieron. Many biographers have intimated he was sacked to accommodate their new female vocalist, but he actually left the band to form **The Nocturnal Babies** well before Tracy Tracy joined. The Cov' band had in fact wanted more of an Iggy Pop type as a vocalist not a female (albeit a rather striking and attractive one), she still got the job. Tracy Cattell was born in Australia in 1967, her peroxide look was to forever equate the band with Blondie. They had more in common musically with The Modettes and Fuzzbox.. Other key members were Paul Court on guitar & vocals, Bassist Steve Dullaghan and drummer Pete Tweedie.

They released their debut single *Thru the Flowers* on their own *Lazy Label* in 1986. Its haunting melodies saw it climb to number one in the Indie' charts, it even got a airing on *The Wogan TV Show!* Their jingle jangle indie style made them the darlings of Radio One, landing sessions for Janice Long, Andy Kershaw and John Peel. More singles followed in 1987 that were to cement their reputation including *Really Stupid and Stop Killing me* another indie number one. Following a European tour Tweedie was replaced by Tig Williams. **The Prim's** then signed their *Lazy Record* label to RCA (Echoes of *2 Tone* to *Chrysalis* there). They recorded the album *Lovely* with The great Paul Sampson producing (SEE THE RELUCTANT STEREOTYPES, SEE THE PINK UMBRELLAS). It's good to know that most of that early stuff was recorded at Cabin Studios on London Road (SEE STUDIOS). The single *Crash* was released from the album and their first single on a major label was an immediate hit at number five. So predictably Tracey became mega trend mag fodder and got on a plethora of glossy covers. Crash really was a fine indie-pop song, sadly the local Cov' press gave them a really hard time (I had hung up my pen by then). It's true to say that **The Prim's** never really had big local appeal, a disgrace as far as I am concerned, support your local band, that's what I say!

The album *Lovely* too got to number six in it's respective chart, shifting some 100,000 copies. The follow-up single *Out Of Reach* faired less well at number 25. Never the less a US tour followed, with bassist Dullaghan leaving at its close replaced (in the studio and for The Japanese tour) by producer Paul Sampson. Until bassist Andy Hobson joined. The next album followed entitled *Pure (33)* (nor counting the compilation *Lazy 86-88*) and singles *Sick Of It* (24), and *Secrets* (49). They released one more album entitled *Galore* produced by The Lighting Seeds mainman Ian Broudie. A pretty good album it was too, including the single *You Are the Way* but it was to be their last and charted at a lowly 58.

When the band finally called it a day, Court and Williams along with Neil Chamion formed **Starpower** (Tracy was also to feature in the project). Other offshoot bands included **The Fixations, Hedy** (who released the single *Superfine)* and **Reverb Inferno**. See See Rider, Nocturnal Babies, The Bensons, Hate, who became **The Hungry I** that included Dullaghan and Martyn Bates (SEE EYELESS IN GAZA). Andy Hobson joined The Pretenders. Tracy appeared on *Never Mind The Buzzcocks* in 2001. Despite the lack of local support **The Prim's** had in their own way cornered a niche in the market and created a sound that was instantly recognisable, something this Coventry band should be proud of.

PUNK

OK when it comes to punk in Cov there can only be one band **Squad** (SEE SQUAD), but hold on a cotton pickin' moment for there were and are others. Original punkers from the mid 70's include **Homicide,** led by Bev the Coventry Queen of Punk. I will never forget seeing her at *Mr George's* (SEE VENUES) on one Thursday 'punk' night wearing just a string vest! If that was punk I thought to myself I want in! Anyway back to **Homicide,** well they were loud, played songs called *Genocide* and *Armageddon* (this track featured on the *Sent From Coventry* Compilation LP) and they could be found mostly playing at *The Swanswell Tavern*. **Riot Act** were another great Cov punk outfit, they never got into the mindless make as much noise as possible punk routine, they put some thought into their music, *Return of the Jets* was once such song, always a great gig starter. With main man Stu Napper leaping around like he was wiring a three pin in the shower, they knew how to work an audience, but in 1978 it wasn't hard. Stu was one of the many Cov muso's that would work in *Virgin Records* in the Arcade (Brad of The Specials was another). **Criminal Class** pretenders to the **Squad** crown? I always thought so. More Oi than punk of course, still going today (like many other original punk bands), Craig St Leon still on vocals (although original members Fred Waite and Mark Braski are long gone). They had a couple of albums *Strength Thru Oi* and *Fighting the system*. Right from the start of the punk movement came **The Pseuds** *Sin City* and *Seventy Seven* were a couple of their songs. They never made much of an impact on the local scene at the time, although drummer John Hewitt went on to be in **King** for a short while and played on *Love and Pride* (SEE KING). Like-wise bass player Mick Gallic joined *Dexy's Midnight Runners* and played on *Geno* and *Come On Eileen,* (speaking of Dexy's, Kevin Rowlands brother Pete was once a teacher at *Caludon Castle School*).

BEV OF HOMICIDE

Others at the time included **White Boss, Solid Action**, (who included Rich Freeman, Dave Freeman of **The Flys** younger brother). **The Filth** (did a great song called *Nay Nay Mr Wilkes*) **Column 88, The Slugs** (both from Rugby)(SEE RUGBY)**,** While Leamington had The **Verukas, The Swell Maps, The Shapes,** *Flack Off* (SEE European Sun), **The School Meals** and **The Defendants** (SEE LEAMINGTON). **The Pot, Rabid, Eoka-B The Pubes, Ikstop** and **Barbwire** were all from the Nuneaton area (SEE NUNEATON). On the fringe were **The Wild Boys** *(SEE RODDY RADIATION),* **The Flys** *(SEE THE FLYS) and* **The Vietnamese Babies** *(SEE VIETNAMESE BABIES)* and **Hazel O'connor** was Queen of punk as the press christened her, though her music wasn't particularly punk. The *Sent From Coventry* compilation album featured a lot of punkers including, **The Wild Boys** (We're Only Monsters & Lorraine), **Solid Action** (Message From a Loner), **Squad** (Flasher), **Homicide** (Armageddon), **Riot act** (Sirens) and **The V Babies** (Donna Blitzen).

PAGE 76   GODIVAROCKS@YAHOO.CO.UK   PAGE 76

Latter day punks in the area have included **3½ Floppy** played at The Bedworth Civic Hall, have now morphed into **The Hunchbacks. The Academy Morticians** meanwhile are from Balsall Common, that's Simon, Dan, Steve and Tom, deriving from the covers band **Soverign** they went on to become **Who Killed Culture 3** then **Doogle** finally becoming the **Academy Morticians**. *Forbidden Curriculum, Shallow Permanence, Consumerism is a STD* and *What Happened* are the bands 4 releases. **XS-Energy** were from Cov, in 1979 they released the poptastic singles *18* and *Use You*. The band consisted of Freddie Voltage (vocals & guitar), Max Headroom (lead guitar & vocals), Nicky Teen (bass & vocals) and Mark Up (drums). **Dave Damage** were a punk/grunge band of 2003, lasted about a year, originally called **Spoofer**. **Crux** were a 'Oi' band from Nuneaton(SEE NUNEATON), released the 12" single *Keep On Running* in the early 80's. **Jellybrain** was a punk record label based in Nuneaton.

Pretty current punkers are **Pigfish**. Formed in 1997 and got some great press with their debut Ska/punk album *Creosote The Baby*. It remains a 'seldom heard' classic to this day. More thrashing guitar music followed with *The Reverend James* EP and the subsequent offering *All snowy On the Pond*. The **Pigfish** name was been well tempered especially in the good old US of A, where they have a cult following (they will shake him off I'm sure). They sadly remain a major cult band if that's not something of a contradiction in terms. With their output regularly getting top reviews from the likes of *Kerrang* and *Metal Hammer*. **Coybito** from the City play a hybrid of punk and techno loops. Like to make out that they aren't very good, but it's a lie, they really are a great little band, there stuff makes you want to smile, and I can actually see it in the charts. **Any Given Day** are from Rugby (SEE ANY GIVEN DAY) and **Malachai, Everescent** are both Nuneaton punk bands. The Business did the track *Coventry* (SEE COVENTRY BY NAME), **Hand and Heart, Climax, Mr.Georges, The Heath Hotel** were good Punk venues in Cov. **Alternative Sounds** (SEE ALTERNATIVE SOUNDS) fanzine was a great place to read about punk bands and gigs.

PINKERTONS ASSORTED COLOURS

Located on the outskirts of Rugby in the early 60's was a place called Clifton Hall (it's still there in fact). This was the base of one of pops most flamboyant characters Reg Calvert (SEE RUGBY). Reg was an impresario, running clubs all over the country. Clifton Hall became a 'pop-school' an academy of beat where new talent could be nurtured and recorded at the halls own recording studios (albeit to only demo quality). Along with the likes of Danny Storm, The Fortunes (SEE THE B LIST) and Screaming Lord Sutch **Pinkertons Assorted Colours** were soon to become part of Reg Calvert's unique empire.

Rugby band **The Liberators** led by songwriter (and top vocalist) Tony Newman had built up a following, not least for their single *Hurts So Much* (produced by Shel Talmy). They decided to approach Reg at Clifton Hall, to ask him to be their personal manager. The deal was done and on December 10th 1965 **The Liberators** were re-invented as **Pinkertons Assorted Colours**. With the new name came the new image, brightly coloured suits were were the order of the day, really putting 'the colour' into Pinkertons. Front man Sam 'Widge' Kempe was re-christened Samuel 'Pinkerton' Kempe and given an amplified auto-harp, this was to become the trademark of the band visually and musically. Although an unusual instrument for a beat band The Lovin' Spoonfull had also experimented with it and Brian Jones of The Rolling Stones was to use the instrument a little later. (Tony Newman places the sound of this unusual instrument close to that of two 12-string guitars in unison). Tony Newman (vocals and guitar) Tom Long (lead guitar), former **Vampires** bassman Barrie Bernhard (SEE THE VAMPIRES) and Johnny Wallbank (drums) completed the line-up. Their first single *Mirror Mirror* was released on Decca at the start of 1966 (produced by Coventry kid **Tony Clarke** (SEE TONY CLARKE), the ever-resourceful Reg Calvert arranged a publicity stunt and the fountains in Trafalgar Square were turned multi-coloured with dye. The record was also constantly played on *Radio City* pirate radio station (that just happened to be controlled by Reg and would soon bring an untimely end). By January 15th *Mirror Mirror* was at number 9 in the UK charts. With it cheerful clanging sound and catchy chorus the song was a sure-fire winner and **Pinkertons** were on the way.

Just as the second single was about to be recorded bass guitarist Barrie Bernhard left to join Jigsaw (SEE JIGSAW), he was replaced by Stuart Colman who had been in the Rugby bands **The Beat-Preachers** and before that **The Cataracts** (SEE RUGBY). *Don't Stop Loving Me baby* the follow-up, managed a number 50 placing in the charts. The next single *Magic Rocking Horse* was a great piece of psychedelic freak beat (indeed it's often forgotten just what a great beat band **Pinkertons Colours** [as they were now billed] actually were, much more than just *Mirror, Mirror*). It should have been huge, but just as it was released their mentor Reg Calvert was to lose his life in a bizarre shooting incident. Who knows if the lack of promotion and the lack of a manager contributed to low sales? Whatever the reason it failed to chart and the guys were to soon have a new manager (Terry King) and a new label (Pye).

Along with the new manager and label came a new producer Tony Macauly, and a new guitarist Steve Jones who was with Coventry unit's **The Peeps** and **The Sabres** (SEE THE PEEPS). After a few unsuccessful singles like *Mum And Dad, There's Nobody I'd Sooner Love* and Kentucky *Woman*. Things were looking decidedly dim, especially after their producer Tony Macauly, was now away having song writing hits with the likes of The Foundations and Long John Baldry. Their drummer Dave Holland also departed to join heavy band Trapeze (that included Glenn Hughes later of Deep Purple), he was replaced by another ex-**Peeps** member Paul Wilkinson. Things then started to look up and the band were invited to contribute the music to the Scottish TV show *Bernadette*. Tony Macauly pulled out all the stops and wrote the song *Smile A Little Smile For Me*. They were all convinced it would bring them the UK hit they so wanted again. It was decided that a new name for the band was in order so **Pinkertons Colours** became **The Flying Machine**. All was ready for the chart onslaught, but nothing was happening (although the Marmalade were charting with a song Tony Macauly had previously written and recorded for them, *Baby make It Soon*). At this point Sam Kempe left to become **Jigsaw's** road manager. Then they discovered that *Smile A Little Smile For Me* had charted in Holland, meanwhile a new single was released in the UK *Send My Baby Home Again*. All their eyes were on this single hoping it would do the business, unbeknown that behind their backs *Smile A Little Smile For Me* was slowly creeping up the American charts!

In 1969 their world turned around and everyone Stateside wanted a piece of **The Flying Machine.** They went back into the studios in no time recording an album *Down to Earth*, the single finally peaked at an amazing number 5 in the US charts! Just as that happened Tony Macauly announced he was leaving Pye records for Bell Records. He asked **The Flying Machine** to join him (he said he had a song especially for them). It was decided that as they had six months left on their contract they would stay with Pye. Macauly was not best pleased and his support for the band was well and truly rescinded. This became evident when their second US release *Baby Make It Soon* was met with the release of 2 other versions from Macauly, effectively diluting the songs success. To make matters worse, that song he had written for them turned out to be *Love Grows Where My Rosemary Goes*. It of course became a global hit, but not for them, for session band Edison lighthouse. Despite this slap in the face they continued to tour, releasing their most progressive song to date *The Devil has Possession of your mind* co written by Coventry's own Johnny Goodison (SEE JOHNNY B.GREAT). After this failed to take off for **The Flying Machine,** they decided to call it a day playing their last gig at the *Forty Thieves* in Coventry June 1971.

Tony was to continue to use the name **Pinkertons Colours** and they enjoyed some success on the country music scene in the 80's, even playing at the Wembley Country Music Festival. Nowadays they still play from time to time with the following personnel. Tony Newman(vocals & guitar), Pete Robbins (drums), Phil Clough Lead Guitar) and Mike Summerson (Bass) As for Stewart Colman, well he went on to be a successful DJ at Radio One. Later moving onto production (his production credits have included, Cliff Richards, Billy Fury, Shakin' Stevens and Kim Wilde). He now works as a producer in Nashville. In 2004 Castle music released a marvellous double CD *Flight recorder* of just about all the output from **Pinkerton's** and **The Flying Machine.** Stuart Colman's in-depth liner notes that accompanies the said CD has proved a very helpful in creating this entry. So thanks Stuart and Tony.

GODIVA ROCKS SOUND BYTE WITH-TONY Newman (Pinkertons Colours & The Flying Machine)

Going back to the early 60's about 63/64 prior to the announcement of PINKERTONS ASSORTED COLOURS who were officially launched on December 10th 1965 with the release of MIRROR MIRROR. Before Pinkerton's the band which consisted of the same members was called the (LIBERATORS). We worked for two really colourful characters both who lived in Rugby at the time.

Quite often on a Sunday night we used to play in the local cinema in Rugby known as the Granada then. A B film and a second rate horror film would be shown, and a pop group would play a set of about 20 mins in between the films every Sunday night. The Manager CHARLIE FIELDS wore make-up for the stage lighting. and when we were appearing, or anyone local would walk on stage and announced that tonight's band show comes from Rugby (in those days that would get applause on its own). Before our performance we would be introduced to Chief, a local character known as (LES PRIOR) who would adjust the level of the PA System, and stress max level would be no more than 6 or distortion would result, as the system was fitted in the 50's. Charlie told us to keep chat to a minimum going straight from one song to another as he put it, keeping it slick. The show would commence and the odd Jack The Lad would call out various band members names during the performance, like good old Kempy whom was the second singer. Charlie would then twist on from the wings and announce the bands last song, much to the horror of the band and insist on counting it in and then immediately twist off again.

The show had finished to adequate applause no time for an encore, as the main film would run late. Charlie had deemed it slick enough and successful enough and he was well pleased. The band would now be treated to a celebration drink in Charlie's Office of cooking sherry. At this point you knew you had made it on the Rugby scene. The other colourful character who was later to be our Manager REG CALVERT who we approached because he ran various venues across the region paying £15 per gig. He ran places such as RUGBY TOWN HALL, NUNEATON CO-OP HALL, KETTERING CENTRAL HALL, MATRIX BALLROOM COVENTRY, BANBURY WINTERGARDENS, HIGH WYCOMBE TOWN HALL, we played all these venues many many times. And I think I could write an entire book on the events that occurred at these venues.

Reg would insist on doing the Hully Gully a sort of current dance at the time, in front of the band on stage at most of these venues. when he was running the night., otherwise his wife DOROTHY would run them being much more laid back than Reg. Sitting at the side of the stage and taking notes of the quality of the act, and entering them into her famous book which she could refer to when bands wanted re-bookings. Reg had many unusual ideas to say the least, one of which was to run a competition and raffles at his venues, where the prizes would consist of a live animal or bird. First it was white mice, then hamsters, later chickens and hens, and various feathered birds.

THE LEGENDARY REG CALVERT (Left) WITH ROBBIE HOOD AT CLIFTON HALL
Photo copyright of Macdonald Queen Anne Press

The festive season was approaching leading up to Christmas, Reg hit on the idea of giving donkeys away at his famous raffles (I have no idea where he got them from). So not only did the band have to transport themselves and musical gear but now a donkey also had to be accommodated in the band van to various venues around the country. We used to sit in the front, the donkey entered the van thro the side leading door, so was in the middle and the gear at the back. You can imagine how surprised the petrol pump attendant was on the A45 en route to the MATRIX BALLROOM, COVENTRY. I believe on one occasion we had to deliver a donkey to the lucky winners address in Bedworth. With Reg there was never a dull moment, when he was around. Both Charlie and Reg were special characters we will never see the likes of again. All I can say is I will always remember those happy days.

RODDY RADIATION

Born Roderick James Byers on 5th May 1955, brought up in Keresley Village his father Stan Byers was a trumpet player of some renound. He was christened Roddy Radiation by his brother Chris during his 'ziggy' days. Started out playing with the club band **Heaven Sent**. Later moving on to Cov punksters **The Wild Boys** that included Roddy's brother Mark Extra on guitar (SEE THE WILD BOYS). Jerry Dammers asked him to join his new band **The Coventry Automatics**, later of course **The Specials** (SEE THE SPECIALS). He would be the second most prolific songwriter in the band penning *Concrete Jungle* (actually written during The Wild Boys days) *Holiday Fortnight, Hey Little Rich Girl* and the number 5 hit record *Ratrace*. Even in **The Specials** his punk persona was slowly giving way to his rock n roll roots, and the song *Braggin' and Tryin' not to Lie* was setting the tone of what was to come. Before the Specials finally split Roddy had formed **Roddy Radiation and The Tearjerkers**. Playing what was referred to as skabilly or reggae meets rock n roll. Another nod of the hat to Coventry's mixed roots and indeed **The Specials** mixed roots. Other hybrids include the natty use of the Jamaican flag stylised with stars to resemble the rebel flag, bringing Ska and rock-a-billy together. The same applies to Hank Jabsco a rock-a-billy version of the famous *2 Tone* Walt Jabsco logo (SEE 2 TONE), clever stuff.

THE TEARJERKERS

The original **Tearjerkers** line-up would include Dave Freeman from **The Flys** (SEE THE FLYS) on guitar, Cov's Pete Davies the former UK-Subs drummer, Joe Hughes also ex-**Flys** on bass and Roddy guitar & vocals and lots of moves and grooves and skabilly shapes. Roddy would leave **The Specials** long before *In The Studio* came out, his only contribution to the album would be a guitar solo for *Racist Friend* lifted from a previous demo. (It would be a period in Roddy's life that would take many years for him to come to terms with, even now he can only just about listen to those **Specials** songs).

The **Tearjerkers** meanwhile were always more a live band than a studio one. Tour mates included Stiff Little Fingers, Elvis Costello, The Bureau and The Modettes. They released one EP and the single *Desire* on *Chiswick Records*. Freeman left the band very early on, while Joe Hughes continued to be a member for some time, eventually leaving and teaming up with Freeman to form **The Lover Speaks** (SEE THE LOVER SPEAKS) they were replaced by Rod's brother Mark Byers on guitar and 'Badger on bass. Pete Davis would also leave being replaced by Tony Lynch. 'Slim' the larger than life one time Boothill Footapper and accordion king would also become a permanent fixture in the band, but after much live giging **The Tearjerkers** broke up, leaving Rod to take stock of things finally launching the Country blues outfit **The Bonediggers**. They would pick up a large following in Germany and release the *album For Those Who Died Trying* and a 12inch EP on *Rimshot Records*. The line-up included Roddy guitar & vocals, Dave West guitar & vocals, Sam Smith bass and Garry Muldoon on drums later replaced by Curly Jim. (a promo video of *Bonediggin'* was recorded for local cable TV). The next incarnation for Roddy was **The Raiders**, where at this point he was to be asked to play on the Desmond Dekker album King of Kings with other ex-**Specials** including Horace Panter (SEE HORACE PANTER), Lynval Golding and Neville Staples. Out of this came the **Specials** reunion tour (*sans* Terry & Jerry) and the badly received album *Todays Specials* followed by the much better follow up *Guilty*, that would include a number of Byers songs. After a two year tour cycle the latterday Specials called it a day (but the similar **2 Tone Collective** would include Roddy and the likes of Ranking Roger & Pauline Black) (SEE HORACE PANTER, SEE PAULINE BLACK,SEE THE SELECTER).

As for now, well his latest rock n roll manifestation is the four piece **Skabilly Rebel**, like his other bands they are a live unit, who play regularly around the local area. He has also seen the release of his anthology album *Skabilly Rebel* that builds on his vast output with **The Specials, The Tearjerkers, The Bonediggers** and **The Raiders** though no **Jumpin' Bad** (another short lived Radiation outfit). It's Rod at his best raw and unsophisticated, well worth checking out. Through it all Rod remains an approachable human being, a regular guy, who can be proud for creating his own skabilly niche in the rock n roll rat race. (SEE THE SPECIALS *for Roddy's contribution.*)

GODIVAROCKS@YAHOO.CO.UK

MARK RATTRAY

A Binley Park Schoolboy who was the last ever person to win on Opportunity Knocks. Originally a nurse at Cov & Warwick Hospital, he was soon to make his mark in musicals. Starting out in *Magic of the Musicals and Musical Magic* A national tour followed, but it was *The West End* where his powerful voice always shone the best. Although he has released the occasional LP including *Mark Rattray Performs Songs of the Musicals (46)* and *The Magic of the Musicals (55)* with Marti Webb taken from the successful show of the same name and was a best selling video too.

1994 and 1995 saw Mark play some 400 West End shows, but still find time to guest as a vocalist on a BBC Radio2 special with The Simon May Orchestra. His touring partners have include Susan Maughan in *Simply Sondheim*, The talented & stunningly gorgeous Melanie Stace in *Magic of the Musicals* (a show that would meander in and out of his career), and Maggie Moone and The Stutz Bear Cats in *The Look of Love*. In the late 90's he was to write and produce the new shows *Summer Musical Magic* and *The Magic of Christmas* (again with Maggie Moone). His list of shows go on and on, like *Music of the Night, Sleeping Beauty, Because You are mine* and *Dick Wittington* (this show broke box office records at Leamington Spa).

1999, was to be a great year for Mark as he starred as the great Mario Lanza in *Lanza-The Last Serenade*. It was created with him in mind, and sanctioned by Mario Lanza's daughter Ellisa. A biographical show written by Dave Dennison. It was to be one of his finest moments. He continues to light up stages in the West End and in North America, and has a large and loyal fan-base second to none. He along with Dave Willetts (SEE DAVE WILLETTS) are undisputed kings of the musical, it's good to know they are both Coventry kids too.

RECORD SHOPS & LABELS

The first Coventry Record shops (called Talking Machine Records in 1900's) were *English Record Co Ltd,* 5 Jesson St, Cov and *Alexander Record Co* in Bishop St both circa1912. Shops around in 1916 were *Charles Askew* in Raglan St, *Cowen & Co* Fleet St, *Midland Gramophones* Hertford St, *Wilsons* in Jordan Well and *William Webb* in Marlborough Rd (he later moved to Paynes Lane). Record shops from circa 1930 included *W.F. Wards* on 203 Walsgrave Road, *Julius Leek Cross Cheaping, Talkie Hits* 3 Leicester Row and *John S Luckman and Co* in Hertford Street selling the old 78's. Pete Waterman talks about a record shop In North Street in his book (SEE PETE WATERMAN). *Fennells* 78 Lower Precinct was a major record seller in the city, it closed in 1979. *Jill Hansons* 8 Market Way small but well stocked and a classical department upstairs, hosted *Jill's Jury* in the Coventry Standard, closed early 80's. *Paynes* Fairfax Street, records and musical instrument closed 1982. *Cranes* had a shop in Gosford Street, I used them a lot, got some well rare stuff from them, and they also had a shop in Barkers Butts Lane. *Barrie Phelps*, 38 Jordan Well, Barrie was the Leofric's musical director in the 60's. Others included *Elliott Electrics* of Albany Road, and *Patels* on Stoney Stanton Road who stocked some great reggae. *Whisky M hle* Records where in *Intershop* in Warwick Row. My area Ball Hill had *Baz Frost* (originally in Marlborough Road then Gosford St), *The Sound Centre* in Clay lane and *Gibbs* on Walsgrave Road. *Hits Misses and Vintage Records* was a great second-hand record shop in Gosford Street, it changed hands many many times. I bought The Larry Lurex (Freddie Mercury) single here for 25p (it's worth hundreds now, I gave it away!).

Then there is *Virgin Records*, not the big mega store we have now, but the one in The City Arcade. I bought tons of stuff from here (so did I, I can hear you say). Brad of **The Specials** worked there, so did Stu of **Riot Act**, (SEE PUNK) as did Chris Long of **The Swinging Cats** (SEE THE SWINGING CATS) and **Tim Strickland** Briefly in **The Coventry Automatics,** more famous for being one of Cov's finest DJ's. He and Chris long also ran *Inferno records* in The Precinct. Upstairs at *Virgin* was Pete Waterman's *Soul Hole* (SEE PETE WATERMAN). Other shops included the great *Spinadisc*, Revolver, *Our Price,* two *HMV's* (the one in Hertford Street gave it's name to *The Dog and Trumpet* (SEE VENUES)

GODIVAROCKS@YAHOO.CO.UK

and *Ray Gun Records* in Cathedral Lanes who now have their own groovy newsletter, a great idea.

Local Record labels include *Data Records* based in Silksby Street, *Panthos Records* from of course *Panthos Studios* in Balsall Common,*Tripping The Light Fantastic Records* a label for local Coventry & Warwickshire talent. *Iguana* from Horizon, *Sonar Records* from Cabin Studios (SEE STUDIOS). Then there was *Lazy Records* from the **Primitives** (SEE THE PRIMITIVES). Of course *2Tone Records* (SEE 2TONE), *Shack Records* and *Rude Boy Records* from **Specials** man Neville Staples (SEE THE SPECIALS). **Lieutenant Pigeon** released the single *Bobbing Up and Down Like This* on here and *21 Guns* by **21 Guns** (SEE LIEUTENANT PIGEON,SEE SQUAD). John Bradbury also of **The Specials** had his own *Race Records*. *Horizon Studios* had logically *Horizon Records (SEE STUDIOS)*. *Coventry Records* release Christian music and are closely associated with Coventry Cathedral (SEE COVENTRY CATHEDRAL) and the virtuoso Paul Leddington Wright. *Take Your Hands Records* are based in Kensington Road, Coventry.

REGGAE

Ok leaving **2 Tone** aside for a minute, here are some other reggae acts that have been sent from Coventry. **Steel locks** often got labelled Coventry's answer to Steel Pulse, perhaps not such a bad thing, but the were always their own people, doing it their way. Indeed the most successful reggae artists have been the ones strong willed enough to do it like that. With a Rasta street warrior image and hybrid reggae punk mix Hillfields based Steel Locks were formed circa 1978 and. An eight piece that included Seymour Angus, Alex Susan and Brinnitte Bailey, Michael Hughes, Tony Bell, Greg Halger and Shaun Kelleher. Their songs included the hard hitting *1980* and the much softer love song *Pretty Bird.* They released the single *Let's Get Together* on *Voyage International Records* in 1980. It was well received and got some gob smacking reviews (I have a cutting from Sounds that called it, ⌈The real spirit of Prince Buster in 1980⌉) despite that it failed to make a dent in the chart. **The People** were a *2 Tone* offshoot. Comprising of Charley Anderson and Desmond Brown from **The Selecter** (SEE THE SELECTER) and Silverton Hutchinson the original **Specials** drummer (SEE THE SPECIALS). They played a great set at the *Rock Against Racism* gig at *The Butts* (SEE VENUES), a single was released on Brad's *Race Records* in 1981 entitled *Musical Man* (a tribute to Rico).

STEEL LOCKS

The Relatives played their own brand of *Upfront Reggae Dance*. An octet that were made up of Trevor ⌈Rockers⌉ drums, Ged ⌈The General⌉ vocals and guitar, Paul ⌈Goldfinger⌉ Aubertin bass, Camille Love vocals, Professor Jack on percussion and sax trio Mark, Lee and Dee. They were the subject of a *Channel 4* sponsored short film entitled *Just Enough Light*. The buzz they created in the 90's seemed to be enough to make them the next big thing from the region. Rightly so their music was well crafted, these guys took their 'sound' very serious indeed. Their lover style beats smoothed over with tender blues guitar riffs gave way to dynamic walls of urban percussion guaranteed to set any dance hall alight. They played a lot out of the area including London, even had a well-oiled management team. Despite having everything right, a major deal never came their way and the parting of the band was inevitable. **Kendell Smith** was a Caribbean Dub Poet based in Coventry his evocative rhythmic poetry delivered with a backdrop of reggae music (what else) was a recipe to fire up any audience. He had been for a short while a vocalist in the Cov' cult band **The Urge** (SEE THE URGE). He later became the manager of Bhangra king Taz eventually joining forces artistically with him and creating **Stereo Nation** (SEE BHANGRA, SEE STEREO NATION). **Sean Paul** the dance hall reggae star who has had smash hits with *Like Glue* and *Baby Boy* (with Beyonce) is of Jamaica by birth but his Grandmother was actually born in Rugby In fact he not only has Rugby blood, but Portuguese and Chinese too. He says, ⌈I have a lot of Love for England my Grandmother's from Rugby, so I was always close to England in the stories I'd hear growing up⌉ Other local reggae stuff include the bands, **The UK Warriors,** took part in *The Barras Club's Best Band Contest*. **Prophecy** an 8 piece who took part in the *All Day Rock Show* at *The Lanch* in 1983. **Rough Beat** used to do a great cover of *Police and Thieves*. **Destiny,** played *Covaid* (SEE FESTIVALS). **Tubilah Dog** were a bit of a hippy reggae outfit who played free festivals, supported Hawkwind, their bass player Tom was once in **UK Warriors. Mo Floppy** are a current band who merge reggae and Hiphop with rock, they have demoed their work at *J10 Studios* (SEE STUDIOS) and have a very Cov sound. Also *Beveley Napier Barrett* was *Mercia Sounds* reggae Queen! (SEE MEDIA). Currently *Club Irie* on the Foleshill Road (formally *The Heath Hotel)* is the place for reggae.

RELUCTANT STEREOTYPES

Guitarist Paul Sampson was with the jazz/rock band **Bung**. Meanwhile clarinettist extrodenaire Steve Edgson had been with the experimental nouveau progressive unit **Analog** (who were regulars at Cov's *Hobo Workshop*). Guitarist Steve Haddon had formed a band called **Ens** and was looking for good personnel. Steve joined first and Paul then came in to replace the great guitarist Peter Bosworth who would leave to concentrate on production, he later died from a heart attack. The line-up was completed by 2 other ex **Analog** members Mick Hartley on bass and Paul Brook on drums. With Peter Bosworth gone a change of direction was called for, a new name was instituted and **The Reluctant Stereotypes** were born. Now before we carry on it's worth pointing out that the **Stereotypes** had 2 distinct periods, really only connected by a couple of members and the name.

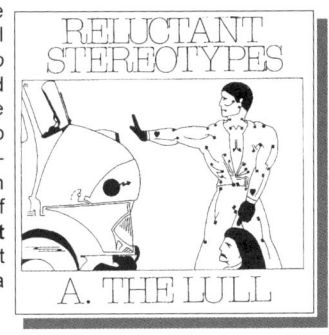

So in 1979 the mark one version began to take shape, with Steve Haddon having ideas of making it a totally instrumental outfit, the vote however went against him an a lead vocalist was auditioned. A certain former Police cadet called Paul King who had been singing at the *Coombe Abbey* medieval Banquets was tried for a few weeks and rejected. Eventually a Nuneaton guy called Martyn Bates came along and his unique vocal style fitted in perfectly. They released their first single on Charlie Gillets *Oval Records The Lull* coupled with *The Rounds* and *Fetch Mr Clifford the Political Boys Are On us*. All were deliciously different quirky jazz influenced pieces. *The Rounds* remains one of my all time favourites, with Martyn Bates (or Salvador Darling as he often known then), providing a vocal line that was just as original as the music he was singing. It was all so inspired, the band took part in a special *Oval Records* night at *Dingwall's* in Camden and began clocking up some great press. But in every dream home a heartache and the musical style was not pleasing everyone. Bates felt the music was too clever and too complex, a second single had to be chosen but no agreement was being reached. Eventually the entire band left leaving just Paul Sampson and Steve Edgson to pick up the pieces. Bates formed the mighty Nuneaton duo **Eyeless In Gaza** with Pete Becker (SEE EYELESS IN GAZA). Meanwhile back at **The Stereotypes** Ex-drama student Paul King (or Winston Smith as he was known here) was re-recruited along with Tony Wall on bass and Colin Heanes on drums.

Phase 2 was beginning, they secured a deal with *WEA records* and released their first single *She Has Changed Not You,* recorded at *Horizon Studios* (SEE STUDIOS). (Made as a duo just before King, Wall and Heanes were recruited. Hence Paul Sampson on vocals). It was easy to see the musical differences, gone was the innovative jazz time signatures, replaced by the then trendy *Coventry Ska sound*. They were just as good, just very different. 1980 would see them release a further three high calibre singles namely *Confused Action,* the rather wonderful *Plans For Today* and *Nightmares.* They also released one well-received album entitled *The Label*, interestingly containing only one of the previously mentioned singles *Plans For Today.* It's testament to WEA's belief in them that they were allowed to release 4 singles and an album. Indeed they had all the makings of a chart band, the songs the style, with Sampson hurling himself about on stage and King with his drama-school mime, not to mention the ever-curious Edgson on the not very rock n roll clarinet. I loved this band, and saw them many times. We all believed they would be the next big thing. They played at The Butts *Festival against Racism* in 1981. Even making it on *The Old Grey Whistle Test* with Adam and the Ants. They played their final gig at *The Reading Festival* also in 1981. They had gone as far as they could go so new pastures were secured. With Paul, Colin and Tony becoming The **Raw Screens**, later **King** and Paul Sampson and Steve forming **The Pink Umbrellas**. (SEE KING, SEE THE PINK UMBRELLAS).

GODIVAROCKS@YAHOO.CO.UK

THE ROLLING STONES

The Stones played 2 shows at the Nuneaton (SEE NUNEATON) *Co-op Ballroom* 15th November 1963, In his book *Stone Alone* Bill Wyman tells of the earlier junior session. It was full of six to ten years old, who were not interested in R & B and proceeded to throw their afternoon tea (cream cakes) at the Stones! Sticky Fingers or what! Next night they played *The Matrix* in Coventry. They also Played 2 shows at Rugby's *Granada Theatre* on 11th Feb 1964 & 13th March 1965 (SEE RUGBY). They played Coventry Theatre (SEE VENUES) on 19th Jan 1964 (2 shows), 17th April at The Locarno 1964, 24th May The Coventry Theatre (2 shows) 1964. Finally playing the venue on 6th March 1971 (2 shows), the first concert has being heavily bootlegged and includes Jumping Jack Flash, Midnight Rambler and Brown Sugar.

11 Schoolboys at a *Woodlands Comprehensive School* were suspended by their headmaster Mr. Donald Thompson in March 1964 for imitating The Rolling Stones hairstyles. He called the style long & scruffy, he told them they could return if they cut their hair like the Beatles! The Brian Jones Fan Club is based in Rugby (SEE RUGBY). Former **Swell Maps** man Nikki Sudden had his mate former Stone Mick Taylor recorded some guitar overdubs for him at WSRS Studios (SEE STUDIOS, SEE LEAMINGTON) produced by John Rivers in Leamington on 16th August 2002, if your interested the songs were *House Of Cards* and *Kitchen Blues*. Mick Jagger recorded the promo video for his solo single *Sweet Thing* (24) at the *Royal Pump Rooms Leamington* on 10th & 11th December 1992. *MTV* attended and interviewed Jagger, producer Julian Temple and Saxophonist supreme Courtney Pine for a *XPO* feature of the single that aired on Jan 16th 1993. Another Stones/Warwickshire connection was of course **The Mighty Avengers** (SEE THE MIGHTY AVENGERS) who's recording manager was Andrew Loog Oldham, who was The Stones manager. Author Charles Bukowski once wrote a novel entitled Jaggernaut based on Michael Philip J, it was published by *Beat Scene Press* Coventry.

Jaggernaut a story by **Charles Bukowski**

RUGBY

Rugby can trace it's musical past back to at least the 1880's and it's famous *Rugby School*, with the likes of Violin master Herr Petterson leader of The *Rugby Philharmonic Society* and Edwin Edwards the organist at the school circa 1895. Famous musicians Sir Arthur Bliss (*master Of the Queens Music*) and Sir Sydney Nicholson (composer of church music) also attended the school as pupils. The school figures strongly in Rugby music and we will come back to it later. **Tom Ward and his Harmo Boys** were the big local stars of the 1930's in Rugby. They were a regular band at *Rugby's Co-op Hall* in Chapel Street. They became **Tom Ward & His New Star Players** in the 1940's, and would continue to entertain in their posh suits and top hats well into the early 50's.

TONY NEWMAN AT 'THE JETTY'

Rugby's first real brush with popular music came in the early 60's with **The Mighty Avengers** (SEE THE MIGHTY AVENGERS) who (thanks to Mick Jagger & Keith Richard) became the first local band to chart with the great song *So In Love* (46) in November 1964. Their contemporaries included **The Beat Preachers** (SEE PICKERTON'S ASSORTED COLOURS). A rockin' good freakbeat mod outfit that included Stuart Coleman on Bass (Stu' would go on to DJ on Radio One and produce the likes of Shaking Stevens). They supported The Who at Cov's Matrix Hall. They released one single in 1965 under the Name **The Carribean** (no not a spelling mistake) *Inside Out*. It's interesting that on the record the writing credits are Benn and Sherriff, obviously a local nod of the hat to Rugby stalwarts *George C. Benn (of Benn memorial Hall* fame) *and Lawrence Sherriff* (the benefactor). Tony Britnell also passed through on saxophone (there's an image) he later joined **Jigsaw** (SEE JIGSAW). Coleman went on to join **Pinkertons Colours** (SEE PICKERTON'S ASSORTED COLOURS). Other 60's bands were **The Ravens, The Reprobates** and **The Surf Cyders**.

Of all the bands of the 60's in Rugby it's **Pinkertons Assorted Colours** (SEE PICKERTON'S ASSORTED COLOURS) who have the biggest story to tell. They began life as Rugby combo **The Liberators** then Reg Calvert took over as their manager he changed their name to **Pinkertons Assorted Colours**. Reg Calvert was a colourful entrepreneur who managed night clubs all over the country, he picked Rugby as his base because of it's central location. He purchased the ramshackled *Clifton Hall* East of the town, and turned it in to a pop school (some 50 years before *Fame Academy* had the similar idea). Even the great Jerry Lee Lewis once stayed the night. Before I tell you just a little about Reg Calvert, It's become a bit of a crusade to get this mans life story made into a feature film. It really has ALL the elements, such was his life, I doubt if any film producers will ever read this humble book, but if you do; go for it!

Calvert nurtured his acts at the Hall systematically sending them off to gig in all direction from his central Rugby hub. Acts like **Vince Taylor & the Playboys, Rory Blackwell, Gullivers Travels, The Clifton All Star, Freddie Flicker and the Knicker Flickers and Robin Hood and His Merry Men**. Then there were the successful ones like **Danny Storm, The Fortunes** (SEE THE FORTUNES), **Screaming Lord Sutch** and **Pinkertons Assorted Colours**. His antics including the giving live animals as raffle prizes as you will read in Tony Newman's hilarious contribution (SEE PICKERTON'S ASSORTED COLOURS). He had a pet chimpanzee that for some reason hated him and attempted to scratch his eyes out every time they came close. His various bands would find it wildly amusing, but he got his own back and often released the chimp on the stage mid-way through a set. Oh what fun to see a band trying to perform while the monkey is swinging from the curtains behind them. Reg also had some imaginative ideas when it came to booking bands, at one point he was parading a band of nobodies as the Irish hit group **Them** (the real band featured Van 'The Man' Morrison). Their manager Phil Solomon was less than pleased on hearing the news, to make matters worse Calvert registered his 'bogus' **Them** as a limited company. Solomon in his retaliation did the same creating bogus bands **The Fortunes** and **Pinkerton's Assorted Colours** and registering them as limited companies. In the end Calvert was powerless and backed down 'hoist with his own petard'.

To promote the bizarre Screaming Lord Sutch (who would famously go on to lead *The Monster Raving Loony Party*), Calvert obtained an old derelict gun tower off the coast at Shivering Sands, Essex. He called it *Radio Sutch*, using the whole station (at first) to promote his most charismatic singer. As time went on Calvert became obsessive with Pirate radio. He eventually launched *Radio City*. Things however were to end tragically. A certain Major Oliver Smedley It would seem claimed that he not Calvert owned the stations transmitter, and demanded 50% of the profits. Reg was absolutely livid, and in a quite out of character fit of pique he forced his way into the Majors house. The Major's housekeeper put up a brave fight and a struggle began. Calvert attacked the woman who was doing her best to stop him going any further into the house. At that point The Major entered the room, shotgun in hand, seconds later one of the pop worlds greatest managers was dead. He left a wife Dorothy, who continued with the business, and a daughter Candy who I believe still lives local. For more information on Reg Calvert get hold of the wonderful book *Starmakers & Svengalis* by Johnny Rogan.

Jigsaw (SEE JIGSAW) emerged from Rugby in the 70's and made a huge impact on the chart with *Sky High*. Before beat-king Billy J. Kramer became famous he nearly took a job with British Rail at Rugby before deciding quite rightly to continue his singing career. He married a Rugby girl in fact his fan club secretary Anne and lived with her at Bilton in the 70's. Punk-wise Rugby had the rather dubiously named **Column 88** and the rather ludicrously named **The Slugs**. **Spacemen 3** of course come from Rugby (SEE SPACEMAN 3). They used to play at *Blitz* in Church Street, *Benn Memorial Hall* and *Imperial Pub* Oxford Street. When **Spacemen 3** split Jason Pierce formed **Spiritualized** (SEE SPIRITUALIZED) and Sonic Boom (Peter Kember) formed **Spectrum**. Sonic attended Rugby Public School. The drugs culture that grew up around these bands led to the music papers dubbing the town Drugby. Sonic still lives in Rugby.

GUY CHADWICK

The Darkside who were signed to *Beggars Banquet* were also part of the **Spacemen 3** legacy (SEE SPACEMAN 3).

Guy Chadwick was from Rugby. He had some success with his guitar-based indie band **House Of Love**, clocking up 8 minor hit singles and 4 hit albums in the late 80's early 90's. His biggest successes was the single *Shine On* charting at 20 and the album *House Of Love* making number 8 in the UK and even getting onto the foot of the Billboard 200 at 156 in the U.S. Guy used to be in the Rugby punk band T**he Flying Teeth** (they played upstairs at the Woolpack). He used to work as a refuse collector for Rugby council. He recently revealed that the first record he bought was T. Rex's *Ride a White Swan* from *Berwicks Records* in Rugby. He went on to form The Madonnas then The Eyedreams finally settling for a solo career. I also discovered a bit of a Rugby/bass/King/ connection going on with Myles Howells a Rugby born bass player with heavy Hull band **King**maker and Slapp Happy the bassman with the jump-jive combo' **King Pleasure and the Biscuit Boys** is also a Rugby lad. Howells is now a journalist in Hull. Current bands include the rather brilliant **Any Given Day** (SEE ANY GIVEN DAY), **Severed State, 8 Miles High, No Remote, The Flanks, The Blanks, The Retards, Attica, Pencilface, The Loaded Hobos, The Shade, Chief Libido, Apex, Oddsods, Howling Tomcats, The Twentyfirst, Head Over Heels, Nutonic, Fap, Paul Martin, Playerone, When The Music Stops, Mesch, Sion, Taverna, Beaverwax** and **Odd Man Out**.

Places to play in Rugby, well many would argue that there has never been a real 'scene' in the town, despite that there has been a few bands from the area, look at the list of current contenders. They have to play somewhere, right. Well there was the old *Co-op hall*, also many big guns played at *The Granada Theatre* including The Rolling Stones (SEE THE ROLLING STONES), they actually played twice in December 1964 & March 1965. Incidentally The Brian Jones fan club is based in Clifton Road, Rugby. Gene Vincent and Cliff Richard have also played The Granada. *The Benn Memorial Hall* still hosts live music (many of the admittedly tribute bands). Other venues are or have been *Blitz* in Church Street, The *Dirty Duck* (Black Swan), *The Peacock Inn* on Newbold Road. Then there is *O'Hagans*, Regent Street, the current fave for live entertainment in the town.

As for songs mentioning the town well apart from Rugby songs cus' they don't count, I can only come up with two. **Pinkertons Assorted Colours** (SEE PINKERTONS ASSORTED COLOURS) wrote a song called *Dukes Jetty* named after the small and insignificant throughway between Sheep Street and High street. It featured on the B-side of their 1968 single *There's Nobody I would sooner Love*, it's pretty psychedelic and turns Dukes Jetty into a real groovy sounding night-club. See photo of Pinkertons Tony Newman at Dukes jetty. The other Rugby related record is the soundtrack to the 1972 musical of *Tom Brown's Schooldays*. Based on the famous novel by Tom Hughes. It was an obvious attempt to do an *Oliver* apparently it didn't work. There are some great sounding songs though, like *Six of the Best*, *The Great White Horse of Uffington* and *Three Acres and A Cow*. Roy Dotrice was the nominal star and played the evil headmaster. It was written by Joan Maitland and 60's popster Chris Andrews.

RUSSIAN GIRLFRIEND

One of the 'current' set much mooted to do big things, i.e. secure a recording contract and sell bucket loads of records. They describe their sound as 'a blend of dark romance and passion with high energy evoking images of another time, another place'. That in my view about sums up their highly inventive sound. It's good to hear bands passionate enough about their music to go out and get their songs recorded and produced to the highest quality (no more will a cassette recorded on a Fostex 4 track be enough). Their sound is well polished and Matt Hanley's vocals are absolutely out of this word! Certainly one of the best singers Coventry has ever produced (just check out *Chameleon Boy* on their website at **www.russiangirlfriend.co.uk**) combine that with the musicianship of Jools on guitar, Dave on drums and Rob on bass, and you have something very (and I mean) very special. The whole band works as one hefty sound unit producing some of the most stunning musical vistas you aural eye will ever witness.

So far they have released an eponymous EP, and have featured in a documentary charting 30 years of *The Leamington Peace Festival* (SEE LEAMINGTON). One of their songs *Butterfly Order* has received intense airplay on digital station *Storm Radio,* and they remain hard giging (especially at **The Jailhouse** (SEE VENUES). More to the point actually seem to enjoy what they do (and believe me I have lost count of the number of bands I have seen who seem bored with the whole music thing). Can it be long before sheer talent takes this band to the A and R department deep in the bowels of some London based record label? Me thinks not.

GODIVA ROCKS SOUND BYTE WITH-Matt Hanley (Russian Girlfriend) "I was not at an age to enjoy the Ska music and the likes of Hazel O'Connor. The first band I saw rise above the grey city skyline was King. After that, nothing happened. The live music scene in Coventry started to fade. The venues vanished and the local bands that played them were as grey as the city. Now, things are changing. The city skyline is brighter and so are the bands being born in the city. There is a brighter future for Russian Girlfriend. Coventry is now breathing art."

THE SELECTER

Neol Davis (that's Neil spelt with an 'o', not Noel), had played guitar with blues band **Cat's Grave** then with **Asgard** and a band named **Mead** in the early 1970's. By 1973 Neol had teamed up with Charley Anderson, Arthur 'Gappa' Hendrickson, Desmond Brown and Silverton in a soul/reggae band called **Chapter Five**. Neol began his education of reggae in this band, something that would serve him well in the not too distant future. **Chapter Five** would take on a certain Lynval Golding in its ranks and become **Pharaoh's Kingdom** then **Earthbound**. At the demise of **Earthbound** Jerry Dammers would poach Lynval and Silverton for **The Coventry Automatics,** (SEE THE SPECIALS) while the rest of the guys would form **Hardtop 22**. Neol had meantime joined a new band called **The Transposed men** (that included the future Urge man Kevin Harrison (SEE THE URGE)). Neol would combine **Hardtop 22** and **Transposed Men** for a line-up that looked like this: Arthur 'Gaps' Hendrickson (vocals), neol Davis (guitar), Compton Amanor (guitar), Charley 'H' Bembridge (drums), Desmond brown (keyboards) and Charley Anderson (bass). Pauline Black (SEE PAULINE BLACK) was the last member to join, she had been singing locally in the folk clubs and had been spotted by Lynval Golding. The band was complete. It was around this time that Jerry Dammers band **The Automatics** had reached critical mass, and had become **The Special AKA** and spent the £700 they had on recording the one track *Gangsters,* they were looking for a cheap B-side. Brad who was with **The Special AKA** at this point mentioned a song he had drummed on with Neol Davis and Barry Jones. Originally called *The Kingston Affair*, the instrumental would be renamed *The Selecter* and grace *Gangsters* B-Side, **The Selecter** were born! Trivia buff may like to know that Brad, would become the only musician to play on the A & B sides of the first and last 2 Tone singles, the last one was his on his **JB All-Stars** project *Alphabet Army*. (With thanks to Jason Weir & Peter Walsh at the great 2 Tone Info website) http://2-tone.info/index.html).

Roger Lomas (SEE ROGER LOMAS) was chosen as producer for **The Selecter's** first proper single (this was fitting as it was at Rogers shed studio that the original *Selecter* track had been recorded) only this time the rather grander *Horizon Studios* (SEE STUDIOS) would be the venue. *On My Radio/Too Much Pressure* became the third *2 Tone* single (SEE 2 TONE), and the third hit, charting at a very respectable number 8 it had cost £1000 to make. They rehearsed at *The Gold Cup Pub* for their tour with **The Specials,** and performed *On my Radio* on *Top Of The Pops* (that show would cement the " Tone ethos as it also featured Madness singing *One Step beyond* and **The Specials** with *A Message To you Rudy).* They duly recorded their first album *Too Much Pressure (*also at Horizon). It was an angry affair that would take the Black and white unity/divide issues another step on (while the bands preach racial harmony sections of their audiences would be hell bent on doing just the opposite). Blacks vocals worked perfectly with the relentless ska machine that was **The Selecter**. There was no room for understatement with these guys. The album made it to number 5, and the follow-up single released in at the start of 1980 *Three Minute Hero* was also charting at number 16 followed by *Missing Words* clocking in at 23. Pauline was the female face of *2 Tone* ska, and was picking up her fair share of press. They also featured in the 2 Tone film *Dance Craze*. They toured the United States, on returning they felt that The *2 Tone* dream was starting to fade and switched to *2 Tone's* mother label *Chrysalis* for their second album *Celebrate The Bullet*. (The single *The Whisper (36)* would be their first offering on the new label). The recording of it was filled with in-band squabbling leading to Desmond Brown and Charley Anderson leaving the band and replaced by James Mackie and Adam Williams. Anderson, Brown and former **Specials** man Silverton would form the band **The People** (SEE REGGAE). *Celebrate the Bullet* was released in March 1981 it showed a progression and maturity and in my opinion their best album. Sadly because of its title, the BBC 'lets take things literally department', banned it in the wake of the assassination of John Lennon and the attempted one on Ronald Regan. It was to fail to reach it's full and rightful potential. The foundation of **The Selecter** was under stress, and Pauline Black would leave followed a little while later by Neol Davis. Pauline would go solo for a while (SEE PAULINE BLACK) before launching **Sunday Best** and later **The Supernaturals.** Like the **Specials** the band would keep returning in various guises with various line-up and *2 Tone* revival packages. It came back with Pauline and Neol to do a tour with Bad Manners in 1990. Releasing an updated version of their past hit *On My Radio 91*. Four albums were also recorded *The Happy album, Hairspray, Cruel Britannia* and *Pucker,* none would be a return to form, many other live and 'best of' packages would also see the light of day. Their new personnel would include former Bad Manners members Nick Welsh and Martin Stewart and Dave Barker former half of the Skinhead Reggae duo Dave & Ansil Collins of *Monkey Spanner & Double Barrel* fame. Culminating in the album *The Kingston Affair* credited as **Dave Barker & The Selecter.** Pauline would leave again eventually reviving the band in an acoustic form with Nick Welsh and releasing the albums *Unplugged For The Rude Boy Generations* and *Requiem For A Black Soul* (excellent stuff). Neol would form the blues band **Box Of Blues** with former **Special** Horace Panter (SEE HORACE PANTER) and Anthony Hearty (former member of The Style Council and **Beachmantango**). Releasing 2 musically brilliant albums, the second *Future Swamp* (credited to Neol Davis) includes The Stones Ronnie Wood on guitar and sees Davies playing such diverse instruments as the sitar, slide guitar and lap steel guitar. Charley Anderson lived in Italy then joined Swedish Ska band **The Skalatones** went to live in Latin America and ended up working for UNICEF.

SENT TO COVENTRY
Just passing through for maybe an hour or maybe year or two.

Sex Pistols Played at *Mr.George's* on the 17th December 1977, The band had created much 'negative' publicity in the press. So they went incognito as The S.P.O.T.S (Sex Pistols On Tour Secretly), to prevent them from being banned. They arrived by train, by all accounts the gig was not particularly good Rotten had flu and there was crowd trouble (never!) Coventry had lost to Arsenal that day and Rotten being a Gooner felt the need to remind the audience of it, not a good move. Sad thing was their visit is more remembered for Sid Vicious smashing up a hotel room at *The Hotel Leofric* than for their groundbreaking music. Apparently head Porter Frank Penlington had this to say, 'I've never seen anything like it, they were all drunk and jumping on the beds. They were the worst band we've had here' The Pistol's Manager Malcolm McLaren calmly paid for the damage (making certain photographs had been taken first) and off they went to seek more adverse publicity. They had actually played in Coventry at *The Lanch* a year earlier on November 29th 1976 and were virtually booed off stage('we must be new wave they'll like us next year' TV Smith).

James Brown Ya All. Yes the Godfather of Soul himself was stranded in Coventry in July 16th 2003 on his way to play the *Summer Pops Festival* in Liverpool. A comedy of errors had ended up with James Brown's train being broken down in Cov station. While he waited for alternative transport to Liverpool, *DP Limousines* to be precise). He delighted the train bound commuters by chatting and signing autographs. 90 minutes later he was *back on the good foot* and in the limo' singing along to his own CD on route for Merseyside. Literally with seconds to spare running from the car to the stage for his performance.

Jimmy James and the Vagabonds Originally from Jamaica, had hits with *Red Red Wine (36)*, *I'll Go Where The Music Takes me* (23) and *Now Is The Time* (5). He would have many line up changes, eventually in the disco 70's becoming an all English group (except of course James). Many of the group would be from Coventry & Nuneaton, including guitarists Chris Garfield (who still plays in Nuneaton) and Rob Manzoli who later went on to be one third of Right Said Fred (the one with the hair) who's biggest hit was *I'm too Sexy*. Right Said Fred made a on tour stop in Coventry a few years ago at *The Ball Hill Diner* on *The Walsgrave Road* (food Highly recommended by the way). The owner Derek kept their plate and mounted it on the wall. Apparently even the great Rick Wakeman has dined there on route to Nuneaton where his Mother used to live.

The Krankies God forgive me putting **The Krankies** in the same section as James Brown and The Pistols. Obviously from Scotland, but Ian and Janette Tough lived for many years in *St Martins Road Finham*. Janette (or Wee Jimmy) was just 4ft 5ins tall, they appeared on *Crackerjack* (please don't say it). Plus loads of other kids TV programmes including their own *The Joke Machine*. They were responsible for giving Lisa Stansfield and Brian Conley their first breaks. They also charted twice (once at number 71 then a re-entry at 46) with the song *Fandabidozi* in 1981.

Terry Hall and Lenny the Lion. Could fate have given Coventry 2 famous Terry Hall's? Well actually no, Terry Hall the ventriloquist of *Lenny the Lion fame* was in fact born in Oldham. He did however marry a Coventry girl Dee Francis, who he met at *the Talisman Theatre* Kenilworth and they settled in the city, although it wasn't till 1984 he got round to playing *The Coventry Theatre*. Music-wise they had a TV show called *Pops and Lenny* that was one of the first to have an appearance by The Beatles (SEE THE BEATLES). Lenny the loveable lion who had trouble pronouncing his R's and had bouts of shyness also appeared on The Ed Sullivan show in America in 1958 singing *I Want A Hippopotamus For Christmas*. He continued the theme in 1959 with the UK single *I Wish That I Could Be Father Christmas*.

Sigue Sigue Sputnik. This publicity hungry pile of futuristic kitsch did a lot of shouting about ultra violence in their trite little pseudo-conceptual songs. They ended up getting some of their very own big time at *The Lanch* in Cov in 1986 when a brain-deficient life form threw a glass at the strutting Martin Degville on stage. He needed four stitches in a cut above his left eye, not exactly a *Love Missile F1-11* then. They would return to Cov however in 2002 to play *The Jailhouse*.

Phil Oakey Famous for fronting The Human league and having the original, "Would you like something on that" haircut. Although synonymous with Sheffield he was actually born in Leicester, and spent some of his growing up in Coventry. I remember when I went to see The Human league in Cov' before they became huge. They were playing to a handful of people at Tiffany's Phil said to the crowd, "Is there anyone here from Wyken? I lost my virginity in Wyken". Whether that was true I know not, but he definitely knew Wyken,. and his brother definitely owned a music shop in the City.

Atomic Kitten, took part in the opening concert for Coventry's *Phoenix Initiative* at *Millennium Place* on Saturday 13th December 2003.

Live in Coventry & Area Some of the people who have recorded live in the area, Include Chuck Berry (*London Sessions* at Tiffs), Specials (*The Specials AKA Live, Skinhead Symphony,* B side only at Tiffs) recorded on the same night was The Selecter (*Carry Go Bring Home,* B-side of *Missing Words* single, and on US issue off *Dance Craze* LP, Tiffs), Thin Lizzy (*Live in Coventry* bootleg, ApolloTheatre), Jasper Carrott (*Rabbits On and On*, The Fletchhamstead), Tangerine Dream (*Ricochet,* Coventry Cathedral), Anthony Braxton Quartet (*The Coventry Concert,* Warwick Uni), Rolling stones (*Live in Coventry* bootleg, Coventry theatre), Siouxsie & The Banshees (*Static Display, Break Up* bootlegs one side only recorded, Coventry Theatre). The Selecter (*Out on The Streets,* The Tic Toc), The Farmers Boys (*The John Peel Sessions,* The General Wolfe), Randall (*Recorded Live,* The Edge). DJ Rap (*Rave 93/94,* The Edge), Queen (*Blitz Coventry* bootleg, Coventry Theatre), The MAYC Orchestra & Singers (*Everything That Has Breath,* Central Hall), John Cale (*Coventry 2001* bootleg, Warwick Uni), Lowdrive (*The Newtz Session,* The Newtz), The Oddsods (*The Shenanigans,* The Wurzel Bush at the Royal British legion Club, Brinklow) and Rob Halligan (*Streets of this Town,* The Jesus Centre, Lamb st), Jethro Tull (*Some Day the Sun Won't Shine For* You, *A Song For Jeffery* & *My Sunday Feeling,* Kelly's Leamington) COBSO (*Facade,* Bedworth Civic Hall).

THE SORROWS

Cov's fave freakbeat band formed in the early 60's. Consisted of former **Hawkes** vocalist Don Maughn, Pip Witcher lead guitar, Phil Peckham bass who had had been in **The Vampires** (SEE THE VAMPIRES), plus Bruce Finlay drums and Terry Jukes rhythm guitar. They wore black on stage and played the blues like they meant it with Maughn's raw vocals setting the local audiences alight. They secured a residency at *The Pilot* in Radford and even played at *Highfield Road*. They were spotted in 1964 by *Picadilly* label manager John Schroeder, and duly signed and were allowed to release their self penned song *I Don't Want To Be Free* as their debut. They played *Ready steady Go*, but the single failed to make a dent in the charts. Meanwhile Terry Jukes left the band and was replaced by Wes Price from **The Unknowns** and **The Autocrats**. The second single *Baby* went the way of the first, there were talks of splitting then up came single number three *Take A Heart*. Originally written by Miki Dallon (aka Mickey Tinsley) for a band called The Boys Blue, **The Sorrows** take on it produced an original piece of blues with a foreboding quality, focused superbly by Maughn's brooding vocals. An appearance on TV's *Ready Steady Go* saw the single rise to number 21 in the UK charts. It was also proved a smash as they say in mainland Europe, especially Italy and Germany where foreign language version were recorded (*Take A Heart* became *Mis Si Spezza Il Cuore* in Italian and *Nimm Mein Herz* in German). Even pre-Slade combo The 'N' Betweens had a shot at it for French release.

Their debut album followed also entitled *Take A Heart*, it's a personal gripe of mine that many only know **The Sorrows** for the one UK hit single. While their album lays mainly unheard, that's a pity because they were more than just one hit single. The album is adorned with standout tracks, check out the superb *We Should Get along fine* and *Don't Sing me No Sad songs,* classic stuff. After various attempts to match *Take A Heart* failed (along with singles *You've Got What I Want, Let The Live Liv, Let Me In* and *Pink Purple, Yellow and Red*). Don Maughn (now reverting to his real name Fardon), left for a successful solo career (SEE DON FARDON) Phil Packam followed and the band worked as a 3-piece for a while. They were offered a stadium tour of Italy on the back of the success of *Take A Heart* and recruited **Clouds** guitarist Roger Lomas (SEE ROGER LOMAS) while Pip Witcher took over on lead vocals. They were huge in Italy, and still having hits with the likes of *Verde,Rosso,Giallo,Blu* the Italian version (not literally though) of *Pink, Purple, Yellow and Red*. They even had their own villa courtesy of *RCA Records* (who looked after them over there). During this part of the bands history they were unofficially known as **The Italian Sorrows**. A new vocalist/keyboard player came in the shape of Chris Smith, from Cov' band **East Side Protection**. More Italian hits followed, with *Per Una Donna....No* reaching number 7. The album that followed entitled *Old Songs, New Songs* was a badly conceived mixture of cover versions and self penned ditties recorded under duress. Members began leaving wholesale and **The Sorrows** hey day even in Italy was over.

Wes Price joined **Indian Summer** (SEE INDIAN SUMMER), Pip Witcher joined Roger Lomas in **The Eggy** (releasing the single *You're Still* Mine a song that Lomas had demoed with **The Sorrows***)* and then joined **The Zips** and **Rog & Pip** (SEE ROGER LOMAS). more recently Pip plays in Torquay's **Brummies's In Exile** (he lives in Paignton). In 1983 **The Sorrows** reformed as a covers band playing at *The Dive* in Cov'. The 90's saw another short reunion take place this time with former front man Fardon in tow. **The Sorrows** leave a legacy that even today sees their songs on mod & freakbeat compilation albums, not bad for a Coventry band who only had one hit nearly 40 years ago!

> **GODIVA ROCKS SOUND BYTE WITH- Phil Packman (The Sorrows), Some Sorrows Trivia...**
>
> Pip's mum called us a sorrowful lot when practising – hence the name "Sorrows". The name Sorrows was covered up on the drum kit as we played at a Jewish wedding in London's Savoy Hotel.
>
> I signed an autograph book for a girl in 1963 at the Coventry Theatre. I married her in 1966.
>
> I noticed a drag link hanging down from the groups Commer van before we left for Liverpool gig. I drove home at only 60 mph. The next morning as the mechanic drove around the garage the wheel fell off.
>
> We were given a birthday cake for Paul Jones of Manfred Mann. During his act the girls shouted did you en joy your cake, what cake said Paul, the girls shouted the {expletive} Sorrows have eaten it.
>
> Pip smashed a guitar to pieces at a Theatre gig while tuning up, because we would not be quiet. Luckily a girl in the audience had one at home and the show went on.

SPACEMEN 3

Formed from the ashes of the Band **Indian Scalp** in Rugby in 1982, with an original line-up of Rugby Public Schoolboy Sonic Boom, Mainliner or Peter Gunn (Peter Kember) on vocals & guitar, Jason Pierce (vocals & guitar) with Sterling 'Rosco' Rosswell on drums and Pete 'Bassman' Baines on bass. It would take time before the throbbing fuzzed-up novae-psychedelic sound we associate with **S3** would be formulated. The band played Rugby's *Blitz* in Church Street, *Benn Memorial Hall* and *Imperial Pub* Oxford Street. They eventually secured a recording contract. Releasing the album *Sound Of Confusion*, with a tip of the hat *to* The 13th Floor Elevators and The Stooges it gave a glimpse of things to come and secured a growing fan base. By the release of album number 2 *The Prefect Prescription* their drug related ethos was well established, and In-fighting between Boom and Pierce would begin to develop (Boom has never made a secret of his Heroin and later methadone dependencies). In 1989 John Mattock and Will Carruthers replaced Rosco & Baines (the latter would form Rugby unit **The Darkside** with Nick Hayden and Craig Wagstaff, releasing 4 albums and 3 EP's including the EP *Highrise Love* and the much-acclaimed album *Melomania*. When they split Sterling 'Rosco' Roswell would go to Italy become a TV presenter and actor and release a solo single *Girl From Orbit)*.

By the time the album *Recurring (46)* was released, the relationship between Boom and Pierce was such that they each recorded their own songs in isolation having a side of the album each for the project. Before the end of **S3** both were working on solo projects (Jason along with John Mattock and Will Carruthers on **Spiritualized**) (SEE SPIRITUALIZED) and Sonic on **Spectrum** originally just a solo album title It charted at 65.When the split finally came both would make these their main bands. (Although there would be a batch of **Spacemen 3** remix albums released posthumously).

Spectrum would let Sonic experiment pretty much unhindered, calling on such influences as Coventry's Delia Derbyshire (SEE DELIA DERBYSHIRE) and the *BBC Radiophonic Workshops*. Sonic would play the musical 'Spectrum', from trance pop to acoustic rock, I personally hear a lot of early Brian Eno influence in his music, but that's probably just me. Boom along with Mike Stout, Geoff Donkin and Richard Formby would release a series of glorious (and collectable) albums including *Soul kiss, Highs, Lows and Heavenly Blows* and *Forever Alien*. Plus the single *True Love Will Find You in the End* that charted at number 70. The band would later be joined by Scott Riley on guitar, Alf Hardy programming and former **Spacemen 3** Peter Bassman. In between times Sonic would also give time to his 'other' project **Experimental Audio Research** or **E.A.R.** a loose guitar based assembly of musicians headed by Boom and including the likes of Kevin Shields (from My Bloody Valentine), Kevin Martin (God) and Eddie Prevost (from AMM). They would also release some eight albums from *Mesmerised* in 1994 to *Continuum* 2003. Of late Sonic works in his *New Atlantis Studio* in Rugby, as well as DJ ing and guesting at concerts (especially in the US). A **Spacemen 3** book is expected shortly.

GODIVA ROCKS SOUND BYTE WITH-Sonic Boom (Spacemen 3, EAR, Spectrum)
You once said that people in Rugby Hate Spaceman 3, did that feeling ever change? No , not really . . I think 'we' or some of us have always stood out as something different to peoples expectations . Its a small conservative place , any deviations from the norm are frowned upon . We were always very open about our lifestyles , and those aren't to everyone's liking .
You're studios are based in Rugby so I assume you are still living there, did you not ever feel like living somewhere else? Yes , I could be happy living in many places . I fancy Palestine for a while . The States would be Ok in the more culturally aware areas -mostly the coasts . Spain would be beautiful . Germany.....Holland......shit the world has so many great places .I live here cus its convenient for everywhere -like Cov .
Your New Atlantis studio set-up looks pretty impressive, do you record other bands there, or is it very much your home studio? I do record other bands - but I'd use Cabin or Planet in Cov - both excellent studios , at fair prices run by cool folks . A very cool situation . I do remixes at home & my own stuff . I've long been a multitracker as opposed to a live band recorder - you learn that you can have the most control that way I think . Most everything in my studio is easy to take to other studios , so................
Do you ever see Jason nowadays (does he still live in Rugby)? No , he doesn't . I've not spoke in 10 + years .i sent him a note a year ago to no reply . so it goes . I don't resent him . i would like to think we could work together again , but i'm not sure he cares to.
What was being a student at Rugby School like, was it character forming or soul destroying? What will be the next major project for Sonic Boom? I would say it was a great opportunity + a very informing and opening experience . I got to have friends from all around the world & there was massive musical + cultural interaction . I had a great time , tho' I wasn't the best student. I left after O's to specialise in Art at Rugby Art College -where I met Jason + formed spacemen 3 . My next projects are a new Spectrum lp i'm in the middle of , and an LP I did in Mississippi with Jim Dickinson of 'wild Horses' , Paris ,Texas & 'Dixie Fried fame . A real mad character . I stayed on his compound in a trailer + we did an LP. some of it is really cool. We did one track about Johnny Ace - A black singer who blew his brains out in a whorehouse , between shows , on Christmas day . Too good to be true - but it is . Jim wrote the lyrics + we wrote the music -kinda' Johnny cash on acid , plus we did some other cool stuff . he was a bear to work with . he had me in bits , but ultimately he's one of the real guys - just ******** nuts .
Spacemen 3, Spectrum and E.A.R all pushed the boundaries of 'popular' music. Was there ever pressure on you to keep it 'mainstream'. Only later on for the last LP -Recurring .That was the most pressure . otherwise no , and I learnt from that too.
Is there a place for Pete Waterman in your world? Man , I was born & bred in Coventry . I 'm from Henley Green -the Council Maisonettes nearly opposite Henley College (as was). I used to hang in Hillfields + Foleshill a lot thru the '80's . Previous to that I was a big fan of the Scene surrounding the Specials - Pete Waterman supposedly financed Gangsters , so hats off there. The Specials were a ******* wonder . Jesus -I saw them at the Locarno/Tiffanys Xmas 79 at the end of there 1st big tour . It was nuts . Neville Staples was swinging round the lighting rig like a maniac , Jerry Dammers ran on the spot the whole gig , Terry Hall walked around pre-gig in his carpet slippers - real Cov Kid style I always thought. Those guys were also really ace to their fans - Not Terry , but Neville , Lynval , Jerry , Noel Redding , Roddy Radiation would all let me hang out at their pads . Jerry lived in Earsldon near Neville in Broomfield Rd. I was like 14 & they were very cool. I saw one of their last ever shows at L'spa spa Centre where I smoked my first proper joint with Rico . He was this crazy looking half Chinese/Jamaican cat - killer trombonist -the best ska geezer -played on all the original stuff too - well , he rolled a big spliff + I asked him for 2's on it . he just looked down & laughed + said summit in patois . I thought -oh well , worth a try , anyway sure enough , a couple a mins later he passed me it with a big grin. I was at Cov station a few years back & I saw the ever cool Roddy Radiation at the opposite platform with guitar case, so I crossed over & went and told him how cool he had been & how I appreciated him letting me hang in Cheylesmore with him (haha).He was total down to earth as ever . I still feel my roots are in Cov . My soulmate Delia Derbyshire & I both grew up within spitting distance of each other on Barker Butts lane , Coundon . I gotta lotta time for Coventry . I'm pleased you asked me to do this. best of luck to an ever fascinating city.

GODIVAROCKS@YAHOO.CO.UK

THE SPECIALS

The ultimate Cov band? Well certainly the best known, more than that of course they launched a whole scene, a whole feeling, made a stand for racial unity and created the *Coventry Sound* Mk 2. Even today their music is used in many a TV commercial, that may not necessarily be a good thing, but it does demonstrate how powerful their legacy was and still is. Despite the mega-Coventry connection only 3 of the band were actually born in Coventry that's Terry Hall, Roddy Radiation and John Bradbury. Lynval and Neville were both from the Caribbean, Jerry was born in India and Horace in Kettering, so a good ethnic mix to build on.

Jerry Dammers met Sir Horace Gentleman (Panter) (SEE HORACE PANTER)) whilst they both attended the Lanch. Dammers had been playing keyboards with the likes of The Sissy Stone Band, Horace played bass with club soulsters **Breaker**. They first worked together on a reggae song Jerry had written for an cartoon film he had created. They then teamed up with Neol Davis (who had previously been in the bands **Cat's Grave, Asgard** and **Mead**) (SEE THE SELECTER) and began demoing Dammers songs. With the recruitment of Silverton Hutchinson (a drummer from **Chapter 5**), Tim Strickland on vocals and guitarist Lynval Golding (from **Pharaoh's Kingdom**) the **Automatics** later **The Coventry Automatics** were formed. They began gigging (using **Ray Kings** PA system) (SEE RAY KING) playing a curious mix of reggae punk, becoming regulars at The Heath Hotel, Hand & Heart and Mr.George's (SEE VENUES). New recruits came in the shape of punk guitarist Roddy Radiation (Byers) from **The Wild Boys** (SEE RODDY RADIATION, SEE THE WILD BOYS) and Terry Hall from Cov punk band **Squad** (SEE SQUAD). **Pete Waterman** (SEE PETE WATERMAN) became ashort-term manager and helped to promote the band, with little success. They struck out to London, and after meeting up with Clash manager Bernie Rhodes secured a support on the *On Parole Tour in 1978*. At this point roadie Neville Staples (SEE FUN BOY THREE) began 'toasting' from the mixing desk and soon became the next member of **The Special AKA** (as they were now called). Although Rhodes was never their manager he did continue to half help them, never in a financial way it must be said, hence they spent many days sleeping and living in their van and experiencing some dodgy situations on their first disastrous French trip (as recounted in *Gangsters*).

At a rehearsal at the *Binley Oak Pub* (once the scene of *Motown House)* in Britannia Street a less than happy Silverton quit the band. Local **Nightease** Drummer John Bradbury (SEE JB's ALLSTARS) was quickly drafted in and *Gangsters* (an already completed song of which Dammers added elements of Prince Buster's *Al Capone* to, making this one of the first ever 'sampled' recordings). Because of their lack of money an old demo was used as the B-side an instrumental track Neol Davis had recorded in Roger Lomas's shed studio (SEE ROGER LOMAS) with Brad entitled *The Selecter*. 500 copies were pressed and the sleeves hand stamped at Horace's flat on The London Road. A new image was also adopted including Crombies coats Harrington jackets, stay-press trousers and pork-pie hats, the Coventry rude boy was awakening. Dammers used the name 2 Tone for the bands corporate image (SEE 2 TONE) and had also created a simple but massively effective logo called *Walt Jabsco*, the black and white 2 Tone man, he based on an early picture of Peter Tosh. Along with a wall of black and white check the image was striking (as was the metaphor) and so was *Gangsters,* it began to make waves, the vague punk reggae of before had made way for a new-age ska sound *Gangsters*. Stalwart John Peel began playing it. Pretty soon **The Specials** (and manager Rick Rodgers) had record companies approaching them to sign (even Mick Jagger). Eventually they signed to *Chrysalis* with an agreement to be able to release 10 singles on their own 2 Tone label a year. Effectively becoming a label within a label.

The Dammed boss Rick Rogers took over as manager just as *Gangsters* was hitting it's peak at number 6 in the UK charts. **The Selecter** was signed, now a real band as opposed to the name only session featured on the *Gangsters* B-side. Madness also signed to 2 Tone releasing their first single *The Prince* that would soon see them sign to major label *Stiff Records*. Work meanwhile was underway on the first **Specials** album produced by star fan Elvis Costello. It was a striking debut that encapsulated a moment in time perfectly, Terry Hall's sardonic vocals duelling with Dammers stabbing organ fills and Panters superb bass runs on par with Brad's rimshot deliveries. *Nite Klub* and *Concrete Jungle* would forever give a bleak reminder of their City (later used to even greater effect on *Ghost Town*). With *Blank Expression, Dawning Of A New Era* and *Doesn't Make It Alright* making compelling listening, and cementing The Specials and their Ska sound in the history of modern music. It peaked at number 7, just as the band along with Madness and **The Selecter** began a 40 date tour that would raise the 2 Tone movement to even higher level (as well as bringing it unwanted attention from the extreme right-wing). Augmenting the band was Jamaican 'bone' playing legend Rico Rodriguez and Dick Cuthell on horn. 1979 saw the release of their second single *A Message To You Rudy* (10), the signing of Birmingham ska band to 2 Tone The Beat who would chart with a ska version of *Tears Of A Clown* (**The Selecter** too were also charting). *The Special AKA live EP* was released in 1980, with the lead track Too Much Too Young becoming the bands first number one (the B-side would include a selection of reggae classics recorded at *Tiffany's* in Coventry). A BBC Arena TV special was aired featuring scenes of Coventry with presenter Adrian Thrills in Jerry's flat in Albany Road, the HQ of 2 Tone. A US tour followed where they supported The Police and received rave reviews. (Though they would never see mainstream chart success Stateside). The tour was not a particularly happy one, arguments began with the band becoming homesick and very tired after playing 2 shows per night. Though the atmosphere was lifted slightly when they were presented with a Radio One award mid-tour via satellite.

Roddy Radiation's *Rat Race* became the next single reaching number five, nation-wide 2 Tone was becoming positively iconic, and the music press loved em'. The Specials began a UK tour with support from The Bodysnatchers. If the US tour had been unpleasant this tour would be hostile, with Dammers and Radiation becoming increasingly unfriendly towards each other. A short Japanese tour followed that would see them in trouble with the Nippon authorities due to unprecedented scenes of Japanese youths dancing in the aisles!. On returning to England they began to record their second album at Cov's Horizon Studios. *More Specials*, more trouble, Jerry was keen to move away from the basic ska music that had been so good to them. He was writing some songs that although still held a message were musically in the jazz lounge sound. The cracks were now beginning to show, on top of that Lynval had been part of a racist attack in London (as would be recounted in the *Ghost Town* B-side *Why?*), and Coventry

THE COVENTRY CANAL BASIN THEN (FROM REAR OF MORE SPECIALS LP).

was also going through a time of racist tension resulting in the deaths of an Asian youth and Doctor. Dammers organised a Anti-racist gig at Cov's *Butts Stadium* (SEE FESTIVALS). More touring followed as the single *Stereotype/International Jet set* was released claiming number 6 in the charts. Their second album *More Specials* (with it's rear cover taken at Cov' s canal basin) was well received despite the slight change of direction charting at number 5. *The More Specials tour* was chaotic to say the least with violence erupting at some gigs coming to a head at Cambridge when Terry and Jerry were arrested being falsely accused of inciting the trouble. Lynval's song *Do Nothing* was released as the bands 6th single making number 4 in the chart.

The band who were now in 'rest' mode as far as the main vehicle **The Specials** was concerned, but Roddy formed his skabilly offshoot **The Tearjerkers** (SEE RODDY RADIATION), while Brad began *Race Records* an Neville *Shack Records*. *(SEE JB's ALLSTARS)*. The ska film *Dancecraze* was also released at this time

PAGE 94   GODIVAROCKS@YAHOO.CO.UK   PAGE 94

including the soundtrack album, it featured all the **2 Tone** bands and Bad Manners. *Ghost town* was released in June 1981, was it about Coventry? Yes but not just Coventry, how many Ghost towns do you know in Britain? It was a massive hit bringing them their second number one. It would also be a defining moment for the band who would fall apart a few months later.

Had **The Specials** split? The rumours were rife, it was confirmed big time when Lynval, Terry & Neville announced their new band **The Fun Boy Three** (SEE THE FUN BOY THREE). After a short tour with Rico, Jerry, Horace and Brad resumed work with **The Special AKA,** as the band was now renamed. Releasing the single *The Boiler* (35) a harrowing tale of rape sung by former Bodysnatcher Rhoda Dakar. Followed by Jungle music attributed to **Rico & The Specials**. As the next single *Racist Friend* was released work began on the third album *In The Studio*. (Recorded at *Woodbine Studios* Leamington (SEE STUDIOS)) During this epic session Horace Panter would leave the set-up (SEE HORACE PANTER) Brad would start work on his **JB's And The Allstars** project (SEE JB's ALLSTARS). The new line-up would be Brad on drums, Gary McManus on bass, former **Swinging Cat** (SEE THE SWINGING CATS) John Shipley on guitar and Rhoda Dakar, Egidio Newton and Stan Campbell (who would leave before them album was released) on vocals. The final album was not generally well liked and Dammers had spent his 3-album allowance on this one album (and nearly 2 years in time). I hated the album at first, but gradually I could see what a masterpiece it was, often understated, often jazzy it sparkled with originality and wit. It probably was Dammers finest moment. The single *Nelson Mandella* heralded the new album and was to become iconic in the genre of protest songs as well as reaching number 9 on the chart. The final single was the rather droll *What I Like Most about You Is Your Girlfriend (51),* ironically the last Specials song was sung by Dammers himself.

Jerry who was still locked in contract, concentrated on political work, like the Nelson Mandella 70th birthday concert at Wembley. He also formed the short-lived band **Jazz Odyssey,** eventually concentrating on being a DJ. Various 2 Tone get-togethers followed like **Special Beat** came and went. Eventually **The Specials** reformed in 1996 albeit without Terry N Jerry (that famous brand of 2 Tone ice cream) (incidentally Jerry has never been happy with the use of the **Specials** name). They toured extensively and releasing 2 albums, the first *Today's Specials* seen as just a cover-version cash-in (it included *Hypocrite (66)* a Bob Marley cover). Followed by the much better album *Guilty,* although still not a 'return to form'. As I write there is the continuing talk of a 'real' **Specials** reunion, to commemorate the 25th anniversary. Including a gig in the new Butts Stadium in Coventry and the reputed offered of 30k each to play at a concert at Crystal Place. The reunion idea has been dismissed by at least five members of the band, and a press release was issued to that effect. So if you want some real live 2 Tone ska go and see **Special Brew** (SEE TRIBUTE ACTS). The talk is that there should be something to commemorate 2 Tone in the city, I agree there should be, but nothing tacky. I say name a street Two Tone Way (SEE INDEX O-Z), but please no statues.

I would like to thank Jerry Dammers for his help in checking the accuracy of this piece.

GODIVA ROCKS SOUND BYTE FROM- Roddy Radiation (Wild Boys, The Specials, The Tearjerkers, The Skabilly Rebels) 1. Coventry has always been a hard town, in terms of hard to please or just plain rough 'n' tuff!! I remember reading that Spike Milligan tried to hang himself after playing to an unappreciative audience at the Coventry Theatre. Yeah...it can do that to ya if you're not on your toes. (That Theatre has since been torn down, like most of my teenage haunts, and replaced by something grey). My first gigs in Cov were at my local Keresley End Youth Club. We played to our friends from school, who also helped us to carry our second-hand guitars and equipment. After playing our favourite Stones, Troggs and Small Faces hits, we would have to make the inevitable walk home through the gangs of Keresley skinheads. Little did I know then that ten years later I would be playing my guitar in front of hundreds of similarly attired young chaps!! In the early 70s the training ground for most would-be pop stars "was at tut-club." I even auditioned for a working men's club band called 'Heaven Sent'. It wasn't very rock 'n' roll but the regular gigs did help me buy a black Gibson Les Paul. **Continued Over**

GODIVAROCKS@YAHOO.CO.UK

Continued Eventually Neville Staples would put that same guitar to good use in a ruck with some National Front supporters.

2. It was with some of these club players I later formed The Wild Boys. We were a sort of Bowie/Lou Reed inspired pre-punk band, playing as often as we could in the dingy back rooms of local pubs such as The Bear Inn, The Golden Cross and The Smithfield (to name a few). Looking back it was a case of "too much too young" I guess? There was also a venue called 'Le Chowmaire' (I can't remember the correct spelling!) which is where The Specials ska guitar player Lynval Golding nearly lost his life in a knife attack in the early 80s. Lynval, Jerry, Horace, Silverton and Tim used to also play at 'The Heath Hotel', which became the place we would go to hear 'The Coventry Automatics' play their weird hybrid of reggae and punk rock. Which was soon transformed into The Specials. The Coventry music scene was, and still is very fluid, in the respect of bands constantly changing members and names in search of that elusive magic band. There were countless very good local bands around Coventry that never made it, whether through a lack of luck, lack of ambition or just too much pop 'n' pot! It's a funny old game...as they say.

3. I guess it's true that The Specials (with The Selecter) helped the local music scene to almost become the Liverpool of The Midlands during the late 70s and early 80s. But that also meant dressing like 'rude boys' and playing that accepted Coventry Two Tone sound. Some of the bands obviously did better than others. Even King were on the scene at that time, in various guises, until they got their ten minutes of fame. These days I find it very depressing to watch how everything has reverted back to the way it was in the early 70s. With few original bands and people opting for the quick and easy pay-out by playing nothing but covers. With Tribute This and Tribute That! I sometimes wonder if punk and ska really changed anything at all? But then every ten years or so the kids want something a bit more REAL and it's all back into those pub back rooms. Local bands for local people all over again.

SPIRITUALIZED

Originally a solo project from Jason Pierce while he was in the final acrimonious stages of **Spacemen 3** (SEE SPACEMEN 3) with Sonic Boom. As **Spacemen 3** came to its premature death, **Spiritualized** became Jason's main project. Consisting of Pierce (or Jason Spaceman) (guitar), and former **Spacemen 3** members Will Caruthers (bass) and Jon Mattock (drums) and Pierce's then girlfriend Kate Radley (keyboards). (She would eventually marry Verve man Richard Ashcroft and be the emotional catalyst of two top selling albums by the two men, in the style of Pattie Boyd). Their dark brooding spatial works were an obvious progression to previous sound. Although their first outing was a cover version of The Troggs song *Anyway that You Want Me,* charting at just 75 (it bore the **Spacemen 3**.logo on it's cover, much to the annoyance of Sonic Boom). They would release many singles throughout their career including, *Medication* (55) in 1992, *Let it Flow* (30) in 1995, *Stop Your Crying* (18) in 2001 and the stunning *She Kissed Me (It Felt Like a hit)*(40) in 2003.Their debut album *Laser Guided Melodies* (27) in 1993, with stand out tracks *Shine A Light* and *Symphony's Place,* sounds like **Spacemen 3** in places, but it would wouldn't it! The lilting melodramatic *Pure Phase (20)* (with it's multi mixes) came out in 1995 (there had been a live album between times), it would set the band up well for their next ground breaking effort, the mighty *Ladies And Gentlemen We Are Floating In Space(4).* From the neat collectable cover that came like a packet of pills complete with the CD's enclosed in a foil pill strip to the perfect music that lay within. It was a winner and a defining moment for the band, check out the anthem-like *Come Together* and *I Think I'm In Love* with its Pink Floyd influences, it even included a cameo appearance on *Cop Shoot Cop* from the charismatic Dr. John. The follow-up *Let It Come Down(3)* for me was a bit of a disappointment, mush less accessible but many swear by this album that is basically is a solo effort from a Jason Pierce (who has a habit of sacking most of his band members). The best of packages *Complete Works Vol 1 and 2,* were released either side of the next album and-. That brings us to *Amazing Grace (25)* another high for Pierce. The album motivates through a drone of fuzz 'n' feedback with Jason's understated distorted vocals searching for the high ground. Nearly every track is standout quality, and that's testament to a man who often single-headedly can still comes up with the goods. In 2004 they played *Glastonbury* appearing strangely in the 'new' artist tent for some strange reason!

STAVELY MAKEPEACE

Rob Woodward had been **Shel Naylor** (SEE SHEL NAYLOR) in the early sixties he would then become part of **The Pretty Flamingos,** eventually linking up with an old friend Nigel Fletcher. Rob (equipped with one heavy reel to reel tape recorder) travelled down to London in 1968 and played Nigel some of his ideas. Rob a gifted musician was keen to experiment with music, much akin to the genius that was Joe Meek, whose creativity with sound was legendary. Nigel loved what he heard and within weeks Guitarist Don Kerr, Steve Tayton on woodwinds and Peter Fisher on bass were recruited and **Stavely Makepeace** with their 'Scrap Iron' sound were formed. Recording in the front room of the Woodward house in Kingsway, they began their epic journey in sound learning on the way. The first single released on *Pyramid Records* in 1969 was *(I Wanna Love You Like A) Mad Dog,* it caused a minor stir, not least for the publicity stunt of sticking postage stamps to the records label to compensate for the rather short (32 seconds long) B-side. A second single was released the lovably bizarre *Edna (Let Me Sing My Beautiful Song)* (on a new label *Concord*) complete with falsetto vocals and yodelling. The guys would perform it on *Top Of The Pops,* with Steve Johnson replacing Pete Fisher on bass. The song would also showcase the mini–piano sound, that would become such a trademark for them (it entailed recording a piano at half speed, then speeding it up to create a manic honky tonk sound). Its release coincided with a upsurge of Coventry artists that summer. With the likes of **Indian Summer, Don Fardon,** The Brotherhood Of Man featuring Johnny Goodison and Stavely all doing their best to promote *The Coventry Sound. Radio One* was divided over *Edna,* some loved it, and others hated it, either way it was unique and it made it into the *Record Mirror* top 50 (though not the official charts we are using here).

They followed it up in 1970 with *Smokey Mountain Rhythm Revue,* earning a spot on the children's pop TV show *Lift Off.* If the lack of success of this single was uneventful the B-side was to have an impact on them that would change their lives. The B-side was an instrumental entitled *Rampant On the Range* .It featured the mini piano sound as the lead instrument, a spark of an idea flashed between Woodward & Fletcher, and **Lieutenant Pigeon** (SEE LIEUTENANT PIGEON) the off-shoot novelty wing of The **Stavely Makepeace** corporation was formed. Meanwhile back at cape Kingsway Makepeace had released the singles *Give Me That Pistol and Walking Through The Blue Grass* uneventful apart from the fact the latter was covered by the bands Red Fox and Slow Dog and they were on a new label *Spark.* The success that **Pigeon**' was having had a positive effect on **Makepeace,** who tracked parallel careers and *Spark* were more that happy to release *Slippery Rock 70's* and *Prima Donna* with the former being released as *Mouldy Old Dough* was number one in the chart! *Slippery Rock 70's* incidentally can currently be found on the very interesting Glam rock compilation CD entitled *Velvet Tinmine.* 1973 saw them on *Decca's* (their label with **Pigeon**) progressive label *Deram* releasing *Cajun Band and Runaround Sue* (with great vocals from Rob in my opinion the best version of this song ever).

There would be a break of nearly 3 years before **Stavely Makepeace** would release another single (on another label) that being *Baby Blue Eyes* on *Unigram,* another non-charter. Things looked better with the intervention of Nigel's friend Don Powell (Slade's drummer of course). They released a pair of singles *No Regrets* and *Coconut Shuffle.* on *Barn Record.* Owned by Slade's manager the late Chas Chandler. Once again two more original songs went a begging (*Coconut Shuffle* would also be released as a remix in 1980 under the name **The Bounty Hunters** get it?) Their last two singles were to be *Songs Of Yesterday* (Hammer Records) 1980 and *Just Tell her Fred Said Goodbye* (on SMA) in 1983. A compilation of the best of **Stavely Makepeace** was released summer 2004 entitled *The Scrap Iron Rhythm Revue,* those not familiar with their music would do well to sample the delights of this unique and forward thinking band, you have a treat to come. The guys tried their hand at many types of music (Rock N Roll, Novelty, Country, Bluegrass and even the sound of the mighty Deltic locomotive) as well as some naughty innuendo songs with yet another offshoot band **Heavy Cochran.** Whatever they did you can bet they had fun doing it, long live the memory of **Stavely Makepeace** a unique experience.

GODIVA ROCKS SOUND BYTE WITH-Nigel Fletcher (Lieutenant Pigeon & Stavely Makepeace). Late in 1968 my old mate Rob Woodward lugged a heavy tape recorder all the way from Coventry to the house in East London where I was living at the time. He'd come to play me some new ideas he'd been working on and coax me into rejoining him in the quest for 'music business success'. His idea was to set up a songwriting/production partnership, put together a recording studio and help establish Stavely Makepeace. It all sounded so fantastic that I couldn't refuse!

Within a few weeks we were caught up in a frenzy of activity working day and night trying to achieve what seemed the impossible. We recruited Coventry musicians Don Ker and Pete Fisher and thus was formed the nucleus of the 'scrap iron' sound of Stavely Makepeace. Soon after we were joined by the urbane Mr Steve Tayton and the line up was complete.

Like our mentor Joe Meek we broke all the rules of studio recording, and that small front room in Kingsway where we set up our recording studio was never idle. Our motto became "If it sounds right it is right" and we learned all about equalisation, compression, echos, reverbs et al as we went along, never really caring much about technicalities. In 1970 bass guitarist Pete Fisher left us to be replaced by Steve Johnson. This coincided with the release of our third single "Edna". Within a few weeks we were booked to play the song on BBC's Top of the Pops TV show. Stavely was established!

Things could only get better in 1971 but all the excitement of the previous year began to stagnate. The fourth single "Give me that Pistol" failed to set the world on fire and by the late summer Steve Tayton had parted company with us leaving a big gap. It was at this time Steve Johnson, myself and Rob decided to form an offshoot band called Lieutenant Pigeon to cater for our 'novelty' and 'experimental' music. One of our tracks recorded in September 1971 was called "Mouldy Old Dough" and the rest, as the saying goes, is history! Recruiting Rob's mum Hilda to play with us became the icing on the cake.

That was 1972 and after 6 years of sustained success with this bizarre quartet we felt it was time to put the Pigeon to roost and turn our attentions back to Stavely Makepeace. We'd kept the band alive as a recording unit during those interim years but now we felt it was time to resume where we'd left off. For a further 5 years we soldiered on but Stavely Makepeace never became the huge success we'd all dreamed about. At the end of 1983, after a total of 13 singles and as many heartbreaks, we finally wound the band down. We remained based in Coventry throughout. It's a great city and ideally placed to reach all the other major cities in the country. Sadly, at the time of writing, only three of us remain here. That's Don Ker, Rob and myself but we might soon have to drag Steve Johnson back from Blackburn and Steve Tayton back from France. This is because in 2004 RPM Records plan to release 22 of the best of our tracks on a compilation CD. Stavely Makepeace lives on!

STEREO NATION

Tarsem Singh, Taz, Johnny Zee or **Stereo Nation**, all these names describe a Coventry kid who had taken his music to another level, a man who has created a huge legacy in his own inimitable way. He pioneered pop fusion as a lyricist, composer, DJ and producer. His first album *Hit The Decks* stormed the UK Asian pop charts and remained at number one for an amazing 36 weeks (eat your heart out Bryan Adams) and has become one of the best selling Asian fusion releases of all time. He crosses boundaries like most of us cross the road, he's never afraid to cross-pollinate his rhythms, be it with UK, US or even African beats. **Stereo Nation** originated when Taz's manager and former dub-poet and **Urge** vocalist Kendell Smith came on board (SEE REGGAE, SEE THE URGE). Mixing Bhangra beats and reggae rhythms they released the inspired *Spirits of Rhythm* and *New Dawn* albums. They went on to achieve a British chart hit in 1996 with *I've Been Waiting* (53), it would also go to number one in the UK Asian charts. With the album *I've Been Waiting* going multi-platinum!

A world tour followed, that would include India, Australia, Africa North America and The UAE (where Taz is huge, and where I have just picked up a the repackaged *Café Mumbai* CD *Apna Sangeet*) The next album *Jambo* was released through *Times Music India,* yet another huge global success. Towards the end of 1999

Taz released the solo album *Nasha (Intoxicated)* further cementing his prime position in dance floor grooves at home and in Europe and the USA. The new Millennium saw a revamped **Stereo Nation**, DJ Kendell had departed and Slave *II Fusion* was released with it's wicked melding of R'n'B, soul, dance and *Bollywood*, shifting some 120,000 units in the UK and US and a staggering 1,4000,000 in India! Because of this massive success Taz was approached by *Bollywood* to visualise a track for the film *Tum Bin,* further advancing his *Bollywood* appeal, culminating in an appearance at *The Indian Oscars* in Sun City performing to an estimated audience of 3 Billion!

In 2001 he hit the UK charts again with *Laila* (44) although it charted in October it had a wonderful summer sound to it, a prefect mix of Asian and western sounds (former **King** (SEE KING) guitarist Jim Landsbury was his sound engineer for a time). The accompanying video was also the first time an Asian artist had used CGI technology in a promo' video. An appearance at *The Royal Albert Hall* for a charity concert for Afghanistan followed, and a performance at the *Richest British Asian Awards* in front of HRH Prince Charles. Next came the classic album *Taz-Mania,* (including the superb dance track *Making Love* showcasing Taz's great vocals and the quite brilliant *Aaja Gideh Vich* and *Love and Devotion*). In 2002 he was awarded Best Music Act by the Guild of British Asians, and nominated for a *Carlton Multicultural Award* alongside Ms Dynamite. More *Bollywood* success came with the song It's magic, sung by *Bollywood* Heart throb Hritik Rosham in the film *Koi Mil Gaya*. Hollywood too has beckoned in the shape of his song *Mehbooba* used in the movie *New York Minute,* look out for Taz the actor pretty soon too. His current album the excellent *Cafè Mumbai* is a further mixture of musical cultures and sounds that demonstrates this guy's ability to stay ahead of the game. It's no wonder that Taz is globally one of Coventry's best selling artist ever.

GODIVA ROCKS SOUND BYTE WITH-Taz (Stereo Nation) Coventry has always been a melting pot of all types of musical cultures which have been very inspiring to myself, especially the 2 tone and ska era blending with the hybrid of reggae. Having grown up with musical influences ranging from traditional Punjabi folk and Bollywood music/Motown Rhythm and blues, I was destined to create a new sound, which I labelled global pop fusion.

Back in the days, Coventry bands/artists seem to have their finger on the pulse and the live scene was thriving which had a major impact on me as an artist. Bhangra in my opinion is a sound that has always been the heartbeat of the Asian community. Finally after all these years of experimentation, the mainstream media had no choice but to recognise and acknowledge this new urban culture. The Asian youth have created a scene of their own, which is not only credible, hip and trendy but also sells bucket loads of records. In my opinion Bhangra blended with the urban sound of hip-hop is a new British sound. Even though it's in it's infancy stage we will see more collaborations between Asian and mainstream acts using this unique sound.

Currently I'm working on signing and developing new acts to my record label 'Cyberphone Records', which specialises in urban crossover music. As well as this I'm putting together my greatest hits album re-mixed, after having nearly 15 years of hits in the music industry worldwide. More recently I've just licensed one of my tracks to a Hollywood movie called 'New York Minute' staring Ashley & Mary-Kate Olson. This year I will also be making my acting debut in a Hollywood movie called 'The Arranged Marriage'.

A GODIVA ROCKS TRIVIA BOX

The most successful UK hit singles by local artist are....

1. I Remember You-Frank Ifield
2. Mouldy Old Dough-Lieutenant Pigeon
3. Lovesick Blues-Frank Ifield
4. Confessin' (That I Love You)-Frank Ifield
5. Ghost Town-The Specials
6. The Wayward Wind-Frank Ifield
7. The Special AKA Live EP-The Special AKA
8. Edelweiss-Vince Hill
9. Love and Pride-King
10. Nobody's Darling But Mine-Frank Ifield

GODIVAROCKS@YAHOO.CO.UK

STEVENSON'S ROCKET

In the heady teenybop days of the mid 70's, when Bay City Rollermania was at fervour pitch. Every self-respecting record company was crying out for their own teenybop band. A certain *Magnet Records* A & R man named **Pete Waterman** (SEE PETE WATERMAN) had crossed paths with such a band at his local haunt *Tiffanys,* instantly Waterman knew he had found his Xerox Rollers.

The guys had begun life as **Chapter Four,** then **TAS Sound** with Alan Twigg on bass, Tim Savage guitar and vocals, Dave Reid keyboards and Steve Bray on drums. This teenage line-up was to play the local club scene until mid 1975. At that juncture most of the band ready to turn the club band into a pro teenybop outfit, except Tim Savage who's vision of things was to continue playing the clubs. By mutual consent founding member Tim left and was replaced by Mike Croshaw guitar, and vocalist Kevin Harris (Tim would continue to play/compere and promote club bands, he now lives in The Isle Of Wight as does Alan Twigg). By the time Pete Waterman had discovered them they were already picking up a large fan base (mainly young and female). They probably have the honour of being Waterman's first 'find' and they even get a small mention in his book *I Wish I Was Me* (on page 95). He describes them as a 'Boy Band' and goes on to say he wrote their first two hits, (despite the fact they only had one, though it did chart twice), he described their sound as a *vocal rock 'n' roll group, playing poppy pop.*

The very 'Rollers' influenced single *Alright Baby* (including Steve Bray's perfect copy of the Tartan ones drum paradiddles) was released in Autumn 1975 and chuffed it's way to number 37 in October of that year, with the band also playing *Top Of the Pops* on the way. As previously mentioned it re-entered the chart a month later and achieved a less pleasing 45. Of course there would be much hype of the boys, who in all fairness were all very capable musicians. That didn't matter as much as a pretty face and some suitable white 'N' flared attire fit for a 70's boy band. The follow up single *Here I Am,* was release in 1976 among a wave of great expectancy (*The Record Mirror* tipped the band for the top in 76, along with Sailor and Smokie). It soon became evident that the material was a little lacking and consequently it failed to chart. They would appear on the chart again though as the backing band for **Pete Waterman's** *Good-Bye-ee* single. That was followed with a rework of the Johnny Tillotson song *Poetry In Motion* was chosen for their third (and final) single featuring Dave Reid on lead vocals, with the B-side *Teenage Guy* written by Mike Croshaw. It was pretty obvious the band had reached it's sell-by date and it was soon all over for the lads, slightly older & wiser. Steve Bray joined Toyah Wilcox's band, and appeared on her two first albums The seminal *Sheep Farming In Barnet* and *The Blue Meaning* (40), and also in the musical film *Urgh! A Musical War*. Kevin Harris meanwhile joined **The Spifires.** As for **Pete Waterman** whatever happened to him??

GODIVA ROCKS SOUND BYTE WITH-Tim Savage (Stevenson's Rocket) As the founder member of the Stevenson's Rockets, I am happy to walk down memory lane some thirty years later and give an insight to how the band formed. Both myself and Steven Bray a life long school friend, had always wanted to play in our own pop band with the Monkeys who were massive in both the TV world and on the pop charts being one of our many influences. Steven always wanted to play the drums and i the guitar, although i could get a tune out of most instruments I picked up. Prior to Stevenson's Rockets both myself and Steve joined our first band called "Chapter four" who also featured school mates the Pembroke boys. At the same time i was heavily in involved with the Church lads brigade, enter Alan Twigg who played side drum in the marching band of which we both were members, incidentally Jimmy Lantsberry later of the band KING lived next door to Alan and often attended the rehearsals of our band band. After several months chapter four ended due to musical differences !!! and the "Tim Alan Steve" Sound were formed (TAS SOUND) this was indeed the forerunner to Stevenson's Rockets.

Dave Read finally joined us several months later to add more musical weight to the band and Stevenson's Rockets were formed. The name was chosen from a large picture that hung in a local working mans club with the image of the great train, strange but true. One of our first gigs as a band was at the Coventry police club, all was going well until our first PA amp blew up, flames everywhere !!! well time's were hard and it did come off a world war two battle cruiser !!!! **Continue over**

Continued. As a trivia point Stevenson's Rockets during my time also became a five piece band when, Robert Savage my older brother joined as front man for a while, he left musical differences again !!!. After a visit to the new Crester club where we met The Rocking Berries a 1960's comedy show band our details were handed on the their management, following an audition Stevenson's Rockets turned professional and we hit the road, I was 15 years old with Dave being the oldest and the only driver. Once again it was working men's clubs and night clubs for us, but management wanted us to follow in the footsteps of The Bay City Rollers who were massive during this time, i guess this is where my time with the band came to an end, I wanted us to sit within the cabaret format as this was my back ground, where the boys wanted to explore the musical world of pop.

The rest is history, two further members were found as my replacement and the band went on to chart success, I followed my cabaret instincts and went on to form a cabaret duo with Chris Cole another Coventry boy, this lasted for more than sixteen years, I still talk to the boys now and then and have no regrets about the path that events lead me down, as the nearly man of Coventry pop I find my self happy and contented as i still work within the entertainment business arranging touring production show world wide. "There's No Business Like Show Business"

A GODIVA ROCKS TRIVIA BOX
Local artist who have enjoyed hits in America include...

Jigsaw with Sky High (3) and Love Fire (30)
Billie Myers with Kiss The Rain (15) and Tell me (28)
The Flying Machine with Smile A Little Smile For Me (5)
Frank Ifield with I Remember You (5)
Don Fardon with Indian Reservation (20)
Panjabi MC with Mundian To Bach Ke (22)

STUDIOS

OK before we start on this section, I mention a lot of artists, so I have cut down on the (SEE 'LINKS'), work them out for yourself here please. The area has its fair share of recording studios. Obviously *Horizon Studios* was probably one of the most well known, where **The Specials, the Selecter** made their historic **2 Tone albums.** Other artists like Bad Manners, The Three Degrees and Steel Pulse have all used the now long gone Warwick Road 24 track. **The Specials** had some promotion photos taken on the roof of the building. Next most famous local studio is the ever-popular *Woodbine Street Studios, Leamington* run by John Rivers (SEE LEAMINGTON). The Specials recorded Ghost Town at the original studios in Woodbine St. **The Special AKA, Eyeless In Gaza** and Steve Gibbons have all been clients. *The Sent From Coventry* compilation was also done here. The studio eventually moved and got a new name *WSRS Studios,* the albums *The Sounds Of Leamington Spa* were recorded here. There were local bands were on it, just a tip of the hat to Johnny's production style, former Stones axe man Mick Taylor has also recorded here.

PAUL SAMPSON AT CABIN STUDIOS

Then we have *Cabin Studios* up on the London Road run by John Lord. The Great Paul Sampson (SEE THE PINK UMBRELLAS) was the in-house producer there, he ran the place looking after the likes of **Sonic**

GODIVAROCKS@YAHOO.CO.UK

Boom, The Primitives, Catatonia and lots of Bhangra stuff. Not forgetting *Rhythm Recording Studios* in Leamington, with Paul Johnston at the helm, it was here the compilation album *The Rhythm Method* was recorded. Paul now runs *j10 Studios* on Fletchamstead Highway, current groovers include the well-mooted **Spotlightkid**, with their Beefheart/Zappa influences and Nuneaton's **Scarlet Phere**. Then at Cash's Lane we have *Planet Recording Studios they* played host to Neville Staples among others. *The Depot Studio* in Coventry part of the City's *Art Council and Heritage Media Service*, for sound and video recording, training and projects. *Fidget Studios* are in Longford. Roger Lomas (SEE ROGER LOMAS) began with a recording studio in his garden shed, he then used Horizon now he has his own **Ro-Lo Studios**. Venue for the recording of the Grammy award winning album *Jamaican ET* by Lee 'Scratch' Perry.

Cov' has some great Bhangra studios including the absolutely brilliant *World Music Recording Studio in* Foleshill. They are custom designed by the owner Bhangra music composer and all round Guru **Baldev Mastana**. I have been in a few studios in my time but these are wonderfully designed, a great place to work. Clients include the outstanding **Shinda Sureela** and **Balwinder Safri & The Safri Boyz**. *Hush Recording Studios* in Old Church Road also specialise in Bhangra the great Jazzy B has recorded there. Then there's Taz's *Laila Studios (SEE STEREO NATION)*. Older studios were *Panthos Studios* in Balsall Common, opened officially by Jimmy Hill in 1965, *Midland Sound Recorders* Bishop Street, was a very popular studio had their own MSR record label used mainly for jazz, folk and local choirs.

Others include *Excel Music*, Leamington, *Gighouse Recording Studios*, Leamington, *Great Central Studios*, Rugby, Ardent Studios, *Backbeat Rehearsal* Studios, ERS Studios, Leamington, *Atrax Studios*, Coventry and Rob Hill's old *Sight and Sound Studios*. Private studios include **Eyeless In Gaza's** *Ambivalent Scale Recordings* in Nuneaton, Sonic Booms *New Atlantis Studios* in Rugby. Also we have for the heavier band *The Sable Rose Studios* run by Andy Faulkner clients include **The 4 Kings, Bolt Thrower** and The Shock. *Ramp Studios* were in Gosford St, the reformed **Specials** Demoed tracks for *Today's Specials* there. **Lieutenant Pigeon** man Rob Woodward's home studio was at 25 Kingsway now just a front-room again!

25 KINGSWAY FORMER 'PIGEON' STUDIO

THE SWINGING CATS

The 'other' Coventry *2Tone (SEE 2 TONE)* band. They originally practised in a small garage that was 'too small to swing a cat'. Played mandatory ska (along with others influences like calypso, Latin and Captain Scarlet) but with an accent on 'fun' rather than political message. Indeed their type of kitsch lounge music was pretty much the way Jerry Dammers would go with the sound of **The Specials** (SEE THE SPECIALS), although in **The Specials** case it would be delivered with a huge slice of allegorical menace.

The Cats' won a contest at The Lanch' the prize was an appearance on BBC's *Look Hear*. They toured with **Gods Toys** (SEE I), **The Bodysnatchers**, **The Selecter** (SEE THE SELECTER), Bad Manners and **The Specials** (SEE THE SPECIALS). Their personnel was forever changing but the 'classic' line–up was something like this. Toby Lyons (Tony El Dorko) on keyboards, John Shipley (aka Vaughan Truvoice) guitar, Wayne Riff bass Jane Bayley (aka Jayne De La Swing) vocals, Paul Heskatt on sax, Billy Gough (aka Dicky Doo) drums and Chris Long (aka Craig Guatamala) on Percussion. Chris worked at *Virgin Records* in Cov, Jane had replaced Val Pussy Perfect on vocals (she was also Jerry Dammers girlfriend) and Paul Heskatt

Who had played on *The More Specials* LP. Their one and only *2 Tone* single was the echo filled *Away* with *Mantovani* as it's t'uther side released in 1981, despite the first twenty thousand copies selling for just 50p, it became the first *2 Tone* flop. Notwithstanding their novelty value and their numerous support slots they remained distinctly second rate, and the Cats would cease to swing. Toby Lyons and Billy Gough would join **L'Homme De Terre** (SEE L'HOMME DE TERRE) Toby would eventually join up with Terry Hall in **The Colourfield** (SEE THE COLOURFIELD). John Shipley would become a member of **The Special AKA** and **The Urge** (SEE THE URGE) and much later Jane Bayley would become a musical comedienne known as *Jane Bom-Bane, Queen Of The Funky Harmonium.*

SQUAD

Cov's prime punk boys started out with Terry Hall vocals, Danny Cunningham guitar, Billy Little drums and Sam McNulty on bass. Terry Hall who was never really cut out for punk left to join a band called **The Specials** (SEE THE SPECIALS). He was replaced by the great Gus Chambers (nice surname name). Gus WAS cut out to be a punk, after seeing **Roddy Radiation and the Wild Boys** (SEE THE WILD BOYS) he was hooked. **Squad's** rock n roll punk style was the kind of dish most punters in the late 70's were looking for. If you didn't move at least a little at a **Squad** gigs then you must have been brown bread. It was always sweaty, loud and enthusiastic with some great laughs thrown in. The line-up changed constantly, with the band becoming a training ground for Cov musicians. Danny Cunningham would leave and form **The Ramrods/ Major 5/Gdansk.** Their drummers would include Mark Hatwood, Rob Hill (SEE THE PINK UMBRELLAS) and Steve Young. Guitarists included Jim Scully (from local band **1984**) and Johnny Adams (from the bands **The Blue Jays**, **RU21**, **Fission**, and **Don't Talk Wet**). With Nigel Mulvey then Nick Edwards replacing Sam McNulty on bass, Sam eventually ended up with **The Giraffes** (SEE THE GIRAFFES).

They released 2 single in their illustrious career, *Millionaire* (where they were hanging out with The Radford Boys) and *Red Alert* with the brilliant 8 *a Week* on the B-side. They also got onto *The Sent From Coventry* compilation with the song *Flasher* (they actually adorn the said albums cover twice see pic courtesy of Rob Lapworth). The singles also appear on *The Anagram* album *Punk Rock Rarities Vol 2*. Songs you were likely to hear at their gigs included *Brockhill Boys (Millionaire B side), Son Of Sam, We Understand, Wrong Date Bang Birds.* and *Bag On Your Head.* They were great I will always remember them singing T*he Bells are Ringing For Me and My Girl* at *The Market Tavern* (except I thought it was *I'm Getting married In the Morning*, till Gus put me right, cheers mate). Whatever the song, whatever the venue be it *The Heath Hotel, The Hand and Heart, The Domino* or *Mr George's*, you knew they would always come up with the goods, great times. As the last pangs of punk rebellion dies in the city, **Squad** members moved on (see above), as for Gus well he joined **21 Guns.** Who released the single *Ambition Rock* on Neville Staples *Shack Records*. Their line-up-included guitarist Stuart Maclean, Kev Tanner and former **Specials** roadies Johnny Rex and Trevor Evans (SEE THE SPECIALS). Gus later moved to America and formed **Sons Of Damnation**, finally joining the no messing high energy metal band **Grip Inc.** They were formed by former Slayer mega-drum king Dave Lombardo. Releasing 3 brooding albums in the mid to late 90's finally coming back with a forth entitled *Incorporated* in 2004 greeted as a true return to form by the critics.

JUNE TABOR

Warwick's most famous daughter and a folk Queen supreme who came 95th in the top 100 greatest singers of all time! Born In Warwick December 31st 1947 attended *Kings School* then *Oxford*. Tried her hand at the restaurant business and for a while worked as a librarian at *Warwick Town Library*, but singing was to dominate her life. She started folk singing in local haunts like Leamington's *Fox & Vivian Public House*. The first songs she ever sang on stage were *Kum Ba Yah* and *Michael Row the Boat Ashore*. Her love for folk (SEE FOLK) was to grow. She released her first solo album *Airs & Graces* in 1976. Later that year she teamed up with Steeleye Span's Maddy Prior as the duo **The Silly Sisters**.

They released two fine albums (though a decade apart) *The Silly Sisters* in 1977 and *No More To Dance* in 1988. Her rich emotive voice would see her release a stunning collection of high quality albums that would transcend her folk traditions and eclipse others music styles including jazz, though she is always at her most evocative whilst singing accapella. Highlights include *A Cut Above* in 1980, *Against The Streams* 1994 and the classic *Echo Of Hooves* in 2003, that would see her surpass her previous best, take a listen to the track *Hughie Graeme* it's the quintessential folk song at it's very best. She would quite rightly win two *BBC 2* Folk awards for this album and the previously mention track *Hughie Graeme*. She has collaborated with the likes of Fairport Convention and The Oyster Band, It's refreshing to note that she is just at home singing a traditional ballad as she is with a contemporary song penned by the likes of Elvis Costello or the genius that is Richard Thompson. As I started this piece I mentioned she was voted 95 in the top 100 greatest singer of all time, it's worth pointing out that she beat the following icons Diana Ross, Tina Turner and Kurt Cobaine. Its good to see that thanks to **June Tabor** folk music is very much alive and thriving.

TALENT CONTESTS

Obviously *Pop Idols* is the current 'big' talent show and Coventry's **Pete Waterman** (SEE PETE WATERMAN) is one of the four main judges. I'm not a fan of the programme I must say, but of course many are, we have all seen it, so mercifully I don't need to explain it here. Anyway the local area has so far not had a big success in the show but **Javine Hylton** who was on *Popstars: The Rivals* has a Coventry born Mother and half her family still live here. Although she never made it to Girls Aloud, she launched a solo career and has charted at number 7 with *Real Things* and 24 with *Surrender Your Love*. She also helped to switch on the Cov' Christmas lights in 2003. Other locals on talent shows have seen the beat group **The Mad Classix** on *Opportunity Knocks* in June 1964. While **The Rickard Brothers** from Coventry won *New Faces* and Leamington band **The Incas** came third on the show in the 70's. **Formula 5** also appeared on *New Faces* (SEE BEVERLEY JONES). Mark Rattray (SEE MARK RATTRAY) was the last winner of *Opportunity Knocks*.

A few local people have represented the area on TV's *Stars in their Eyes*. Bedworth singer **Nick McCullock** got through to the finals as Neil Diamond. Then there's 14-year-old Woodlands schoolboy **Ryan Waite** from Eastern Green appeared on the kids version as Gareth Gates. Despite his tender years, he has already recorded a single *Love is A Treasure* when he was only 11 and has appeared on *Songs of Praise* as well as appearing in local productions of *Anything Goes* and *Me and My Girl*. Then there is Coventry's **Tracey Shields**, who has made a profession out of impersonating Celine Dion after appearing on the show as the Canadian songstress. Sarah Tuson from Heath Road also did well on *Stars in their Eyes* as Lisa Stansfield. She made it to the final in 2000 losing out to a Freddie Mercury sound-alike. She now goes under the name of **Sarah-Jane** and has signed a record deal, *Reverence* is her first single. Not forgetting **Sofia Kearns** a Coventry singer who got to second place in the singing contest *This Is My moment*, she is currently featured on the **Retox** single *Why Can't We See*.

TERMINAL TEARS

From the ashes of *Stoke Park School* bands **Wolf** & **Stoney Road** came **Wishful Thinking**. A wonderful manager by the name of **Pete Chambers** (it is me) came in circa 1984 and re-christened them **Terminal Tears,** and gave them a new look. Such was the trend of the time image was important especially with the likes of **King** (SEE KING) who were the big fish at the time. I chose a curly guitar lead motif for the guys and the dictums *"The Hard Edge of Pop and Follow The Lead"*. The band were Rob Home (vocals and guitar), Anthony Quinney (drums), Rich Piorkowski (guitar), Al Trickett (keyboards) and Nigel Kefford (bass). They had already produced a great demo as **Wishful Thinking**, Rob Home was a quality songwriter (and singer), my favourite lyric from him was from their best song *Tower Of Silence*, "Who can picture what I'm thinking, when I think nothing at all". Simple but blooming genius. I took them on because I really believed in them. (I also had an offer of management from their archrivals **Still Life** (SEE NOISE LIKE NOISE)). The lads had a larf', but could turn it on when they had to... Rich was a gifted guitarist and Anthony was the archetypal mad but brilliant drummer. Their second demo was recorded at *Cabin* (SEE STUDIOS) we even did a jingle for *Mercia Sound*. With my A & R connections we did a tour of the London studios, never got signed but it was fun. We filmed a video, I started *The Network* a sort of a fanzine based fan club. I got out when I knew it wasn't going anywhere, they split a few weeks later. A new band called **Car Party** was promised it never happened. Rich (my then son-in-law) and I formed the studio-based duo **Exhibit A**, got some good reviews from Paul Robinson of *The Coventry Citizen* (and he went on to be a producer at Radio One). Rich later joined pub band **Betty Swallocks** I heard that Nigel is now a policeman. If any of you guys read this I would love to hear from you.

THORIA

The Mighty **Thoria** seemed to have picked up the baton of Coventry hard rock and kept on running. Although they have already done 10 years together, their lack of a major record deal seems to have just inspired them on to greater thing rather that deflating them. Their somewhat satanic-laden music has pricked up the ears of *MTV* who made their *I Got Satan* promo' *A Most wanted Video track*. Heavy mag' Kerrang too have taken to the 4 piece and awarded their *Love Sick* album 4 out of 5. Their first mini album *Worry Dolls* (produced by Paul Sampson) (SEE PINK UMBRELLAS) spawned the first single Keep 'Em In The Attic (both on their own *Red Crust* label) that gained much *Radio One* attention. That was followed by the post-grunge classic *Love Sick*, (complete with pavement pizza cover) further cementing their hold on the market despite their B.U.R.B status. New songs like *The Craft* (an absolute classic) is still to come, whatever Martin, Mike, Tom and Mike get up to in the future you can bet it will be good 'n' loud!

TRIBUTE BANDS

OK not really what this book is about, but they are local and they are music (quiet at the back), so here goes. **Dark Side of the Wall**, of course a Floyd tribute band from Coventry. **The Jamm** are a Leamington Jam tribute band, they have actually sang in front of Paul Weller's mother! **Paul Leegan** does a tribute act to Lonnie Donegan, he also has the distinction of being an understudy to the great man when Donegan played his last ever concert. **Barbed Wire Man** from Rugby do a tribute to U2 and REM. **Special Brew** are supposed to be a *2 Tone* tribute band, but in their defence they are really a fun ska band in their own right, and are apparently well looking out for.

2 TONE

The label that put Coventry on the music map, with talk about us being the new *Motown* (like Detroit we were a motor town and we did have our own brand of music). It was great at the time, people talked about Cov, bands came to record here because it was trendy (yeah, Cov was trendy). I have a cutting about Hereford band The Photos, it says, "Remember that Hereford's near enough to Coventry for the Photos to have developed a ska beat of their own". That's how it was, every UK band wanted to be from Cov, and every Cov band wanted the Coventry Ska sound. When Jerry Dammers and **The Specials** (SEE THE SPECIALS) started their own black and white label, little did they know just how influential it would be. The boardroom (if you could call it that) consisted of all **The Specials** and **The Selecter** (SEE THE SELECTER). *2 Tone* was just a label and a musical feeling, there wasn't any real *2 Tone* base, the nearest thing was Dammers house in Albany Road. Dammers created the famous *2 Tone* man logo Walt *Jabsco* (the name appeared on an American bowling shirt owned by Jerry), based on an early picture of Peter Tosh. Along with a wall of black and white check the image it created a brilliant metaphor, in the 80's the black and white check was everywhere, even the checkerd bands on police uniforms had been reclaimed by *2 Tone*.

Other *2 Tone* artists were London's Madness, Brum's The Beat, Cov's **The Swinging Cats** (SEE THE SWINGING CATS). The Bodysnatchers, Rico,The Apollinaires, The Higsons (with *The Fast Shows* Charlie Higson), The Friday Club and JB's Allstars. There was also Elvis Costello's withdrawn 2 Tone single *I Can't Stand Up For Falling Down,* now worth a small fortune. The label produced 28 singles proper (excluding Costello's aborted single, a 2 Tone EP and a Ghostown revisited 45). 19 of them charted including two number ones, and another 8 top ten placings plus 6 charted albums (excluding compilations). Not bad for a Coventry cottage industry.

PAGE 105   GODIVAROCKS@YAHOO.CO.UK   PAGE 105

GODIVA ROCKS SOUND BYTE WITH-Jerry Dammers (The Specials and creator of 2 Tone).

My first live band in Coventry, when I was about 15, was called "Gristle", Roddy Radiation had been in it briefly, but it turns out he always thought it was called "Rissole"! By the time we did our first gig Roddy had already left. I'd just gone over the handle bars on my bike and knocked my front teeth out so I had a big brace and stitches in my face. I was playing drums and I was hit in the face by a full can of Coke lobbed all the way from the back of the hall at Green Lane Youth Club-very painful. You could tell Coventry was a boom town-anywhere else they would have drunk the Coke first!

The very first fore taste of things to come was probably in about 1971/2 when I managed to persuade the school rock band I played drums in, to play some reggae. Don't get me wrong, I'm not making any claims, I use "band" in the widest possible sense of the word! It was called "The Southside Greeks"(just that) and was about as rubbish as it gets- doing bad covers of Faces and Stones songs- without a singer. At that time, Reggae was regarded as a moronic novelty music by rock fans and the rock press, it was completely unheard of for a white rock band to play reggae. I think some of them thought it was a joke, but I did get the band to do a terrible version based on Liquidator/007.

Then I went off to art college, where Prince Buster's Golden Hits was the perfect record for freaking out flared cheese-cloth eared Yes fans at student parties. I wasn't exactly your normal art student- after my foundation year at Nottingham my first choice of college was Leeds. I didn't take any paintings to the interview. I tried to pull a "Pete Townshend" type scam, I told them I was going to create a "pop art" band instead of doing any paintings! I said it would be like "a modern version of the Who"- all I had was a tape of me singing "Little Bitch" (which the Specials ended up doing about 4 years later).The professor doing the interview just laughed and shook his head in disbelief and showed me the door! I had to come back to my second choice of college, Coventry, where I showed them my paintings and got in. If it hadn't been for that bold and crazy move at the first interview I might have actually got in at Leeds college - and there would have been no Specials and no 2 Tone as we know it !

While at college in Coventry I decided to put off my band masterplan until after I'd finished my course, and pay my dues playing in various club bands:.... teddy boy rock'n rollers "Ricky Nugent and the Loiterers", "Lane Travis' Country (and western) Trio", "The Ray King Soul Band" with Neol Davies -we did "Hot Chocolate" covers! -along with some half decent reggae and funk covers- but Ray wanted to keep it commercial. I got a bit frustrated with the Coventry music scene and went further afield to reggae and funk clubs in Brum and Bristol, I joined "The Cissy Stone Band"- a funky soul band from Brum . When punk rock happened, like Kevin Rowland I thought "that should be me". I knew it was time to stop doing covers, and finally put a band together to do my songs, (like I'd always planned from the age of ten). I also played keyboards in Coventry's first strictly reggae band, "Hard Top 22", around that time.

Once I'd put the Specials together I managed to talk our way onto a nationwide tour with the Clash, then we got fed up with their manager Bernie Rhodes, and came back to Coventry, where we got our ska direction and image together. The image wasn't Bernie Rhodes' idea at all as has been reported, we had completely parted company with him by that time. I suppose I should also say sorry, but "The Selecter" track on the B side of Gangsters wasn't an influence on the Specials' decision to play ska either, as has been implied in certain quarters. The original track "The Kingston Affair" was a great Neol Davis disco dub track (not ska), with a bit of a Rico vibe, which was on the shelf gathering dust. We (the Specials) had also recorded demos (with Pete Waterman) around the same time I think and we all knew Rico's music. It was my idea to add the ska beat to "Kingston Affair", and liven the track up a bit for the B side of "Gangsters" (which was already finished as a ska track). What the hell, ska was invented in Jamaica anyway, it was a great track and it was from Coventry! The rest is history.

Finally I'd like to big up the late great Delia Derbyshire, probably Coventry's best (pop?) musician (she did the Dr Who theme and lots of top electronica for the B.B.C.) if you don't believe the "Bristol sound" came from Coventry originally, listen to the first track on the "White Noise- An Electric Storm" album she did with David Vorhaus - Massive Attack a full 25 years earlier - absolutely incredible!

URBAN

With apologies to all you *groovemeisters* of dance, for I have put Hip Hop, Techno Dance and Fusion all in this one section, remember I'm old, and the subtle differences tend to blend in as one for the likes of me who was born in the 50's. Also (SEE BHANGRA).

The Eclipse *Lower Ford Street* circa 1991, became a major venue on the national circuit. Playing host to top DJ's like Sasha and Top Buzz. Became **The Edge** and it still attracted the likes of colossus Carl Cox. Even the clubs flyers and cassette covers have become collector's items. The great **Doc Scott** was born in Coventry. An influential DJ and producer playing rave and Hardcore, before moving onto Jungle. Worked under The Amnesia banner at *The Sky Blue Connection.* He eventually gave up his job as a telephone worker in 1991 and went pro. His recordings for Absolute2 and Surgery saw him emerge as a leader in the Hardcore scene. Joined up with **Reinforced Recordings Crew** (including Goldie, Mark Mac, Dego and 4 Hero). His track *Here Comes The Drumz* was to set the scene for darkside drums 'n' bass. (he would update the track for a later venture **Metalheadz** in 1994). **Banco De Gaia** the master of Chill Out resides in Leamington (SEE BANCO DE GAIA). **Shiloh Clarke** from Earlsdon a chill out musician who has toured with Imagination's Leee John. Released the track *The Gift* as a single on *The Cafe Del Mar Label* in 2004. **Paul Morrell** is another top Cov DJ who has the residency at *Ikon* in Coventry and *Bangin' Tunes* was the place for drum 'n' bass. Top DJ **Lisa Lashes** is a Coventry Lass, and one of the best female DJ's in the country.

LISA LASHES

Kenilworth born Hiphop DJ and artist **Rob Life** and **The Breaking Bread Collective** has become a main event in London, he has taken part in the *Godiva Festival.* **Off Licence** Hiphop/garage crossover including Lex Eye and Pro-Jay and Sunny MC, recorded at Cov's *j10* studios. The areas most established hiphop crew are **C.O.V.** (or **The City of Villainz**). They have appeared on the underground hiphop video *Corner 2 Corner Volume 1.* Basically created by filmmaker I J Oshin to showcase new UK hiphop talent and give some insight into what makes British street culture 'tick'. The crew have appeared at the Godiva Festival and are making tracks at *j10* Studio. **Hillz Yungsterz** from *'Beverly' Hill Fields* these two guys are one of my local hiphop faves, their songs *So Fine* and *From Da Hood* are both refreshingly original, and these boys can sing in harmony too, excellent stuff. Another top class act also from *Hillfields* are **YBR** I saw recently performing in Cov City centre, powerful stuff. Other Hiphop acts are **Defcom 3** (from Coventry), **Dang 2** (2 Nuneaton girls who do R&B too) and **Phoenix Knightz, Phoenix Crew** and **Infinite Dark**. We have some great home grown urban talent here in Coventry.

YBR

URGE

Formed in 1978 with an original line-up of Dave Wankling on vocals, Kevin Harrison guitar & synthesiser, Lynda Harrison vocals, John Westacott on Bass and former **Squad** (SEE SQUAD) drummer Billy Little. John Shipley would also play guitar for a short while before leaving to join **The Swinging Cats** (SEE THE SWINGING CATS). Claimed they refused to jump on the 'ska' bandwagon, then released the virtual ska single *Revolving Boy in 1980.* It made them a lot of fans especially DJ's John Peel and Kid Jensen who made it his record of the week! They supported The UK Subs and **The Specials** (SEE THE SPECIALS) on their European tour and appeared on *The Sent From Coventry* compilation with the track *Nuclear Terrorist*. Harrison would also release the solo tape *On Earth II* on **Eyeless In Gaza** (SEE EYELESS IN GAZA) *Ambivalent Scale* label. In August 1980 the band signed to *Arista* releasing a second

GODIVAROCKS@YAHOO.CO.UK

single *Bobby* and appeared on TV in the show *Look Hear*. John Westacott left to be replaced by another ex-**squad**ie *Nigel Mulvey*. After a tour supporting **The Selecter** *(SEE THE SELECTER)* they called it a day.

This was a band who wouldn't lie down and die, so **The Urge** mark 2 were formed, again with Lynda (now) Novak and Harrison, but also new blood like Dennis Burns (keyboards) and former **Mix** (SEE DAVE PEPPER) man Dave Gedney on guitar. After initial experiments with a drum machine proved less that beneficial they took on drummer John Hill and later Rick medlock (former **I**) (SEE I) and sax man Pete Jordan (ex *L'Homme de Terre*) (SEE L'HOMME DE TERRE). The played a lot at The Whitley Abbey pub, but it would seem that their chance had come and gone with the original line-up and once again the band split. Harrison did some solo work The LP *Inscrutably Obvious* on *Cherry Red Records* and the 12 inch single *Fly* (featuring former **Specials** Horace Panter on bass) and medlock drums. They came back one more time, with yet another line-up including Kendell Smith on vocals (who went on to join **Stereo Nation** (SEE STEREO NATION)) plus Harrison, and Medlock and Lynda now Harrison. They recorded one session at *Woodbine Studios (SEE STUDIOS)* including the songs *Pressure Drop* and *Style & Fashion*. They finally split for good in 1993. Kevin Harrison still records and releases albums (like *Epiphany* 2001 and *Velvet Galaxy/Spider Mill* 2002). Gedney would join The **Skabilly rebels** for a while (SEE RODDY RADIATION).

THE VAMPIRES (with Vince Martin & Johnny Washington)

Influential Rock n roll band in the area one of the first formed in 1959 fronted by the dynamic Vince Martin (later Holliday) and Johnny Washington (formerly Hounslow). Also included Barry Bernard on bass, Alan Palmer drums and guitarists Johnny Buggins and Robin Bailey. When they headlined *Nuneaton's Co-op Hall* (SEE NUNEATON) their support band was The Beatles (SEE THE BEATLES) Despite their success they never actually 'cut a disc' as they say. Vince began an entertainment agency (*Big three Enterprises later JRD Entertainment's* in Albany Road) booking the likes of Cilla Black, Shane Fenton, Lulu and local bands like The **Sorrows, the Matadors** and managing **Peppermint Kreem.** (SEE THE SORROWS, SEE THE B LIST, SEE THE PLAGUE). Johnny Washington ended up working in America and Barry Bernard joined **Pinkertons Colours** and then **Jigsaw** (SEE PINKERTON'S COLOURS, SEE JIGSAW). The band (sans Washington) all got together for a reunion in 1994. Vince went on to be a travel agent (well you would with a name like Holliday).

VENUES

Of all Coventry venues, the most revered without doubt was **The Coventry Theatre** (**Coventry Hippodrome**). Since it's demise it has risen to almost shrine-like status, although that may be a slight exaggeration, it never the less has a history that certainly in Coventry is second to none. Built in 1937 for £140,000, it has played host to anyone and everyone. Coventry's own **Reg Dixon** (SEE REG DIXON) opened the stage musical *Zip Goes A Million* there in 1951. Laurel and Hardy, George Formby, The Beatles, Elton John, the Rolling Stones and **King** (SEE KING). To name but a few have all played there, it even had it's own broadcasting Orchestra led by Charles Shadwell (who went on to lead the BBC Variety Orchestra) and later Bill Pethers (who's signature tune was *I Want To Be Happy* and regularly broadcasted on the world Service). It was sad to see it go, but in truth we all knew that it died spiritually when it became a bingo hall! Barbara Dixon was the last act to play at Coventry Theatre on 6th June 1985. Her last song was *We'll Meet Again,* in the style of Gracie Fields. No amount of protest was going to save the dilapidated old girl from the slaughter that awaited her. (That's the theatre I'm talking about now, not Barbara Dixon) Sad then when the City had gone to the trouble to build The Sky Dome on the old GEC site, they have never used it to it's full potential.

GODIVAROCKS@YAHOO.CO.UK

You see I always thought of the **SkyDome** arena as the obvious updated replacement for the Hippodrome. Reasonable acoustics sort of reminded me as a mini NEC main arena. It's an ideal venue for the sort of acts Leamington gets, but Coventry doesn't. Why not? It's built and ready to use, yet apart from a few concerts here and there (notably Daniel O'Donnell) it remains the sole preserve of Ice Hockey. For heaven sake, let's start using it, so we no longer have to travel to Leamington or **Warwick Art Centre** for our gigs.

I'm not knocking the Arts Centre, I've seen some good concerts there, but there really isn't a great deal to say about it as a venue (SEE JAZZ). I suppose **The Lanchester Polytechnic**, or just *"The Lanch"* as it was known, was the prime gig for me. Every Friday and Saturday night you knew you would have a great time, see a band, drink cheap beer and buy some cut-price vinyl in the upstairs bar. Go home without a hint of trouble (well maybe a little). We all freaked out to the sounds of the Who, Roxy Music, Bowie, Led Zeppelin, Budgie and so on. When we weren't listening to records, we were watching live the likes of, Thin Lizzy, ELO, ELP, Stone the Crows, Caravan and generally drowning in a sea of progressive rock. The Lanch was the chosen venue for **Covaid** (SEE FESTIVALS) and **The Specials** (SEE THE SPECIALS) filmed the video for the single Rat Race in the main hall, and socialist MP Dave Nellis was the regular DJ there for many years. **Specials** Horace Panter and Jerry Dammers got their art degrees at *The Lanch* (Jerry never bothered to pick his up). Pauline Black studied Bio-chemistry here. John Kettley of the single *John Kettley is a weatherman* by The Tribe of Toffs attended the Lanch as an applied physics graduate. Jethro Tull axe-man Martin Barre also attended the Poly in the 60's.

When researching for this book the most mentioned venue however was **Tiffanys**, (or **The Locarno** or Rockhouse). With it's strange glass entrance tower dominating the City's Precinct (sadly now of course gone, when the main building became the home of the new central library), a good night was pretty much guaranteed for all. The revolving stage turning to the sound of Green Onions is a powerful memory for many. So was **Pete Watermans** (SEE PETE WATERMAN) DJ stints at the venue (he recorded his **14-18** album here). Before him was DJ/compere Frank 'Chick' Pritchard. Although mainly a disco/dance hall venue (Coventry's first all nighters happened here in 1970), it did play host to some top notch acts. Led Zeppelin played there during a bomb scare. Mott The Hoople, Cockney Rebel, Madness, **The Selecter** (SEE THE SELECTER) and **The Specials** (SEE THE SPECIALS) all graced it's stage **The Specials** recorded the B side of their number one *Special AKA live EP* here. Not forgetting the heats of Miss World and the BBc's *Come Dancing*.Then there's a little matter of a Ding A-Ling (SEE CHUCK BERRY). The City was never quite the same when it was closed down. Look out for Roy Pargetter's book on the subject entitled *Rockhouse Nutter*.

The General Wolfe, a major Coventry venue for local talent, probably the MOST important venue in the City. One name springs to mind when you talk about the Wolfe that's **Ken Brown**. Ken's a convivial bloke from Enniskillen, and a huge Van Morrison fan, and a 'king' in the promotion of local talent. His importance on the local scene can not be overstated. His long stint at the 'Wolf' saw a plethora of bands on its small but perfectly formed stage (even U2 played there in September 1980). Although Ken moved from the Wolfe many moons ago (to the Dog and Trumpet then Browns) The Wolfe will always be synonymous with Ken. Even rock god Robert Plant has played and attended the venue. For a time the Wolfe even had it's own splendid in-house fanzine called The Wolfe, well it would be wouldn't it. It has seen good times and recently some bad times, as I write I sadly learn of its demise as a live venue once again.

The Belgrade Although extensively a theatre for drama and musical theatre The Belgrade has had over the years its fair share of local music acts, especially during its Festival weeks. Theatre stage Director **Trevor Nunn** began his illustrious career at The Belgrade. Coventrian (and big Sky Blues fan) **Bob Carlton** started out at the Belgrade, although he is probably best know for creating the musical 'Return To The Forbidden Planet', he has also directed for TV including *Emmerdale* and *Brookside*. **The Orchid Ballroom/The Tick-Toc Club/The Colosseum** It's good to see that this building in Primrose Hill Street is once again hosting and more importantly promoting new talent from the area. As the Orchid Ballroom this building was a corner stone of 60's music in Coventry. Run by soon to be legendary Larry Page, along with Denmark Productions, Larry was able to promote a batch of up and coming talent at the club. These included the girl group

THE ORCHID

The Orchids Named after the venue (SEE THE ORCHIDS). **Shel Naylor** (who would grow up to be **Rob Woodward** of **Lieutenant Pigeon**) (SEE SHEL NAYLOR, SEE STAVELY MAKEPEACE, SEE LIEUTENANT PIGEON), Johnny B.Great (real name **Johnny Goodison**) (SEE JOHNNY B GREAT) **Beverly Jones** (SEE BEVERLY JONES) and Little Lenny Davis. Page went on to manage The Kinks, The Troggs and create the Page One record label. The building eventually became a bingo hall until in the 1980's it opened it's doors to live music once more as the Tic-Toc Club (Tic-Toc standing for "Theatre in Coventry, Theatre of Coventry" the name of the theatre group that owned it). Finally becoming the Colosseum, and still promoting live music in Coventry today. **The Matrix** on Fletchamstead Highway played host to many acts, including The Beatles (SEE THE BEATLES) the Who, Steppenwolf, The Kinks and The Small Faces. **The Hotel Leofric** in Broadgate has also seen some live action, in the shape Chris Farlowe, Jimmy Cliff, Jeff Beck, Spooky Tooth, Taste and reggae ace Jimmy Cliff. The R & B Sunday Sessions were also popular there in the 60's. **The Jailhouse** (along with The Coliseum) (SEE ABOVE) is a current favourite in the City, manager Gaggs has a refreshing view of the scene, he's a man who cares passionately about the music, hence the calibre of his venue. He still feels however that bands & punters could do more to prevent the City becoming a ghost town again. His view is, "Use them or loose them" sounds like sense to me.

ALL THAT REMAINS OF THE MERCERS ARMS

Here's a list of Cov venues past and present. The Depot, The Dog and Trumpet, The Dive, The Climax, City Centre Club, Busters, The Domino, Hope and Anchor, City Centre Club, Mr George's (great for punk and cheap whisky, the Pistols played here) Golden Cross, The Colin Campbell, The Market Tavern, The Walsgrave (even playing host to a young Rod Stewart), Henley College, Butts College, The Stoker, The Zodiac. White Swan, Mercers Arms (once a great jazz and R&B venue, Pete Waterman had his *Floorboards Club* here, Shotgun Express that included a young Rod Stewart played here), Hand and Heart, The Pitts Head, The Spencer, Hare & Hounds Keresely and The Jailhouse (the last 3 all current favourites).

GODIVA ROCKS SOUND BYTE WITH-Larry Page (legendary Coventry entrepreneur and manager of The Troggs & The Kinks) Regarding Coventry in the 60's, it was just waiting to wake up as was Birmingham, and the Orchid Ballroom was the perfect venue to attract new talent. It was very much a team effort with everybody getting involved, from the bouncers to the performers, we all plastered the town with posters - many of which were illegal - and on more than one occasion we sealed telephone boxes by mistake with posters that were put on the wrong side of the phone box.

I started writing a page for the Coventry Echo doing record reviews etc. and this helped attract people like Johnny Goodison who of course then became Johnny Be Great. We had problems early on keeping the rough element out, so there was the occasional fight breaking out, but the bouncers were fantastic and on more than one occasion when Johnny was performing and a fight broke out that I was involved in, the music would stop and as I turned I'd see Johnny by the side of me thumping somebody with the words 'Are you alright Lar?' My instructions were always if a fight breaks out play the National Anthem. It seemed to work in those days, but I don't know which anthem you would play today.

When I first saw Rob Woodward (Shel Naylor) I thought he was the closest thing I had ever seen to Elvis Presley and so talented, and it was very important to me to try and get him off the ground. We had no trouble at all getting public reaction, but nationally and record-wise it certainly wasn't easy in those days. I suppose the idea of dressing groups up i.e. The Kinks and The Troggs, stemmed from Coventry and I believe the first one I tried it on was a band called "The Hangmen" and I had a noose constructed for the stage, but I must say I can't remember too much about that. So the first of the costume brigade were definitely "The Pick Wicks", and we had them dressed up in frock coats with top hats at the ready. Great little band and they came in all shapes and sizes, and as I'm dictating this I can see them in my mind's eye. We did some very good records and I suppose the value of the records now will be the fact that I had Jimmy Page playing on them.

The Orchids were so good for three little schoolgirls and the sound they came out with was tremendous. In America we had to change their name to The Blue Orchids because it clashed with an already existing band. We did many trips down the motorway to London trying to set up deals which we succeeded in

---

PAGE 110   GODIVAROCKS@YAHOO.CO.UK   PAGE 110

Continued doing. Of course there was a lot of politics that went on behind the scenes but they all had a shot at fame and they were all released in the US as part of the British invasion. It was never easy getting a recording job and it isn't today. That's why eventually I started my own label and produced all my own records, so that I had total control. Regarding The Troggs and The Kinks, The Troggs were fun in the early days and I produced many hit records with them which will live on and on. When you see the film 'Love Actually' and you realise 'Love Is All Around" was originally The Troggs hit, then re-recorded by Wet,Wet,Wet, you realise the value of a good song. 'Wild Thing' of course stands out on its own and you can go into any pub around the world and there is a fair chance someone's going to be playing it.

I was lucky enough to manage Sonny & Cher during their big successes and they were wonderful to work with. The Kinks were another ball game. Ray Davies is so talented but not easy from a managers point of view. But I did manage them again late 80's/early 90's and it's one of those sad situations where he is surrounded by people who agree with him, and that's not always the best way to achieve success and I certainly never did it. Going back to The Orchid as you may be aware, the big competition and certainly a bigger ballroom was The Locarno Ballroom, which was about four times as big and held a couple of thousand of people I think, so I decided to print flyers and send people in there. It was like a military operation but all you could see was Orchid Ballroom flyers all over the place, and it certainly did the trick. Please give my regards to everyone who I was ever connected with for I have a very soft-spot for Coventry as that was where it all kicked off big time.

GODIVA ROCKS SOUND BYTE WITH-Ken Brown (Manager of The General Wolfe, The Dog & Trumpet and Browns) I Came over in 1965 , I got my first pub in 1970 The General Wolfe was my 3rd pub . I had that between 73 –83 Wolfe. I've always liked my music, so putting bands on just seemed natural especially as we had a big room not really being used a lot.

What's the best band to come out of the City? There were a lot of good band to come out of the town obviously The Specials, Selecter but there were other very good bands notably Hot Snacks Gods Toys Paul King's original band the Stereotypes. Stan Campbell had a band Channel A, he of course finished up playing in The Special AKA to do the Nelson Mandella single.

What was the most satisfying moment as Wolfe manger?
I suppose one of the unique things to happen to us when U2 were about to release their first album, they were just starting out and you could see just what the potential was, the were just unbelievable. They had it then as they have it now. It was all there you could see it in each individual member of the band. Actually you could always tell the bands who were really good during the sound check, as apposed to the guys that were playing around at being superstars.

What other major bands did you have at The general Wolfe? We had Aztec Camera, The Thompson Twins, Annie Lennox's Eurthymics, Joboxers Tandoori Cassette. Eric bell, played on the early Thin Lizzy records, he was a regular. Of course Friday night was blues night. Once the news spread, about the venue promoters record company all called me to put their bands on. Talk Talk had never done a live gig before, their first was at the Wolfe.

Did you notice particularly during the height of 2 tone, that everyone wanted to play in Coventry? Actually it was quite funny if the phone was red hot in the day with people checking about who was playing you knew you were in for a full house. One thing that sticks with me during the Toxteth riots in Liverpool we had Pete Wylie and the Mighty Wha on, he always brought a crowd from Merseyside. Somebody came into the pub and heard all these Liverpool accents and thought they were here to stir up trouble so they called the police. The next thing I know the police turn up.

Did you think there was an actually Coventry sound? It definitely existed, the 2 Tone thing was unique, there were lots of people playing it in the area after the Specials. It was a unique blend of Ska and punk, some bands have the magic blend then they split and try to recapture it, but it's gone, the elements aren't there anymore. We used to have two West Indian guys who used to play bluebeat at the Wolfe, funny enough they had the same surname as me Brown. They were the brown Brothers. They were very secretive of their music they never let anyone find out who it was, because they wanted to keep it to themselves. So obviously Jerry (Dammers) and the boys were heavily influenced by that, adding their own punk and rock elements to it.

WARWICK

The Midnights were the Warwick beat group of the time back on 1963/64, they played *The Coventry Theartre* (SEE VENUES) in 1963 and released a single *Show me Around* on *Ember Records* in 65 and appeared on TV's *Thank Your Lucky Stars*. They included Paul 'Mitch' Mitchell, Rick Robbins, Peter Sykes and Keith Sandall. **June Tabor** was born here (SEE JUNE TABOR). **The Edgar Broughton Band** who are also from Warwick (Edgar & brother Steve were both born here while Arthur Grant is a Leamatonian) and were once banned from playing an open-air concert In the Town so as a protest they played from the back of a moving lorry down Warwick's main High street! (SEE THE EDGAR BROUGHTON BAND). The town has also spawned **The Hangover Blues Band** fronted blues harp maestro Sam Powell who also plays in **The Steve Walwyn Band** (SEE THE DT'S). Warwick parties and function band **Bitter Tears** had a residency at *The Waterman Inn* nr Hatton 1986. Then we have the concerts at *Warwick Castle* (Cliff Richards, Donny Osmond) and *Charlecote Park* (Simple Minds). **Porifera** are a current Warwick band, but heaven knows where they play, probably Leamington. Because there certainly isn't any 'scene going on in this County Town.

Warwick University. Yes I know it's nowhere near Warwick, but it fits nicely on this page. So here goes Sting went to the Uni but dropped out after one term. DJ Simon Mayo and Rock god Timmy Mallett also attended. Rock critic and sociologist Simon Frith was a professor here. Folk band **Waterfall** (SEE FOLK) was formed here. The University has bestowed Honorary degrees to violinist (doesn't seem enough just calling him a violinist) Stephan Grappelli and percussionist Evelyn Glennie (she went on to get around another 12 of them from various other Uni's). Opera diva Dame Kiri Te Kanawa also has an honorary degree from the Facilty as does jazz man Humphrie Lyttelton (SEE JAZZ).

WARWICKSHIRE

Stratford Upon Avon's most famous son's music-wise are Simon Gilbert and Neil Codling both members of **Suede**. The most famous son of all William Shakespeare had the title of his plays used a few times in chart songs, like *As You like It* (Adam Faith), *Winter's Tale* (David Essex) and *Romeo & Juliet* (Dire Straits) and BA Robinson used the famous soliloquy *To Be Or Not To Be* in his song title. William Shakespeare also had a go at writing himself with songs like *Bee Sucks* and *Full Fathom Five* they were adapted by Benjamin Britten, Michael Tippett and Arthur Sullivan. Then there were the girls of Shakespeare's Sister (and the Smiths song). Current bands from the town are **Kontiki, Entity, Kharma, Man With Van, Mark Roberts and the Cosmic Crew, The Snugglewhippers, Thegurthcontrol, Sten** and **the...and Not Affected**. Apparently Screaming Lord Sutch got 209 votes stood for election with the *National Teenage Party* in 1963 in the town. **Long Marston** was the venue for *The Phoenix Festival*. Kenny Everett lived at Old Red Lion in *Shipston-on-Stour* in the 70's. *Tanworth-In-Arden* was the home of the iconic Nick Drake (Brother of Gabriel). **Smile** come from *Alcester*. Atherstone is home to the mighty **Stairway**. These Christian rockers have been going since 1993 they sound like all my fave's of the 70's rolled into one (Wishbone Ash, Purple and Uriah Heep). They have 3 albums under their belts *No Rest, No Mercy, Bleeding Heart*, and *On hallowed Ground* and a Japanese release of the *No Rest, No Mercy* saw it chart at 48, wonderful Stuff. Finally *The Warwickshire Lad* was the name of a song and an album by folk purist Martin Best in 1974. The song originates from the 1769 and was written by David Garrick for the *Shakespeare Jubilee Festival*. It has been adapted as the regimental march of the Royal Warwickshire Regiment. The bells of St Mary's church Warwick play the song every Friday. The *Warwickshire Keeper* is a song recorded by Stratford folk band Willows Folk on their *Songs and Music of The Midlands & Warwickshire*.

STAIRWAY

PETE WATERMAN

Not many people can claim not to have heard of this man (well in the UK at least). The City's most famous son? Certainly a contender. Born in Burlington Road, Stoke Heath, Coventry on Jan 15th 1947. Worked at the GEC until he gave it up to be a full-time (and very influential) DJ at the Locarno and other Cov haunts. He would make a name for himself as his knowledge of music would rise above the norm, giving tips to many top bands on what they should be listening to and recording. Was the vocalist & guitarist in the soul band **Tomorrows Kind** in 1967/68. He ran The Soul Hole upstairs of Virgin Records in City Arcade. (I often went there with my good mate Malc Coombs. A walking encyclopaedia of 'black music'. He opened a door for me into the world of the Ohio Players, Norman Whitfield's Temptations and The Jimmy Castor Bunch). Pete's fame began to spread and he Would soon become an A & R executive for *Magnet Records* and have his first hits with Peter Shelly and Gee Baby and later Coventry's **Stevenson's Rocket** (SEE STEVENSON'S ROCKET). He was to chart under the name **14-18** with the World War I classic *Good-Bye-Ee,* something he isn't keen to talk about now, but it did chart at number 33. It also spawned an album of similar war inspired sing-a-longs recorded at *Coventry's Tiffany's*. He was the first to discovered **The Specials** in Cov and promoted them, to an unready world (SEE THE SPECIALS) .Becoming restless he left the safety of Magnet records and after stints laying concrete and working at *MCA Records* he started his own *Loose-End* Productions promoting Musical Youth and Divine.

By 1984 he had teamed up with fellow Coventrian **Matt Aitken** (who was born in the City moving to Manchester at an early age), and Mike Stock. Together as of course **Stock, Aitken and Waterman** they would become one of the greatest production companies in the world ever. Producing Hi-NRG glossy pop songs for Dead or Alive, Nik Kershaw, Bananarama, Mel & Kim, Princess and their own single under the name **S.A.W** *Roadblock(13)* (Issued originally as a phoney old 'rare groove' record in an unmarked sleeve to prove to doubters that they could make records that didn't necessarily sound like **Stock, Aitken and Waterman**).They won The *Songwriters of the Year* awards for 3 years running and the Hit Factory just couldn't lose. Pete got to host his own pop show *The Hitman and Her* with Michaela Strachen (not bad for a guy who in his own words was barely literate). 1988 gave **SAW**'s its biggest artists they were of course Kylie Minogue and Jason Donovan. By 1993 their production partnership had ended with Stock and Aitken claiming two-thirds ownership of the company (it would take until 1999 to be finally settled in Pete's Favour). Never the less the Ferrari collecting train mad Waterman continued unabated and set up his own *PWL* company and went on to have huge success with Steps. Then later as the second most outspoken judge on TV's *Pop Idols*. In 2001 he received an honorary degree from *Coventry University*, for his contribution to popular music.

While his success and influence in the world of music cannot be denied, there are those who would argue that his music is 'throwaway pop pap' with as much integrity as a beer mat! Others claim that Waterman takes himself a little too seriously (it's hard to argue with that when his website was previously called *Pete Waterman The Pop Phenomenon*). Whatever you think of him, he has done it all as a Coventry Kid, and I highly recommend his very entertaining autobiography *I Wish I Was Me*.

DAVE WILLETS

Dave's big break came when he was performing a play at Kenilworth's Priory Theatre (where Dave is still a patron) and was spotted by *Cov Telegraph* reporter Paul McGarry. He had been a manager at an engineering company in the City, all that was to change when he was recommended to *The Belgrade Theatre*. By 1985 he was appearing in The Shakespeare's version of *Les Miserables* at *The Palace Theatre* in London under the direction of former *Belgrade* Director Trevor Nunn (SEE VENUES). He then played *The Phantom* In Lloyd Webbers famous musical *Phantom of the Opera* . Dave became the only person to play the leading role in both these landmark productions.

Other shows included *Someone Like You* (opposite Petula Clark) and Tim Rice's *Tycoon,* and *Jesus Christ Superstar*. His concert tours and Musical reviews are always well supported by Dave's massive fan base (especially the favourite *Magic of the Musicals*). He's no stranger to radio and TV, and like Vince Hill (SEE VINCE HILL) he has been the subject of *This Is your Life*. His albums include *On & Off Stage* and the eclectic Timeless (a CD where Dave tackles such favourites as Tears *In Heaven* and *You Took the Words Right Out Of My Mouth,* it is highly recommended and is produced by Mike (Mick) Roberts ex-**King** (SEE KING)). His CV runs like an encyclopaedia of musicals including *Cats* and *Seven Brides For Seven Brothers* where he played Adam Pontipee. Of late he has recently returned from yet another successful tour and 2003 saw the release of the album *The Musicals Unplugged*. He lives in Baginton village and has recently voiced his opposition to the Airport expansion plans there. His contribution to the stage is an unequalled one and he remains one of Music Theatres most enduring performers.

GODIVA ROCKS THE 'B' LIST

A Band Called George a folk unit from Cov/Leamington appeared on Midlands Today released the single *NCB Man* on *Bell records* in 1973.

Martin Bell Leamington violinist (also plays banjo, mandolin, accordion and guitar), played with **Van De Hoog's Elderflower Remedy** (with *Warwick Uni* graduate and fellow fiddler Martyn Oram)(SEE FOLK), also **The Mix** & **The Mosquito's,** (SEE HORACE PANTER) before becoming 'Fiddly' in the Stourbridge indie darlings The **Wonderstuff,** Who had hits with the songs *The Size of A Cow* and *Dizzy* with Vic Reeves. Martin has also played with Boy George, The Albion band, The Men They Couldn't hang and Kirsty McColl. He also wrote the original score for the film *Small Time Obsession.*

Declan Bennett A huge talent from Coventry, he writes his own music, acts and can play many musical instruments and on top of that he is known to be a bit of a heart throb. Began in the *Youth Operata Group* in Cov and appeared in the likes of *Jesus Christ Superstar* and *Boyband*. That was handy because in the 80's he was one third of the boy band **Point Break,** who had the proud distinction of writing their own material. They had five hits in all they were, *Do We rock* (29), the rather good *Stand Tough* (7), *Freakytime (13), You (14)* and *What About Us (24)* plus the album *Apocadelic (21).* They toured the world and built a huge fan-base. On leaving he was to land a role in Boy George's stage show *Taboo,* something he would leave and rejoin over the years. He currently fronts the band **Sumladfromcov** and has aptly enough appeared at the Godiva Festivals. A new album *The Painters Ball* is due out soon, with more than a little help from Declan's mentor *Boy George.*

DECLAN

Birdland many state they were from Cov, I say they were from Birmingham, I have included them here just for arguments sake. They had a punk attitude, and died blond hair (and resembled a David Sylvian look-a-like contest). They sounded a kin to Jesus and Mary Chain and were very much in your face. Had five hit singles between 1989 and 1991, the biggest being *Sleep With Me* getting to 32. Also hit with the album *Birdland* (44) in 1991.

Chevy from Leamington, fronted by Martin Cure. His pedigree looks like a veritable who's who of local bands. From **The Sabres, The Peeps, Rainbows, Still Life** (SEE THE PEEPS) to Cupids Inspiration Joining them in 1971 after their hit, *Yesterday Has Gone*. He went on to form **Chevy** with Paul Shanahan who had been in the band **Jalopy Ride** along side *Rhythm Studios* mainman John Rivers (SEE STUDIOS). Forever living under the banner of the New Wave Of British Heavy Metal (or N.W.O.B.H.M). With Paul Shanahan and Stephen Walwyn's twin guitar sound, the comparison with Wishbone Ash was inevitable. Chevy were always much more than that though. Lining up as; Cure (vocals), Steve Walwyn (lead guitar, vocals), Paul Shanahan (guitar, vocals), Bob Poole (bass, vocals) and Andy Chaplin (drums) they wooed the rock fans and pulled off support slots to Space rockers Hawkwind (playing at Cov's Tiffanys in 1980) and the worlds fastest axeman Alvin Lee. W. Gaining a prize spot on the EMI *Metal For Muthas Vol 2* album with the track *Chevy*. Their first album *The Taker* on Avatar Records was awaited with anticipation but never really lived up to the promise of their live performances. After two singles, *The Taker* and *Just Another Day* and personnel changes the band split in 1981. The nucleus of the band became **Red On Red** along with Rob Jackson (SEE ROB JACKSON). Steve Walwyn and Andy Chaplin later formed R n B band **The DT's** (SEE THE DT'S).

Tony Clarke born in Coventry 1941. Took up the bass guitar obtained some session work at Decca Records. Became a writer (he wrote *Our Song* performed by both Jack Jones and Malcolm Roberts) and eventually a producer. His first production was for Rugby's **Pinkerton's Assorted Colours** with their first single *Mirror Mirror* (9) (SEE PINKERTONS COLOURS). He also produced the number one hit Baby come Back from The Equals. Though he would be best known for his work with The Moody Blues. He was considered the sixth Moody Blue by the group, their George Martin if you will. He produced everything for them (including solo efforts) from *Fly Me High* in 1966 to *Octave* in 1978. That includes the singles *Night's In White Satin, Question, Isn't Life Strange* and *I'm Just A Singer In A Rock N Roll Band*. Also the classic albums On *The Threshold Of A Dream, A Question Of Balance* and *Seventh Sojourn*. He also produced the song *Simple Game* twice, once for The Moodies and then for The Four Tops who had the number 3 hit with it in 1971. His later work includes Clannad's *Legend* album and The Everly Brothers *Reunion Concert* LP. He remains a giant in the world of production!

Crocodile Tears or Christopher Sidwell. Ernsord Grange based muso', had been with the ground breaking **Evil Winds** and **Digital Dinosaurs**. He was joined by **Pink Umbrellas** drummer Robin Hill, and released an album of his own unique style of pop songs in the 80's.

Faya Largeau (were **Jump The Gun**) Trio comprising of Paul Whitehead, Roger Clarke and Eddie Broadly. *Operation 'Y'* and *Dreaming* were stand out tracks for me.

Fiori won *The Godiva Festival Battle of the Bands* in 2002. No amount of make-up and posturing can hide the talent this 4 piece obviously have. Arthur Gatfield, Dave Ryder, Steve Harris and Paul Watson combine to create something gritty and good.

Fineline Won *Cov Festival Battle of the Bands 2002 and Sennheiser unsigned artist's battle of the bands*. Got to play in Virgin in Coventry and at Glastonbury in 2003.

FIORI

Matt Fisher a refreshing sound of one man and acoustic guitar, especially as Matt doesn't try to sound like anyone else. Played Cov Festival 2004, music from the heart.

Ivy Fitton Coventry singing teacher, trained the likes of **Vince Hill** (SEE VINCE HILL) and his sister Valerie Marston (who along with Shirley Pemberton was a member of the singing club duo The Lynettes).

The Flying Tortellinis including former Style Council and **Beachmantango** multi-instrumentalist Anthony Harty (who also played on the Grammy award winning album Jamaican ET by Lee 'Scratch' Perry). Plus former **King** keyboard player Mick Roberts (both had been in the band **The Walnut Conspiracy**). They play contemporary country music with a twist. Released the CD True Believers. Harty was also part of the Neol Davis Horace Panter blues unit **Box of Blues**.

The Fortunes Despite their obvious Cov' connection they were ostensibly a Birmingham band. Managed by Reg Calvert at Clifton Hall (SEE RUGBY). They provided the song *Caroline* that was used as a jingle and theme tune for pirate radio station *Radio Caroline* and like so many of their songs featured multi-part harmonies. Their first hit was *You've Got Your Troubles* (2) followed by *Here It Comes Again* (4) both in 1965. They also chart in The US with *You've Got Your Troubles* (7), *Here It Comes Again* (27) and *Here Comes That Rainy Day Feeling Again* (15). They were also the voice of the Coke commercial *It's The Real Thing* in 1972. They would go through many line-up changes. Finally re-inventing themselves on *Capitol Records* in the 70's any enjoying a second career with the hits, *Freedom Come, Freedom Go* (6) and *Storm In A Teacup* (7). Rod Allen a founder member is still with the band, along side newer guys Paul Hooper (drums), Bob Jackson (vocals, guitar and keyboards) and Michael Smitham (guitar). Hooper and Jackson were both in **Indian Summer** and **The Dodgers** (SEE INDIAN SUMMER, SEE THE DODGERS). Michael, Rob and Paul all grew up in Coventry. The band continues to tour extensively.

FX had a lot of ideas, probably too many, I believe that Rob Hill drummed with them for a while, guitar based they recorded a demo featuring the tracks *Down To The Beaches* and *Sunburn LA Melodrama*. Some of their members went on to join political band **Tubilah Dog** who played the festivals and became part of the Hawkwind family.

John Hanson It's a little known fact that this singer/actor best known for his portrayal of The Red Shadow in *The Desert Song* was in fact born in Coventry November 28th 1920. He would leave England at an early age and settle in Canada. Appeared on The Royal Variety Performance in 1982 and many big West End productions during the 50's & 60's. *The Desert Song* enjoyed a record-breaking revival at Drury Lane Theatre in 1967. He appeared on the album charts on 3 occasions with; *The Student Prince* (17) in 1960, *The Student Prince/The Vagabond King* (9) in 1961 and *John Hanson Sings 20 Showtime Greats* (16) in 1977. He passed away in 1998.

Harvey and the Wallbangers Popular circuit band of the 80's, with an emphasis on humour and rock 'n' roll. Led by Harvey Brough, who was educated in Coventry (as was his double bass player Richard Allen). Harvey was also trained at Coventry Cathedral (SEE COVENTRY CATHEDRAL). Their first album was released in 1984 entitled *Allez Bananes!* After some six years hard touring they split (having played at the likes of The Lanchester, The Albert Hall and Sadlers Wells). Harvey then worked as a composer for TV, radio and stage. He won the *Andrew Milne Award for Jazz Composition* for his *Requiem in Blue.* His talents as an arranger have been used by the likes of Kim Wilde, Spiritualized, (SEE SPIRITUALIZED) Terry Hall (SEE TERRY HALL). In 2000 he formed the band Field of Blue formed with singer Jacqueline Dankworth performing a mix of jazz, blues and pop.

The Hawaiian Surgeons dressed the part in Hawaiian shirts, and were generally manic on stage, released a single in 1985 entitled *1001 Better things To Do.*

Nat Jackley Born in Sunderland in 1909, this rubber-necked physical comedian lived in Styvechale Coventry for many years. Began his career in a clog dance troupe **The 8 Lancashire Lads** (a certain Charlie Chaplin was once a member). He was to star in his own show *Nat's In the Belfrey* in 1956. His odd voice and looks won him many small character parts through his long career. Including cameos in the films Yanks and Mrs Brown You've Got a Lovely Daughter, also on TV in Minder and Juliet Bravo. However it was his appearance in The Beatles *Magical Mystery Tour* as Happy Nat (the rubber man) he was probably most known. He died in Coventry September 1988.

NAT JACKLEY

Jason John member of disco pop trio **Big Fun**. He was born in Cov' on 18th March 1967. Produced by **Stock, Aitken & Waterman** (SEE PETE WATERMAN), they had hits with the Jackson's cover *Blame It On the Boogie* (4), *Can't Shake The Feeling* (8), *Handful Of Promises* (21) and *Hey There Lonely Girl* (62). They also teamed up with Sonia for The Childline Charity with the James Taylor song *You've Got A Friend* (14). Their album *A Pocketful Of Dreams* made number seven in 1990. Their biggest claim to fame was having three simultaneous top 15 hits in Spain.

The Little Darlings a Cov freakbeat/mod band made up of Allan Waites (guitar), John Gilroy (guitar), Barry Eaton (drums), Malcolm O'Sullivan (vocals) and Terry Twigger (bass). Originally called **The Pines**. The legendary Joe Meek was their recording manager. Cut the now collectable *Good Things Are Worth Waiting For* in 1966 on *Fontana*. Became **The Sensations** in late 66, their first (and very psychedelic) single *Look At My Baby* was *Radio London* Record of the Week in May 1966. Apparently Sonny & Cher were fans. They became **The Good Time Losers** in 1967.

Lowdrive current Cov trio who are Steve Jones (guitar & voice), Greg Schofield (bass & voice) and Tim Bowes (drums). Their guitar based indie rock sound has been used to good effect on their two EP's especially on *Turning Circles*. They are all committed Christians and their music quite rightly reflects their beliefs. Their acoustic version of *Skydiving Grace* (recorded live on *Kix 69*) is sublime. No wonder they are picking up lots of good press, they played the main stage at The 2003 *Coventry Festival*. They were also The BBC band of the month in June 2004.

The Matadors actually from Hinckley, but played so much in Coventry people thought they were from here. Known as 'The Midlands Beatles'. Recorded with the great Joe Meek and released the single *A Man's Gotta' Stand* on Columbia records in 1966 (as **The Four Matadors**) but they were not happy with Meek's creative ideas'. So left and courted some interest from Andrew Loog Oldham and Tony Hatch. Became 8-piece soul band **Magazine** in 1967 with the addition of a brass section. Split in 1975. Their drummer Harry Heppingstall formed the band Wave with **Dando Shaft** man Ted Kay.

Moon London Pub rockers had members from Coventry and London. The Cov contingent included Bob Jackson from **Indian Summer** (SEE ROB JACKSON, SEE INDIAN SUMMER), bass man Ron Lawrence (from Cov folk band **April**), and guitarist Loz Netto (who attended *Coventry Drama School* as did **Paul King**). Released two albums on *Epic Too Close For Comfort* and *Turning The Tide* (both mid 70's). Loz Netto and Ron Lawrence joined cult new wavers **Sniff N the Tears** who had a number 42 on *Chiswick* in 1979 with the superlative *Drivers Seat*. Lawrence went on to become a bass session player his credits include The Kinks 1978 album *Misfits*. Bob of course would join *Badfinger*.

Caz Moore Born in Wolston, a hard working local singer. Released a single called *Shine* with Mick Roberts ex-**King** (SEE KING) in 2001. Has worked with **Taz**, the Bhangra music star (SEE STEREO NATION) as well as a host of local club circuit bands. Her website can be found at www.cazmoore.co.uk/.

Nektar although based in Germany they were a bunch of ex-pats, including Coventry man Roy (now Roye) Albrighton who had been with a plethora of local bands including **The Plague Peppermint Kreem** and **Rainbows** (SEE THE PLAGUE, SEE THE PEEPS)). Formed in 1968, theirs was a blend of art and progressive rock. using lights and films at their shows to complete the overall experience. Their classic album was their debut *Journey To The Centre of the Eye*. While the US debut *Remember The Future* went top 20 Stateside. The group understandably moved to America in 1976. Other offerings like *A Tab In the Ocean* and *Sound Like This* would sell to a less extent, the band finally split in 1978 (although Roy had left the previous year). By 2001 they had reformed, releasing *The Prodigal Son* and in 2002 Roye put out the solo album *The Follies of Rupert Treacle*. They embarked on a extensive US tour in 2004.

Ning were an odd Coventry band that were a bit of a mystery (they never gave interviews), they released the single *Machine* in the UK on *Decca* and in America on the *London* Label in 1971. They played Prog soul-rock and had a very energetic stage act. The single was written and produced by Mike Berry, and they included former **3AM** guitarist Derek Wilson. They played 7 nights a week below a Café!

Oskar Kokoshka hard gigging Cov band, liked to look eccentric, played keyboard-based songs like *Kissing Fences*.

Peppermint Circus Many believe that they were another incarnation of Cov band Peppermint Kreem (SEE THE PLAGUE), they weren't. This 5 piece originally recorded on the Swedish label *Olga* next on *Polydor* then on *A&M* and and released five singles in all. They had a vocalist was called Paul Thomas. The singles were, *All The King's Horses* (a Bee Gee's song), *I Won't Be There*, *Please Be Patient*, *One Thing Leads To another* (got to number 35 in Germany) and *Let Me Go* (produced by Mike Batt). Thanks to Paul Cross at at SFA for this info.

The Plague Coventry beat group included the Albrigton brothers Arthur (Modie) and his brother Roye (SEE THE PEEPS). Both are now located in Germany, but their roots are firmly entrenched in Coventry and it's music scene. Modie a top class guitarist and blues harp player began with the local band **Makeshift**. Before moving onto **Peppermint Kreem** a 5 piece rock band that headlined a memorial park concert in the mid sixties. They even recorded their own rock opera Revelations 2001 (at Time Machine Studios Earlsdon). Members included founder Paul Kennelly, Tom Ryan, Dave Fairclough and Ray Haywood. Modie went on to join the likes of **Nuts and Bolts, Crossfire and Heaven Sent** a club band that would include Rodney Byers in its ranks (SEE RODDY RADIATION). Modie still lives in Germany and is associated with Falcon recording studios and hosts a fantastic website on Coventry bands. Check it out at **www.coventry-bands.de/**

Clint Poppy. Born Clint Mansell in Coventry November 7th 1963. Became guitarist, vocalist and frontman for the mid 80's indie chart favourite's **Pop Will Eat Itself** (or **The Poppies**)(their name came from an NME headline they had previously been The Wild And Wondering). They would chart with what they called 'Grebo' rock' on no fewer than 15 occasion's, with the bigger hits being *X,Y and Zee* (15) and *Get The Girl! Kill The Baddies!* (9). Their hip-hop infected music would prove influential, with tracks like C*an U Dig It?* (38) and *Def. Con One* (63) and they would also chart with their classic album *This Is The Day...This Is The Hour...This Is This!* (24 UK and 169 in America) Their body of work would see that the **PWEI** legacy burnt bright for many years. Finally Clint went on to work with Nine Inch Nails among others, and has written numerous film scores including *Darren Aronofsky* and *Murder by Numbers*.

Julianne Regan Born in Coventry moving to London at 19, she fronted (and still does) the Goth band (that's Goth with a small g) **All About Eve.** They managed to rack up some 13 hit singles from 1987 to 92 (although only the super-atmospheric *Martha's Harbour* actually reached the top 10 in 1988). However their self-titled album reached a very credible 7 in 1988. She has also worked with Bedworth born Tim McTighe in the band **Mice**. Julianne recently revealed that she rarely visits her hometown much anymore. now that she no longer has any family here. Her worst moment was on *Top Of The Pops,* when the song was being heard but not by a un-singing Julianne.

Resound great current band from Coventry shame that their vocalist wants to sound like Noel Gallager. Capable of playing some astounding blues, remind me of The Yardbirds. Have release two E.P's namely *Delayed* and *Give The Boy A Medal*.

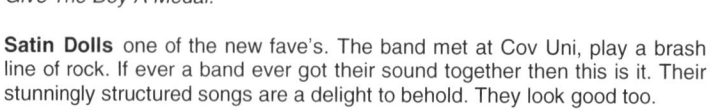

JULIE OF THE SATIN DOLLS

Satin Dolls one of the new fave's. The band met at Cov Uni, play a brash line of rock. If ever a band ever got their sound together then this is it. Their stunningly structured songs are a delight to behold. They look good too.

Sheer Pride a real product of the 80's, with King and Duran Duran overtones, played The Wolfe loads of times, *Virgin Dancer* and *Too Late* were two of their best songs. Mainman Martin Keatman wrote books about psychic Phenomena. They appeared on Paul Johnson's *Rhythm Method* compilation album with the track *Peace Of mind*. They also played *Covaid*.

Sonic Harmony German based dance fusion band with a female vocalist from Coventry.

Spider Murphy Blooming great 80's band, lead by now session guitarist Steve Madden, appeared at *Covaid* and on the *Rhythm Method* LP (as **Murphy's Law**) with the best track *Days Gone By*, stunning stuff.

GODIVAROCKS@YAHOO.CO.UK

Splash With Sonya were a young band formed at *Stoke Park School* in the mid 80's, by Niall Carson, had some great ideas on music and image. Did a wonderful demo that included the fab song *Crashdive*.

Ian Steadman influential A & R executive for *Tommy Boy Records*, born in Cov, moved to London as a child then to Canada in 1982. Attended *Harvard University*, has promoted the likes of De La Soul and Naughty By Nature.

Sue & Mary two 13-year-old *Cardinal Wisemen* schoolgirls who were overheard by their teacher singing a song in the playground that turned out to be written by the girls. With the intervention of guitar legend Burt Weedon they signed to *Decca Records* in 1965 and released the self-penned single *Traitor In Disguise*.

Dave Swarbrick 'Swarb' is folks (SEE FOLK) finest fiddler lives in *Stoke, Coventry* although he was born in London (in 1941). He moved to Yorkshire as a young child, and began learning the violin at the age of 6. Later settling in Birmingham then much later Coventry. Some of his earliest folk appearances were with the great Ewan MacColl. He joined The Ian Campbell Folk Group in the early 60's later teaming up with Martin Carthy, both becoming kingpins of the contemporary folk scene. It was his next move that was to be the most dramatic however as a member the legendary folk group Fairport Convention. Where he clocked up 5 chart albums (including the seminal *Unhalfbricking*) and even a hit single with *Si Tu Dois Partir* (a French version of Dylan's *If You Gotta go, Go Now* (21)). His place a folk's greatest fiddle player was secure. He left Fairpoint in 1984 forming **Whippersnapper** with Cov's Kevin Dempsey (SEE DANDO SHAFT) before joining The Band Of Hope, and in 1993 moving to live in Australia for 3 years forming a duo with Alistair Hulett. Dave returned to Coventry, he contracted the lung disease emphysema (although he would still continue to tour for a time with oxygen canister in tow). In April 29th 1999 *The Daily Telegraph* ran an erroneous obituary to him of which they later apologised for, typically Dave remarked, "It wasn't the first time he had died in Coventry". Now unable to play because of his illness, he awaits a lung transplant, his mates Kevin Dempsey and Martin Carthy among others have organised *SwarbAid* to help him financially through these hard times. Dave has always been one of folks most endearing characters, so it's fitting that he should win *The Lifetime Achievement Award* in The BBC2 *Folk awards 2004*. I wish him all the very best.

Tina and the Hotstrings Beat group that included Tina Sedgley (vocals), Graham Rodgers (guitar), David Walls (guitar) and John Casey (drums). Recorded a version of Marianne Faithfull's *Come And Stay With Me* at *Panthos Studios* in 1965 (SEE STUDIOS). Signed to *Polydor Records* in 1967 and called themselves **Orange Flavour.** Released the single *Baby's Gonna Cry* in 1968.

20 Days (so named because the three were born 20 days apart) came out of the four piece **The Time** (when Martin Burke left). As a three piece they consisting of Simon O'Grady (vocals & bass) Peter Burke (drums) and John O'Sullivan (vocals & guitar). Had a brand of high-energy guitar based rock, they played regularly at *The Rose and Crown High Street*. Released a four track 12inch EP in 1985 on Cabin's *Sonar Label (SEE STUDIOS)*. With *Freefall* as the lead track (nice back cover photo taken by a guy called Pete Chambers, I also did the one here, one of my favourites). In 1989 they morphed into 'superband' **The Hungry i** when former **Primitives** Steve Dullaghan and ex-**Eyeless In Gaza** Martyn Bates joined (SEE THE PRIMITIVES, SEE EYELESS IN GAZA). They released 2 EP's in 1991, *Falling Orchard* & *Second Step,* and recorded an album at Cabin Studios, but it never saw the light of day. John O'Sullivan would also play on Bates's solo tours. When Bates departed and **The Hungry i** became a trio again, O'Sullivan, O'Grady and Burke formed **My Favourite Things**. Who were a beat group for the Zen Generation apparently. They recorded the singles *Fruit Machine* and *Syd* (the latter a collaboration with Cov favourites **The Nocturnal Babies** (SEE THE PRIMITIVES) They supported INXS in 1996 then split a little later. John O'Sullivan would later join **Primitives** off shoot band **Starpower**, (with Paul Court) who released the singles Turn *My world* and *Drifter* (featuring **The Prim's** Tracey). **Starpower** then became **Hedy** and released a single *Superfine* in 1996.

THE V BABIES

The Vietnamese Babies played on the edge of punk towards the pub rock side of things. I did a photo session with these guys once, they were absolutely barmy, great lads, just out of their minds. *The Hope & Anchor* seemed to be their spiritual Mecca. They recorded *Donna Blitzen* for *The Sent To Coventry album*. They were slightly more PC then as the **V Babies**. They always pulled in a crowd because they were well good live.

Vin Lloyd and His Mounties. Have the distinction of being Coventry's first big pop group. A nine-piece skiffle band who met at *The Coventry Technical College* and all came from Wyken. They were auditioned on *ITA* for *The Carroll Levis Show*, supported *The Kirchins* on a tour in Scotland. When they played Nottingham they took 3 coach loads over from Coventry. They were Vincent Lloyd, Lorraine Sawbridge, Gordon Cattell, Peter Tanner, Ron Turner, Janet Sawbridge, Derek Swoffield, George Newton and Bob Garrood. I loved the idea of skiffle, it was so beautifully obvious where mid 50's garage music was all heading. A mixture of bluegrass, blues, folk and country would see that while kids were spending five to fifty pounds on that precious guitar for a skiffle band they would soon be playing rock 'n' roll outfits.

The Wild Boys Originally Roddy Radiation's first band and the city's first punk band (SEE RODDY RADIATION). **The Wild Boys** included Roddy's brother Mark Extra on guitar, Rob Lapworth (bass) and Tony Lynch (drums) and when Rod went to join a band called **The Specials** (SEE THE SPECIALS) Johnny Thompson (guitar & Vocals) came in. When Rod left he would continue to write for them including the songs *Lorraine* and *We're Only Monsters* (this featured on *The Sent From Coventry album*). They were always a great live band, with great songs like *Confusion* and *Personal Gift*. Rob Lapworth left to become a photographer (his work includes **Attrition** and on the cover of T*he Sent From Coventry* album). They provided 2 songs for Ron Hutchinson's production of *Risky City* at *The Belgrade Theatre* (they were *Risky City* and *Death of Eddy* it was released on cassette only single, I still have mine). When they split Extra and Lynch joined up with Roddy in **The Tearjerkers**

WITH HUGE THANKS TO THE FOLLOWING PEOPLE....Julie Chambers my project co-ordinator. Kev Monks, Horace Panter, Jerry Dammers, Bob Parsons at Coventry Council, Glen Bachelor, Dougie Woodward, Marvin Wall, Denis Murphy, Vince Hill, Jack Hill, Rob Woodward, Nigel Fletcher, Rob Jackson, Alan Hartley, Mick Hartley, Kev Johnson, Barbara Folan, Rob Armstrong, Shelagh Monks, Jean Gardener, Peter Frame, Sarah and Matt Nicholls, Boo, the staff at Central Library, Coventry Telegraph archives, Coventry & Rugby Observers, 2 Cov website, Arly, Carol and Brenda Grove. John Ashby, John Collis, Larry Page, Clive Scott, Paul King, Frank Ifield, Paul Sampson, Windows on Warwickshire, Tony Newman, Arden Shields Recruitment, Kevin Dempsey, John Miles, Shel Talmy, Clare Panter, Hazel O'connor, Neil O'connor, Maureen Simpson, Viv at PWL, Southall punjabi com, Joe Kerrigan, Baldev Mastana, Shel Talmy, Tim Savage, The Boy Slim, Ken Brown, Roddy Byers, Gus, David McGrory, Dee Harris, Anne and Bob Myers, Bev Jones, Darren Jones, Jane Howard, Sonic Boom, Colin Armstrong, Vince Holliday and for all the retail outlets selling this book and the many other kind people who have helped in any way.

and especially these 4 stunning Coventry Music sites without whom….PLEASE check them out.

The Perfumery from Rex Brough at http://www.rexbrough.pwp.blueyonder.co.uk/coventry.html

The Broadgate Gnome at http://www.broadgategnome.co.uk/bands01.htm

The Cov Music site at http://www.fortunecity.de/kraftwerk/hotrats/151/page15.html

Tim James at http://www.timjamesblues.com/lists.htm#top

THE GODIVA ROCKS 'C' LIST
Here's a mega-list of all those others who also served, not a complete list it never could be, please excuse any duplicates.

ACORN, ADRIANS WALL, AFRICAN GRASS, DAVID ADDIS, THE AGENTS, THE ANGSTROMS, THE ANTACTICS, APRIL, APRIL THE FIRST MOVEMENT, ARCHIMEDES PRINCIPLE, THE ARROWS, BLOWN FUSE, BLAZE, BARREL HOUSE BLUES BAND, THE BATMAN, BRIDGES, BEAUTIFUL PEOPLE, THE BIG IDEA,THE BLACK DIAMONDS, BLUES PENTATHLON, BLUE JAYS, BOOTHILL SIX, BOOTS, THE BOYS BLUE, BREAKDOWN, THE BLACK MARIAHS,BACCUS, BITTER TEARS, ,THE BRETHREN,BRITISH STANDARD, BATTLE JUMBO MUSHROOM,THE BROOMDUSTERS, BUMBLE, CLIQUE,CHAPTER 5, THE CIRCLE, CLOSE TO TEARS,CROSSFIRE,CARDINAL,THE CARDINALS,CAROL AND THE ELECTRONS, CARL'S FABLES,CATARACT,CATHEDRAL,CATS GRAVE, CAT WEASEL,CENTRAL SOUND,THE CHADS, THE CHALLENGERS,CHANGIN SCENE,THE CHARIOTEERS,THE CHEETAHS,CHEYENNE AUTUMN,CHICAGO HUSH, CHICAGO LINE,CHICANES,CHILDREN,CHRIS JONES AGRESSION,CLEAR LIQUID,THE CLIFF COWLING TRIO, ,COCONUT MAT,THE CONCERT, THE COMPLEX,COYBITO,COUNTERACT,THE CONCLUSIONS, CONCRETE PARACHUTE,CONFEDERATES, CHIKINKI,CIVIC SERVANTS,COSSACKS, CROMWELL SOUND, CROSSFIRE, DINOSAURS, D.S.BAND,DENSA, DRIVER SIGHT,DONWARD EDGE,DOWNWARD EDGE, DRIVER 8,DIGITIAL DINOSAUR,DETOUR,DELTOID,DROPS OF BRANDY,DIGITAL LABOUR,DUMDUMS,DANDELIONS,THE DARKNESS, DECEMBER,THE DEBONAIRES,THE DESPERADOS,DWEEB,DECCATONE, DRIVER 8,DUSK,THE DICTATORS,THE DIRECTORY, THE DISTINCTIONS,DON'T PICK A FLOWER,DON'T TALK WET,DOCTOR SLAGS CONFESSION.END, EYES OF BLUE, THE EDITION,EVIL WINDOW,EVIL WIND,THE EARTH,EVEN FLOWERS KILL,EARTHQUAKES,EAST LIGHT,EAST SIDE PROTECTION, THE EBONIES,THE ECKO FOUR,THE EDDY JAMES SOUND,THE ELEGANTS SET,THE ELEMENTS, ELF, ELI, ELIAS, ELIJAH'S PEOPLE,ESTABLISHMENT, FRAUD,FUME,THE FINX, FADER,FIVE MINUTES TO MIDNIGHT,FINELINE,FACTORY,ELYSIUM, FALLING LEAVES,ROD FELTON,FISSION,FISTY,FIVEWAY ADAPTOR,FIFI AND THE FRENCH BOYS, FAT RHINO, 4TH FRONT,FIORI,THE FLAGGS,FLASHBACK SCENE, FIRST OFFENCE, THE FLOWERS,FLOOD,FLYING CIRCUS,FOLKLORE,FORULA ONE,THE FOUR ACES,FOUR CLUBS, FREE SOCIETY,FROM THE SUN, 4 FORTY,GOLDSMITH,GUARANTEED UGLY,THE GAELS,GRIM REAPER,THE GAZELLES,GEORGE AND THE DRAGON,GDANSK, GYPSY KISS,THE GOOD TIME LOSERS,GASH,GRASSHOPPERS,THE GREGORY JONZ,GROUP 66,THE GROWTH,HOUSEHOLD, THE HEARING,HEAVEN SENT,THE HEARING, ,HADES,HAMPTON COURT,HARD ROCK,HAYWOOD,THE HEARTBEATS,HELICOPTER,HELLS BELLS, HELLS ANGELS,ROB HALLIGAN,HIGH BROOM, THE HOT BLOODS, INTERNATIONAL MEGASTARS,IS MARY HOME, IGNITION, THE IMAGE,THE IMAGINATION,IOLA,IN YOUR HEADLIGHTS,IMMEDIATE PLEASURE,INSTONE,THE INCAS,THE INSIDEOUT. THE INVADERS, I SPARTACUS,JESSIE BOY 5,JUSTINE,JANET AND THE THREE SPIRES,JOJO COOKE AND THE PROTECTION RACKET, JESUS DELUX,JOHNNY NEALE AMALGAMATION,THE JONESES,JOURNEY OF A LIFE TIME,JUG,JUNKHOUSE, JOHNNY CLIFFORD AND THE PRESIDENTS, KINGSTON MEWS,THE KERRIES,THE KHAYYAM, KING SIZE KINGS,KISS OF LIFE, THE KLEEK,THE KOBALTS,LLEASE,LINEAR,LOW DRIVE,LOST CHILDREN,LEECH LAMENT,LOOPHOLE, L'HOMME DE TERRE, LADY JANE AND THE ROYAL TEE,THE LAST FAIR DEAL,THE LIBERATORS,THE LITTLE DARLINGS, LEVVITY,LOS CIMMARONS,LOVE AND KISSES,THE MAKESHIFT, MIDNIGHT CIRCUS, MIX,MACHINE, MONSTER MAGNET,MY BOY ELROY,MERCURIAL, MEN IN FROCKS,MY FAVOURITE THINGS, MAD CLASSIX,MAGAZINE,MAGIC BOX, MONTANA,THE MATADORS,THE MEAD,THE MEGADONS,MERCURIAL, MIDNIGHT MOOD,THE MIDNIGHT,THE MILD,MOBY DICK,MONDAYS CHILDREN, MONEY JUNGLE,MONEY SPIDERS, MURPH,MOODOOS,THE MOONACTS,MORNING DEW,THE MOTION, THE MOTORISED GRAPES,MY FAVOURITE THINGS, MR BENN,NEWMATICS,NEW CITY SOUND,NATURAL GAS, THE NEW BREED,NEWCASTLE BROWN,NIGHTEASE,NINA,1984,NUTS AND BOLTS,THE OLD NUMBER 7 BAND, OCHRE DAYDREAM,OPTICAL ILLUSIONS, ORANGE FLAVOUR,THE ORANGE PIPS,ORPHAN CLYDE,OTTOMAN, OUR DOG WINSTON, PURPLE HAZE,PURITON,THE POISE,PROTÉGÉ, PEOPLE, THE PACIFICS,PAHANA,PANDORA'S BOX, PARIFINALIA, PENNY FARTHING, THE PEPPERS MACHINE,PRODUCT,PERFUME GARDEN, PHASE 3,THE PIG BIN,THE PINES,THE PIPS,PLATFORM 1, POP N ORA,PRIDE AND PASSION, PRIVILEGED FEW,PSYCHO, THE RING, THE PLAN,PROFILE, PSHYCOTIC REACTION THE PUNCTURE OUTFIT,RING,THE RE;OFFENDERS, RUBBER PUPPY, RED SPHERE,RAINBOW, RA HO TEP, RUFUS REBELS, RADICALS,RARESET, THE RAVENS,THE REACTIONS,THE REASON, RED WHITE BLUES,RENEGADE,RENO,REPROBATES,REPRODUCTION ROCK LTD,REVOLUTION,THE RIPPERS, THE RIVALS,RUBBER GLASS,RUPERT BEAR,STEEL LOCKSSTILLETTO, SEDATION,SPINSILVER, SEAGULL,SCARLET PHERE,SIAK REDEM,THE SENSES,THE SESSION, THE SHAKES,THE SEANCE METHOD,SIKA REDEM,SOMETHING SPECIAL, THE SWAINS, SILICON BABY,SLYBOB,THE SAMBASSADORS OF GROOVE,SOME KINDA EARTHQUAKE, THE SUNFLOWERS,SATORI,SUPER FLY BLUE, SABINA,SACRIFICE,SAM SPADE AND THE GRAVE DIGGERS,THE SEA, THE SEED,SPIDER MURPHY, STAR POWER,THE SENSATIONS,STUNTMEN,SHARRONS,THE SHOAL,THE SLY,SIX APPEAL TAKE ONE, SKINDEEP, THE SILENCE, THE SMALL CHANGE,THE SEQUINS,SUGERFIX,SHYLO, THE SMOKSTACKS,SNEAKS NOISE,THE SOUL EXPRESS, SOUL SET,SOUNDCASTERS, SWAMP DONKEY,SOVEREIGNS,SPARKLING,THE SPIRAL,THE SPRING,THE SQUARE, THE STRAKE, THE SUNBEATS, THE SUN GOD,SUN TROLLEY,SWEENEY TODD,TOP ARC,TEQUILA,TORY PARTY,TOMORROWS KIND,TRACER,TEAM23,TEQUILA STUNTMAN,3AM,THREE SPIRES,TEASET, TEDDY BEARS,TRACER,TIERNEYS FUGITIVES,TOBACCO ASH SUNDAY,TIME,OBIAS HEAT, THE TRANE,THE TREND MEN,THE TRENDSETTERS, THE TRITONS,THE TWILIGHT ZONE, UNDERDOGS,UNDER THE HAMMER, UNREQUITED, REVERB,ULTRASOUNDS,UNKNOWNS, ,VOCALS,VOX,VIABLE,VOICE,VINYL STATE, ,WASTED DAZE,THE WAY,

INDEX A-O

14-18, 113
2 Tone,93,94,95,105
20 Days,119
21 Guns,103
3½ Floppy,77
A Band Called George,114
Academy Morticians,77
ACME Patent Electric Band,39
Adorable,5
Adventures in Reality,5
Ak Band,,46
Alternative Sounds,5
Analog,83
Any Given Day,6,86
Armalite,49
Armpit Jug Band,30,40
Armstrong, Rob,6
Asgard,87
Attic Dressers,74
Attrition.6
Autocrats,90
Bait,7
Banco De Gaia,7
Beachmantango,116
Beat Preachers,78,84
Beatles,7,8,9
Bedworth,63
Belgrade Theatre,109
Bell, Martin,114
Bennett, Declan,114
Berry, Chuck,10,11
Bhangra,11,12
Black, Pauline,12
Blitz Kreig Zone,73
Blue Orchids,66
Blues to Go,70
Bolton, Polly,13,21
Boom, Sonic,91
Bounty Hunters,97
Box of Blues,70,116
Bradbury, John,41,93,94,95
Breaker,69,93
Bridges,51
Broken Dolls,13
Brolly, Bob,15
Bron Area,26
Brough, Rex,36
Broughton, Edgar (band),13,14,112
Brown, James,88
Brown, Ken,111
Bung,83
C.O.V.,107
Coventry Automatics,93
Cabin Studios,101
Calvary,15
Calvert, Reg,85
Carribean,84
Cat's Grave,87
Cathedral,34
Chadwick, Guy,85
Chainsaw,54
Chapter Five,87
Cheeky Chappies,48
Chevy,50,115

Clarke, Tony,115
Classical,14,15
Clifton Hall,85
Clouds,54
Colosseum,109
Colourfield,16
Conway, David,20
Co-op Ballroom Nuneaton,63
Coutiers of Fashion,72
Cov City F.C.,19
Covaid,27
Coventry Automatics,93
Coventry Cathedral,18
Coventry Ska Jazz Orchestra,70
Coventry Theatre,108
Coybito,77
Criminal Class,76
Crocodile Tears,115
Cure, Martin,71
Curtis, Lynne,60
Dakar, Rhoda,12,95
Dando Shaft,21
Dammers,Jerry,93,94,95,102,105
Decker, Carol,21
Derbyshire, Delia,22
Destiny,82
Dixon, Reg,22
Doc Mustard,23
Dodgers,54
Dorrian, Lee,34
Dragster,23
Drops of Brandy,34
DT's,24
Dunville, T.E.,23
E.A.R,91
Ebrahim, Omar,14
Eclipse,107
Edge,107
Editors,49
Eggy,44,54,90
End,72
Ens,83
European Sun,25
Exceptions,66
Eyeless in Gaza,25
Eyes Of Blue,15
Fardon, Don,27
Faya Largeau,115
Ferneyhough, Brian,14
Festivals,27
Fiori,115
Fineline,115
Fisher, Matt,115
Fitten, Ivy,115
Flack Off,25
Fletcher, Nigel,52,53
Flying Machine,78
Flying Tortellinis,48,116
Flys,29,55
Folk,30
Four Kings,31
Fresh Maggots,63

Fun Boy Three,31
Furious Apples,32
Fx,116
Gdansk,73
General Public,70
General Wolfe,109
Giraffes,32
Golding, Lynval,31,93,94,95
Gods Toys,36
Goodison, Johnny,44
Grip Inc',103
Hall, Terry,16,33,93,94,95
Hangover Blues Band,112
Hanson, John,116
Hardtop 22,87
Harvey and the Wallbangers,116
Hawaiian Surgeons,116
Hedy,76
Heavy Rock,34
Hells Angels,43
Hill,Vince,35
Holloway, Robin,14
Homicide,76
Horizon studios,101
Hot Snax,23
Howells, Norman,15
Human Cabbages,49
Hungry i,25,119
Hyare, Mitch,12
I,17,36
Idiot Grunt Band,6
Ifield,Frank,37
In Embrace,25
Incas,104
Incredible Kidda Band,63
Indian Scalp,91
Indian Summer,39
J10 Studios,102
Jackley, Nat,116
Jackson, Bob,39,40
Jailhouse,110
Jalopy Ride,50
James, Jimmy,89
James, Tim,41
Jazz,39
Jazz Odyssey,95
JB's Allstars,41
Jigsaw,41,85
Jimmy Jimmy,43
John, Jason,117
Johnny B Great,44
Jones, Beverly,43
Joyce McKinnely Experience,50
Jumpin' Bad,80
Kember, Peter,91
Kenilworth,46
Jazz,39
Jazz Odyssey,95
JB's Allstars,41
Jigsaw,41,85
Jimmy Jimmy,43
John, Jason,117
Johnny B Great,44

Jones, Beverly,43
Joyce McKinnely Experience,50
Jumpin' Bad,80
Kember, Peter,91
Kenilworth,46
King,46,47
King Size Kings,49
King, Ray,49
Krankies,89
L'Homme De Terre,49
Locarno,109
Lament,46
Lanch,109
Lazy Eye,57,64
Leamington Spa,50,51
Liberators,77
Lieutenant Pigeon,52
Little Darlings,117
Locking, Brian,63
Lomas, Nigel,44,54
Lomas, Roger,54
Lover Speaks,55,80
Lowdrive,117
Ludicrous Lollipops,56
Lyons, Toby,16
Machine,23
Major 5,73
March, Andrew,14
Martin, Vince,108
Martyn, Beverly,56
Mastana, Baldev12
Matadors,117
Matrix,110
Matthew, Brian,56
Mawda,51
Mead,87
Megahype,64
Midnight Circus,29
Mighty Avengers,58,84
Mix,69
Mob,17
Moon,117
Moore, Caz,117
Mosquitoes,69
MP's,47
Mudsliders,32
Mummy Calls,50,59
Music Box,6
Mustangs,60
Mustangs,46
Myers, Billie,60
Nags,63
Napalm Death,34
Naylor, Shel,61
Nektar,117
New Modern Grunt Band,6
Nightease,93
Nocturnal Babies,75,119
Noise Like Noise,62
Nuneaton,63
Oakey, Phil,89
O'Connor, Hazel,64
Orchid Ballroom,109

INDEX A-O GODIVAROCKS@YAHOO.CO.UK INDEX A-O

O
O'Connor, Hazel,64
Oakey, Phil,89
Orchid Ballroom,109
Orchids,66
Out of the Blue,43
Over, Simon,14
P
Page, Larry,109
Panjabi MC,68
Panter, Horace,69,93,94,95
Pardesi, Silinder,11
Paris,34
Partners In Rhyme,11
Pat Gisane Show Band,15
Paul, Sean,82
Payne,Jack,39,50
Peeps,70
Penfold,51
People,82
Pepper, Dave,72,73
Peppermint Kreem,118
Pharaoh's Kingdom,87
Pickwicks,73
Pierce, Jason,96
Pigface,23
Pigfish,77
Pilgrims,32
Pink Umbrellas,74,83
Pinkertons Colours,77,85
Pips,54
Plague,118
Polak,5
Poppy, Clint,118
Porifera,112
Prestons,43
Pretty Flamingos,97
Primitives,75
Pseuds,47
Punk,76,77
R
Radiation, Roddy,80,93,94,95
Rainbows,71
Raindrops,35
Ramrods,73
Randall, Alan,63
Rattray, Mark,81
Raw Screens,46,83
Razzle,34
Red on Red,115
Reggae,82
Regan, Julianne,118
Relatives,82
Reluctant Stereotypes,74,83
Renagades (Leamington band),51
Renagades (Cov band),54
Resound,118
Rhythm Recording Studios,102
Riot Act,76
Rolling Stones,84
Rough Beat,82
RU21,103
Rugby,85,86
Rugby Granada,86

Russian Girlfriends,86
Rythm Recording Studios,102
S
Sabres,70
Satin Dolls,118
Scarlet Phere,64
School Meals,50
Selecter,87
Sex Pistols,88
Shapes,50
Sheer Pride,118
Sigue Sigue Sputnik,89
Singh, Tazsem,98
Ska Billy Rebels,80
Skalatones,88
Sky Dome,109
Smackee,15
Smith, Kendell,82,99,107
Sonic Harmony,118
Sorrows,90
Spacemen 3,85,91
Special AKA,87,93
Special Beat,95
Special Brew,105
Specials,80,93,94,95
Spectrum,91
Spider Murphy,118
Spiritualized,85,91,96
Squad,103
Stairway,112
Staples,Neville,31,93,94,95
Starpower,76,119
Stavely Makepeace,52,97
Stevenson's Rocket,100
Steadman, Ian,119
Steel Locks,82
Stereo Nation,98
Stevenson's Rocket,100
Still Life (signed band),71
Still Life (unsigned band),62
Studios,101,102
Sue & Mary,119
Sumladfromcov,114
Supernaturals,88
Supernaturals,12
Sureela, Shinda,11
Swarbrick, Dave,119
Swell Maps,50
Swinging Cats,102
T
Tabor, June,103,112
Talmy, Shel,68
Targets,49
Team 23,72
Tearjerkers,80
Terminal Tears,104
Terry Hall and Lenny the Lion,89
Terry,Blair and Anouchka,33
Thoria,105
Tic Tock Club,109
Tiffanys,109

Tina and the Hotstrings,119
Tony Martin and His Echo Four,73
Transposed Men,87
Tubilah Dog,82
U
UK Warriors,82
Urban,107
Urge,98,107
Vampires,108
V
Varukers,50
Venues,108,109,110
Vietnamese Babies,120
Vin Lloyd and his Mounties,120
W
Walnut Conspiracy,48
Walt Jabsco,93
Walwyn, Steve,24
Ward, Tom,84
Warwick,112
Warwick Arts Centre,109
Warwick University,112
Waterman, Pete,100,113
Whippersnapper,119
White Noise,22
White, Bubs,6
Wild Boys,80
Wild Boys,120
Willets, Dave,114
Willow, Pete,30
Wills, Dr Arthur,14
Wonderland,62
Woodbine Street Studios,101
Woodward, Rob,52,61
X
X-Certs,72
Y
Y.B.R.,107
Z
Zips,90
Zodiacs,44

This book was written and designed by Pete Chambers, from January to July 2004.

No claim is made for the use of any copyright material that may have inadvertently been used in this publication.

TWO TONE WAY
LEADING TO RAZOR BLADE ALLY AND ORANGE STREET

JERRY DAMMERS AT COVAID

INDEX O-Z   **GODIVAROCKS@YAHOO.CO.UK**   **INDEX O-Z**

1